MASTERMINDING THE STORE

National Retail Federation Series

The National Retail Federation Series comprises books on retail store management, for stores of all sizes and for all management responsibilities. The National Retail Federation is the world's largest retail trade association, with membership that includes the leading department, specialty, discount, mass merchandise, and independent stores, as well as 30 national and 50 state associations. NRF members represent an industry that encompasses more than 1.4 million U.S. retail establishments and employs nearly 20 million people—1 in 5 American workers. The NRF's international members operate stores in more than 50 nations.

The National Retail Federation Series includes the following books:

Competing with the Retail Giants: How to Survive in the New Retail Landscape, Kenneth E. Stone

Credit Card Marketing, Bill Grady

Dictionary of Retailing and Merchandising, Jerry M. Rosenberg

The Electronic Retailing Market: TV Home Shopping, Infomercials, and Interactive Retailing, Packaged Facts, Inc.

FOR 1996: Financial and Operating Results of Retail Stores in 1995, National Retail Federation

Loss Prevention Guide for Retail Businesses, Rudolf C. Kimiecik

Management of Retail Buying, 3d Edition, R. Patrick Cash, John W. Wingate, Joseph S. Friedlander

MasterMinding the Store: Advertising, Sales Promotion, and the New Marketing Reality, Donald Ziccardi with David Moin

MOR 1996: Merchandising and Operating Results of Retail Stores in 1995, National Retail Federation

Practical Merchandising Math, Leo Gafney

Retail Store Planning and Design Manual, 2d Edition, Michael Lopez

Small Store Survival: Success Strategies for Retailers, Arthur Andersen

The Software Directory for Retailers, 5th Edition, Coopers & Lybrand, L.L.P.

Specialty Shop Retailing: A Guide to Starting Your Own Store, Carol Schroeder

Value Retailing in the 1990s: Off-Pricers, Factory Outlets, and Closeout Stores, Packaged Facts, Inc.

MASTERMINDING THE STORE

Advertising, Sales Promotion, and The New Marketing Reality

Donald Ziccardi

WITH
David Moin

JOHN WILEY & SONS, INC.

New York · Chichester · Brisbane · Toronto · Singapore · Weinheim

This text is printed on acid-free paper.

Copyright © 1997 by Donald Ziccardi and David Moin
Published by John Wiley & Sons, Inc.

This publication is designed to provide accurate and authoritative information in regard to the subject matter covered. It is sold with the understanding that the publisher is not engaged in rendering legal, accounting, or other professional services. If legal advice or other expert assistance is required, the services of a competent professional person should be sought.

Library of Congress Cataloging-in-Publication Data:

Ziccardi, Donald.
    MasterMinding the store : advertising, sales promotion and the new
    marketing reality / Donald Ziccardi with David Moin.
        p.   cm. — (National Retail Federation series)
    Includes index.
    ISBN 0-471-13910-6 (cloth : alk. paper)
    1. Retail trade—Marketing.   2. Advertising.   3. Sales promotion.
    I. Moin, David.   II. Title.   III. Series.
    HF5429.Z45   1997
    658.8'7—dc20   96-30258

Printed in the United States of America

10 9 8 7 6 5 4 3 2 1

This book is for my two sons,
Evan Lewis and Alexander Ian,
and dedicated to the loving memory of
my father, Donald A. Ziccardi.

Credits

Editor:	**Ruth Mills**
Project Director:	**Jeffrey R. Jackson**
Project Editor:	**Kathryn Daniels**
Associate Project Editor:	**Jackie Wein**
Contributors:	**Joe Fontana** **Louise Charles**
Financial Planning:	**Allyn Salpeter**
Art Directors:	**Susan P. Black** **Tracy Brennan**
Cover Design:	**Vicki Woliver**
Cartoon Concepts:	**Joe Fontana**
Cartoonist:	**Renée Pappo-Moy**
Art Production Supervisor:	**Lisa Sonkin-Hasson**
Art Production Coordinator:	**Robert Henick**
Art Production Staff:	**Daniel Zahor** **Nassos Gnafkis** **Denley Hung**
Computer Production:	**Chris Benjamin**
Proofreader:	**Deborah Hay**

Acknowledgments

I've always disliked reading book acknowledgments because they remind me of insincere Academy Award acceptance speeches. However, in writing this book, I now realize that acknowledgments are indeed unavoidable occupational hazards for authors. Writing a book takes a lot of sweat and very few of us can do it without a great deal of help from supportive colleagues, family, and friends.

Acknowledgments are necessary, but I'll keep them brief. And, at the expense of the many people who play an important part of my success going unnoted, I'll limit my attributions to those who have made the writing of this specific book even remotely possible.

Thank you, all mentioned on the credits page, for the unrelenting tenacity and hard work that went into the production of this book; the staff of Ziccardi & Partners, for believing in dreams and driving so hard to make them come true; all our special clients, who challenge us every day to move forward and never rest on laurels; members of the media, who work with us to always position our clients in the best possible way; our production vendors, who understand the meaning of quality and economy and the importance of outstanding customer service; Herb Gallen, for all your wonderful support and wisdom; Linda Allard, for being Linda Allard; Paul Carlucci, Deborah Aiges, Janis Donnaud, Maryann Palumbo, Paul Fedorko, Jack Laschever, and Glenn Palmer, for your endorsements; Bruce Gerstein, Ken Gross, Lenny Shapiro, and Billy Regen, for all the invaluable financial and legal advice; Martin, Rosemarie, Joe, Jimmy, C.C., and Gwen, for your special support; Elizabeth, Rod, Rob and Donna, Jackie, Lois, Tony, and Sheilah for helping with the important things in my life; thanks, Mom and Johnny; and the law of dharma, which says that by expressing your unique talents and fulfilling the needs of your fellowman you begin to create whatever you want, whenever you want it.

Preface

In business, it's not what you sell that counts. It's how you sell it. Whether you're running the corner mom-and-pop grocery, or operating a mega-sized hypermart in a suburban supermall, whether you're selling bananas, books, basketballs or manufacturing bridge sportswear, the same principles for successful marketing apply. Even though the products and the selling formats may differ, the rules don't change.

That's actually one of the best-kept secrets in the business community. Few executives are aware of all that links them with those from other industries. I learned about the universal principles of successful marketing, and how to apply them to different products, over the course of my career—first in retail marketing and then running my own advertising agency. It's been a long, hard learning process. This book can help you dramatically speed up the process. It's a quick, breezy read that lays out the fundamentals, as I see them. Read this book and you're on the road to becoming a masterful marketer.

But what makes this book so special? Why listen to me? Because I've been there. I've been a key player in some of the great successes and great failures in recent retail marketing. And I've learned from them both. When I joined B. Altman in 1988 as senior vice president of marketing, I was part of a team masterminding the resurrection of the Altman flagship on 34th Street in New York City. It was the vision of Australian real estate developer George Herscu to build giant malls across the United States using the Altman, Bonwit Teller, and Sakowitz nameplates as anchors, and I was drawn into the vision. It was a vision based on some wonderful ideas but little insight into the turbulent real estate and retail industries. The proper research, planning, and marketing wasn't there. The rules were

PREFACE

skirted. And Herscu's ambitious but risky scheme ultimately dragged the corporation into bankruptcy and the man himself into obscurity.

I was vice president at Macy's in 1978 when we launched the Cellar in Herald Square, a groundbreaker in housewares and foods presented with all the panache and excitement of Broadway. I learned about focusing a concept, selling new kinds of products, and advertising it all. It was powerful marketing, top to bottom. And it was retail theater at its best. The store thrived, talent flourished, and the bounds of success seemed unlimited.

Unfortunately, management became overly smitten with success and, years later, decided to stage a leveraged buyout of Macy's, taking it private. I was among the "select" executives asked to cough up some capital. For a mere $25,000, I could in five years be a millionaire. I was excited by the prospect of winning retail lotto, but not convinced of it. I analyzed what some investment bankers were saying. I did my homework, following one of the key principles of smart marketing, which is to examine the risks and the requirements of any plan. I learned that awesome sales were needed for us to pay off the debt and make the LBO work. The Cellar was a miracle on 34th Street, but now we needed another one. I thought miracles just don't happen that often. I packed my bags and joined the May Department Stores as senior vice president, director of marketing, for their Robinson's division.

Eventually, I opted to escape the retail mayhem. I wanted to take control of my fate. So when an opportunity arose to leverage–buy out an advertising agency specializing in publishing, I seized it, but not without much trepidation. I remember asking my investment bankers after the deal closed, "What do I know about publishing?" Or about book covers, bookmarks, or promoting authors, for that matter? It seemed as if I were entering an entirely new world.

I soon found that I wasn't in totally foreign territory. I discovered that the fundamentals for successful advertising that I had learned during my 10 years in retail marketing promoting hundreds of different products could be applied to books and the publishing industry as well as to other businesses. With that understanding, I proceeded to expand the scope of my advertising agency to other sectors, among them fashion, jewelry, hotels, magazines, and cosmetics. It worked! Our diverse client list includes Ellen Tracy, the Millennium Broadway hotel, *TV Guide,* Random House, South Sea Pearl Consortium, and *Departures* magazine.

This book has been seasoned with many case studies and anecdotes from my own experiences and those of others to illustrate the common ground—the problems and solutions that are relevant to marketers of all sizes, shapes, and colors—and provide lessons of how to achieve a marketing grand slam.

In addition, there's a nitty-gritty side to the book: the rules and procedures for developing solid advertising campaigns are fleshed out. I have found that many companies do not follow these guidelines. Often, they lack the essential understanding that, before developing advertising and promotional elements, a wealth of information must be compiled and analyzed and a marketing plan written. Unfortunately, many advertisers construct strategies without being fully prepared. The company's products, strengths, weaknesses, and goals; the customer's behavior and the demographics; and the competition's strengths, weaknesses, and strategies—all of these must be researched before a dynamic and targeted advertising strategy can be devised.

The first section of the book, "MasterMinding the Store," shows in the opening three chapters how to conduct an analysis of your company, its customers, and the competition and how to essentially compile a comprehensive business analysis. Armed with that information, you'll be able to write the marketing plan for the company—a plan that serves as a blueprint for masterminding the store. The process of writing this plan is covered in Chapter 4, the final chapter of that section.

The second section of the book, "Advertising, Sales Promotion, and the New Marketing Reality," is a thorough discussion of the art and mechanics of creating advertising, promotions, and publicity. It's really the definitive model for building a successful advertising and sales promotion campaign.

Combined, the two sections deliver a comprehensive how-to strategy for winning at the marketing game, regardless of the nature of your business.

Contents

CONTENTS

SECTION II
Advertising, Sales Promotion,
and the New Marketing Reality

CONTENTS

Introduction

Welcome to the age of mega-marketing. Or is it marketing miasma? Marketers are taking action not only to satisfy the needs and desires of consumers, but by spending big, running cross-promotional campaigns, and exploiting the power of the media, they're also creating a market for things that people never knew they needed. Bloomingdale's did it in the 1970s when they sold pet rocks. Volkswagen did it in the 1960s with its "think small" campaign, sparking a great countertrend to America's fixation on large, gas-guzzling cars.

But in the 1990s, it's not enough to be quirky, cute, or creative. In today's difficult economy, marketers are bottom line–oriented, selling to wider audiences, seeking to steal share from the competition, and they are less willing to gamble on a fad. How do they do it? Marketers blitz the public with an inescapable barrage of pre-release advertising, publicity, and merchandise tie-ins, so that people don't just go to movies anymore. They succumb to cinematic events.

After a movie, who goes to a diner these days? Theme restaurants— decked out in glitzy Hollywood trappings, hawking T-shirts, caps, mugs, celebrity endorsements, and hamburgers costing twice what one would expect to pay—have replaced diners.

Businesses are budgeting big to create an aura around products, to re-build corporate images and icons, and to sell to populations previously overlooked. Thus, Campbell reworks its classic soup can. Ralph Lauren shops become "the world of Ralph Lauren," filled with home products, fragrances, and apparel collections for lounging around the mansion, for black-tie evenings, or for boardroom meetings. Chrysler takes an ethnic urban appeal by sponsoring a broadcast—the *Hoop Dreams* documentary—about African-Americans and basketball. After years of missing out on the fashion market, Sears is spending approximately $500 million annually selling its "softer side" and soft-selling its macho side.

Jeans manufacturers have made their products into objects of curiosity using statements of rebellion. When Calvin Klein pushes the limits of permissiveness with jeans ads depicting teenage models in suggestive poses, conservatives protest, magazines drop the ads, the FBI investigates, and all the fuss generates record sales for Klein.

Even the long-disbanded Beatles have been tapped for mega-marketing. Now you can "Meet the Beatles"—again. Capitol Records teamed with ABC to produce a six-hour, three-part TV special on the rock group and a CD anthology in a huge campaign carrying a nostalgic, multigenerational appeal, even to those who were not yet born when the Beatles toured. The group is back on the charts 25 years after breaking up.

MARKETING TODAY

Pervasive as it has become, marketing to many remains an abstract idea; few understand the dynamics. It's not some foggy notion of pinstriped executives or polyestered flimflam people selling hype over substance. It requires the right tools and the right information.

Marketers must carefully monitor the environment, changes in the economy, demographic shifts, new lifestyles, and consumer debt levels. If the city or state is cutting back on employment, your business could be seriously affected.

Successful marketing—bringing the right products and services to customers when and where they want them—requires a collaborative effort by all departments of a company. The best way to ensure that the company is in sync and speaks with one voice is to develop a strategic marketing plan.

A NEW GENERATION OF MARKETERS

The marketing plan is crucial, particularly in light of today's uncertain economy marked by slow growth, cost cutting, and ongoing corporate restructuring. Enormous job insecurity among blue- and white-collar workers, frenzied stock trading, and rapidly changing demographics compound the situation. Amid the calamity, a new generation of marketers will emerge as retail, entertainment, banking, transportation, and consumer-product industries reconfigure and search for innovative advertising and marketing strategies. More and more careers will be made in database manipulation, sophisticated marketing procedures, and management economics. It's all just on the horizon.

By probing the computer data, businesses will discover a new frontier of information on how the market ticks. Buying habits, hobbies, family histories, favorite brands, color preferences, and, of course, whether she's a size 8 or 10 can all be learned through sales transactions and market research. Armed with this information, marketing programs and strategic long-term marketing plans can be tailor-made.

Marketers must also monitor the competition. Is Macy's breaking prices on swimwear early in the season? Is Isaac Mizrahi spending more time in his studio or in the MTV studio? Is The Gap launching a new division, with lower prices and an army/navy type of store format? Is Neiman Marcus redesigning its catalog? Who will be shopping tomorrow at Today's Man?

How should your firm respond to these new challenges? Hire someone from the competition? It's been done, but that's not necessarily the best answer. Get in on what's happening now, and before the store next door gets there first. Think big and get big. Focus on what's real, not potentially real five years down the road. Think about technology that provides fast data and fast delivery: tangibles.

The new millennium once held the promise of a new world—a world of interactive selling, boundless consumer choices, high-speed delivery, and a perfect marriage of supply and demand. The mall would come to you.

But the year 2000 is fast approaching and the signs are pointing in a different direction. Technology is advancing and industries are changing. Those companies that survive and thrive won't be the ones on the cutting edge. They will do the cutting, shed the waste, and conquer the competition—companies that think big and get big. The worlds of fashion and retailing will be dominated by the Wal-Marts, Macy's, Gaps, Ralph Laurens, and Levi's with little left in between and few real signs of creative ingenuity. Street smarts will win out because there is really nothing new under the sun. Those that take a sound idea, already tested, and run with it will prevail. It's the new marketing reality.

Whether you are a student or a veteran of industry, this book is your guide. Initially, we deal with assessing your company, setting its mission, determining the character of the competition, and targeting consumers. These are the prerequisites. Then, through accounts of real campaigns that provide valuable lessons, you'll discover the nuts and bolts of moving your advertising and promotional efforts forward.

MASTERMINDING THE STORE

1 Getting Started

"OK. Heads, we're upscale fashion;
tails, we'll do hardware."

Unless they're totally rash, most businesspeople don't flip a coin to decide on a business field or a target market. Decisions have to be made so that you can market, advertise, and sell products effectively, not thoughtlessly, and profile your company to really focus on its "core" business.

That's precisely what I did when I acquired Sussman & Sugar, the ad agency that grew into Ziccardi & Partners. Sussman was a premier agency in the world of book publishing with a respectable $25 million in annual billings—until a large, global agency with poor management purchased it and dragged it down to $1.8 million in billings. The day after I bought the agency, one of the two remaining clients suddenly left, billings took another dive to $800,000, and the future looked dim.

I knew the only chance for survival was to refashion the business from the ground up and to begin by drawing a clear picture of the agency's goals so that I could articulate my vision to others and have a sharp focus. In what industries would we specialize? Who would our target clients be? Could we define the agency more broadly—draw a new profile—and include industries besides publishing? I examined the competition, its strengths, weaknesses, successes, and failures. Before I could even think of developing a marketing and promotional strategy for the agency, there were scores of hard questions that needed to be answered.

My agency grew to $50 million in billings because I took the right first steps on the road to developing a marketing plan. Ironically, these steps had virtually nothing to do with the hard-core elements of marketing. So, as this chapter advises, forget advertising and sales promotion—for now. You're still a long way from that stage. The getting-started phase means you're in a period of reflection, not action.

THE PLANNING BEGINS

Think of the marketing plan as your corporate constitution—a forceful written document with more impact than a verbal statement or a thought passed along during a board meeting or company picnic. It is an organic document that's shared in the organization for compliance and commentary from employees.

The marketing plan can form a significant part of a 5- or 10-year business plan at a time when a company is formed, when new management arrives, when new directions are sought, when a company is trying to emerge from bankruptcy, when it merges with another company, or when the competition is stealing your share of business and it's time to launch a counterattack. It is something the workforce can rally around to help accomplish new goals.

The marketing plan also helps you develop effective advertisements, which on the surface look easy to create. Some appear downright simple. How hard can they be to put together? The answer: excruciatingly so. That's because the businesses of advertising and promoting are volatile. What seems like a good strategy from inside the four walls of your office can be offensive to the public or simply irrelevant. Styles fly in and out of fashion in a matter of months, sometimes weeks. What's in vogue one season can be passé the next. Some products have a short shelf life. Tastes change. Attitudes change. Conservative values take over. And technology and society seem to move faster as time passes.

With advance research, commonsense planning, and effective execution, a company can determine where it is, how it got there, and where it wants to go. But the first step is writing the business summary.

DRAWING THE COMPANY PROFILE

Initially, it's a mundane process. The basics must be recorded: the names, addresses, and phone numbers of principals and company facilities, such as its offices, store sites, warehouses, and design studios. The role of each principal in the company must also be described. From this, a picture of the company's operations, players, and purpose will emerge, giving you a clear sense of what the company is about and an ability to describe it to others.

Avoid Missteps

Drawing the profile provides a clear plan with a clear focus. Focus has become the key to surviving in the current business climate. Many companies have failed or are failing because of a lack of focus. Some say Kmart went awry when it shifted focus from its core discount stores and began developing specialty businesses, such as Sports Authority. Sears Merchandising Group lost focus, too, but regained momentum after shedding its insurance, real estate, and financial subsidiaries.

Getting on the right path can take years and generally comes after making a few false moves, undergoing intense self-analysis, or subjecting your company to outsiders looking in. The Limited, Inc., for example, has had several divisions seeking distinction. Divisions such as Limited Stores, Lerner New York, and Express cannibalized sales, copied each other's merchandise, and floundered in the first half of the 1990s. It took a string of poor quarters before the corporation recruited new talent from firms like Saks Fifth Avenue and Bergdorf Goodman and reorganized its leadership in an effort to put some sizzle back into its fashions.

The Company Definition: Use Broad Strokes

There's another hurdle here that ties into getting focused: defining the business of the company in a broad but accurate way. For example, Ford could define itself as an auto company. More wisely, it's in the transportation business.

By broadly defining your company, you give it room to grow and change as the needs of your customers change and competitive challenges arise.

If Walt Disney had considered himself merely a cartoonist rather than an entertainer, he never would have nurtured amusement parks and movies, nor would future Disney managers have launched Disney stores, started a Disney network, and taken over Capital Cities/ABC. Disney has become a factory for churning out innovative entertainment and thrilling its audiences time and again.

Does your company have a motto or a mission statement? If so, include it in the description of the company. Include the company's history. Who started it? What was its original intent? How have its products or services evolved? Are any originals still being marketed?

5

VISIONS AND DECISIONS FOR A BETTER FUTURE

From this analysis, you should be able to review decisions of the past to discover which ones paid off and which ones didn't. Evaluate those that may have been too hasty, such as a major acquisition or expansion strategy.

Infamous Decisions

One of the most infamous decisions was R.H. Macy & Company's purchase of Bullock's and I. Magnin in 1988. It was the vision of then Macy CEO Edward Finkelstein to build a greater Macy presence on the West Coast, and that made sense considering the power of the Macy name. But the California economy went sour, retailing slowed in many parts of the country, and Macy's business couldn't support the added debt. Macy's already had a huge debt load from its leveraged buyout of 1986. The end result: Macy's filed for bankruptcy in January 1992 and was taken over by Federated Department Stores in December 1994. Ironically, the new Macy's management is doing what Finkelstein dreamed of doing—spreading Macy's on the West Coast.

On a smaller scale, Merry-Go-Round fell into the trap of overexpanding, and like Macy's it had its eye on acquisitions when things seemed great. In the early 1990s, it became the nation's hottest specialty chain for urban, teen apparel and gobbled up other chains, including Chess King. The strategy backfired. MGR found itself stuck with a lot of weak locations, and the junior market dried up. Merry-Go-Round plummeted into bankruptcy in 1994 and liquidated in 1996.

Correctly reading the market is crucial to the marketing strategy, but there are as many cases of failure in this as success. Toys "R" Us set the standard for everyday low pricing, but Dillard Department Stores and Sears Roebuck got burned when they tried it. They learned the hard way that their shoppers were too conditioned to shop markdown days.

Decisions that were spectacularly wrong and those just not quite right all have to be reviewed. This assessment helps you focus on who your customers are, what they expect, and what plans are right for your company.

The Vision Thing

Once you know where the company is and how it got there, it is time to consider new directions: a different plan for the year, a 5-year vision, a 10-year vision. That timeline helps you translate your long-term goals into your short-term plan for the next year.

Each year should represent an incremental step toward the 5-year and 10-year vision. Each year, the plans involving growth, new products, and all of the marketing should be updated to reflect the extent of achievement and the success of the company. Good strategic plans start with a definition, a sense of history, and a vision. A clear and solid vision can unite your workforce to work toward a common goal. A good vision can come from an individual, upper management, or the workforce and from top-down planning, bottom-up compilations, or a combination of the two.

Entrepreneur Wayne Huizenga's vision was to combine the fragmented video rental industry into a giant national video chain called Blockbuster. Leslie H. Wexner had a vision of creating a major business out of selling low-priced trendy sportswear. He modeled The Limited after Milton Petrie's.

Perhaps one of the greatest visionaries in corporate history was Sam Walton, the legendary retailer. His aim was to create a national chain of country stores for rural America with a broad assortment and low prices, known as Wal-Mart.

Frederick W. Smith had a vision: to create a new system of fast and reliable door-to-door delivery. Execution was key. When he started Federal Express in 1973, employees used their own cars and rented vans to take packages to their destinations and to the company's fleet of about a dozen Falcon jets. Previously, a package had to pass through a network of handlers from different companies before arriving at the destination. Federal Express became the first company to promise overnight delivery and to have its own aircraft, air crews, and ground staff. It was also the first delivery company to track packages by computer. This is one example of a vision that paid off: During the eighties, Federal Express became—and still is today—a major force in the overnight-delivery business.

Bill Gates, the chairman and CEO of Microsoft, has been a heavy advertiser and marketer. But what has also spurred his company is an imaginative vision of the future. In this vision, the masses on both sides of the globe will be connected electronically through high-speed communication networks, and families will have technologies at home that make their lives simpler and easier. All the information consumers get from books, movies, advertising, and TV will be available on demand through pocket-size computers that are easily transported. Gates's vision also entails broadening Microsoft's scope beyond software into such areas as health care and banking.

Allen I. Questrom, the chairman and chief executive of Federated Department Stores, had a vision to spread Macy's nationally and make it the country's largest department store chain. Questrom says that when Federated fell into bankruptcy in 1990, "people were saying that department stores were really a dying breed. The attitude out there was very negative and debilitating for our people. It became our vision to create an attitude that department stores had a future. We put down on paper what needed to be done for department stores to be the right concept for the 21st century. Not dinosaurs. There were many issues to work on, but our overall challenge was to provide better merchandise—fashion forward but not leading edge—to appeal to the broad middle class, unlike discounters and specialty stores. In essence, we would become category killers in the malls for customers shopping apparel and accessories, kids' merchandise, and home goods under one roof."

The mission also included recasting Federated, which operated such chains as Bloomingdale's, Rich's, and Burdines, from "a series of autonomous divisions competing against each other to a united team acting as one," Questrom says. Federated pulled out of bankruptcy in 1992 and a new vision emerged. In 1994, Federated acquired Macy's and took a big step toward forming a cohesive operation. Federated's Abraham & Straus and Jordan Marsh divisions on the East Coast, Bullock's division on the West Coast, and other divisions would all become Macy's, the one department store with true national brand recognition and enormous untapped potential. Besides exploding Macy's stores nationally, Questrom's vision entails possibly creating a national Macy's catalog and a Macy's home shopping TV channel. "Different channels of distribution are emerging, but no one channel will be omnipotent," Questrom says.

A New Pair of Jeans: The Right Fit, the Right Decision

In the early 1980s, jeans companies such as Sasson, Bonjour, Jordache, and Gloria Vanderbilt were doing high-profile advertising and marketing campaigns portraying jeans as sexy, fashionable, and must-have items for the wardrobe. Jeans were no longer simply something you wore for backyard gardening. They became acceptable for social situations, even hip. The jeans business, in total, was on the rise.

Lee, however, was not riding the wave. It lacked vision. Its distribution was not ballooning, and rivals Levi Strauss and Wrangler were perceived to have better products. Lee had some regional discounter distribution to chains such as Bradlees, Hills, and some department stores, including Macy's, Dayton's, and Hudson's.

Lee was faced with a two-pronged dilemma: Other jeans were cutting into sales and Lee didn't have the image of being upscale or hip. With its back to the wall, Lee conducted an ambitious positioning project that cost an estimated $100,000, researching consumers to find out how they perceived the brand. It discovered that it had a frumpy, blue-collar image, with no fashion profile.

In came Kathy Ferguson, a woman of vision in search of the perfect fit. A women's merchandiser at Lee, she engineered a new jean with a new fit, incorporating a U-shaped crotch. It fit better and felt more comfortable, compared with the standard V-shaped crotch that was used for both men's and women's jeans.

Lee developed a marketing strategy that focused on the social acceptability of the jeans and the new fit. The print ads depicted women wearing jeans in social settings. The campaign is considered the first jeans campaign to focus solely on women. In contrast, Wrangler was the heavy sponsor of rodeos and showed cowboys in its ads.

Lee's revenues exploded from $300 million to $800 million in a couple of years, and the company became the volume leader in women's jeans. There was a launch of the new product at a New York disco, point-of-sale efforts, changes in all of the tags, and rounders (circular clothing racks) at a time when few people were doing them. The sales force grew. Bozell Worldwide handled the advertising.

The strategy was dead-on. Everything Lee did said fit, fit, fit, and the product served it up. "Most advertising was designer/image driven. We had a real product benefit," said Ferguson.

THE PERFECT MATCH: PRODUCTS AND CUSTOMERS

With a definition and a vision of the business in hand, the next step is to state the types of products and services you offer, where they are available and at what prices, and how you plan to advertise. Write it down in simple but complete terms. Call it a mom-and-pop operation, if it's a single-unit, family-run business. Or call it a five-and-dime store, if the offerings are sundry, budget priced, and varied; or a major fashion chain, if there are multiple locations and an overwhelming percentage of apparel. Those definitions are fairly specific and narrow. In each case, the character of the product mix must fit into the corporate identity.

From here, determine whether your perception of the company matches your customers'. This goal requires market research, including consumer surveys, focus groups, and exit interviews. The process is time-consuming on the first attempt. However, the effort that is made now will pay off later. For example, those consumer groups initially used to gather perceptions of your business and trends can be recalled six months or two years later, after new marketing strategies have been implemented. Compare the data from the two focus group meetings to see whether perceptions have changed and to measure the efficacy of the new strategies.

Collecting the information doesn't have to be expensive, either, and you can do it yourself. A Ziccardi & Partners client, Island Hotels, needed to heavily promote its newest specialty hotel in the Blue Mountains of Jamaica. The company did not have a lot of money for research, so we conducted it in-house, putting together focus groups of travel agents, heavy travelers, and light travelers. We called friends, family members—anyone we knew who fit the categories and was within the right demographics.

What we learned from this research was significant in developing the right creative message for the hotel. Because Jamaican resorts are typically beach resorts, there had to be other reasons to go high up into the Blue Mountains for a vacation. We found them by visiting the property. While secluded, it offered the accommodations of a four-star hotel, the solitude of a retreat, and an authentic look at Jamaican tradition. This was a place where wealthy travelers would go for a different kind of vacation experience.

"Retreat into the heart of the Blue Mountains, and into Jamaica's past . . ." When we gave this line to the focus groups, they all sparked to it. The consensus was that finding a place that was truly unique was a strong selling point to the upscale traveler. The whole research process cost a mere $300, but it gave us the information we needed to present a focused idea to the client.

Identifying the Target Market: Gray Panthers or Grunge

Identifying your customers is important. Identifying the customers of your competitors is just as important. Using this information put Warner Brothers Studio stores on the right path.

As Peter Starrett, president of Warner Brothers Studio stores, recalls, "We saw the success of the Disney Store, but the thing that concerned us was there was a number of other stores in the same genre—Sesame Street, Ringling Brothers, Hanna Barbera. As we looked at entering the marketplace, we didn't want to be the fifth store in the market, and as we talked to developers, we found that's what they didn't want, either. They perceived it as a cluttered marketplace.

"We did a lot of research with consumers. Warner Brothers had a strong appeal to kids, but a stronger appeal to adults, 20 to 45. We did focus groups on both coasts, in Los Angeles and New York. As we began to determine our niche, we realized to break through the clutter we would really have to go at a different target market. Primarily adults. Kids would be secondary. Clearly, toys are 100 percent for kids, but that is a relatively small portion of the business." Warner Brothers decided to gear about 75 percent of its total goods to adults but also included some children's items.

Warner Brothers stores took a novel approach. The company did its homework to determine who would actually be its customer. Would that customer be an impulse buyer or someone entering with a definite purpose in mind?

Companies doing research need to ask customers questions that allow the companies to form better descriptions of buying habits. Customer needs in terms of products and services should be at the top of the list. Service can be the linchpin in pulling together the total image of the store and set you apart from the competition.

Service: A Great Differentiator and Image Maker

What services do your customers appreciate? There are myriad possibilities. Ikea, the European home furnishings chain expanding in the United States, includes a play area for children and a cafeteria with Swedish meatballs. Many new or remodeled Bloomingdale's stores provide wider aisles, designed so that mothers can easily wheel baby strollers without colliding into other customers or displays. More stores are offering private shopping nights planned to make preferred customers feel special. By providing discounts and a few hors d'oeuvres one evening, it's possible to make up last week's sales shortfall.

For its best credit customers, Saks Fifth Avenue has a program offering points based on dollars spent, which can be used for rebates on future purchases. Original Levi's stores offer custom-made jeans, with computerized fitting. Sharper Image lets you test the electronic massagers at its stores.

Enterprise Rent-A-Car uses expanded customer service to gain advantage in the nonairport market of the car rental industry. Their $22 million "Pick Enterprise. We'll pick you up" campaign has aggressively promoted the fact that they will pick up customers at the repair site or at home. Offering this value-added service has helped Enterprise to distinguish itself in the highly competitive car rental market.

Even insurance companies are beginning to understand that improved customer service means improved market opportunities. Olympus Insurance Agency in Salt Lake City provides services that most insurers don't. Agents offer regularly scheduled meetings with customers to review exposures, to update and remarket coverages, and to discuss industry trends.

Numerous stores offer personal shopping, valet parking, free alterations, and gift wrapping. Many catalogs, including L.L. Bean and J. Crew, have 24-hour operator service during the holiday rush so you can get through quickly if you call late at night.

L.L. Bean goes the extra yard in service. Ordering is toll-free. The company guarantees 100 percent satisfaction; otherwise, it will replace an item or refund your money. Purchases are shipped within 24 hours after ordering. Customers can choose from a variety of ordering options to speed delivery; orders can also be faxed. There are special devices so that deaf customers can order by phone, and a guide is provided in the front of the catalog for quick reference. The company will also send swatches to customers who want to see and touch fabrics before a purchase.

Caterpillar, the truck and tractor manufacturer, had a reputation for being slow to repair its engines, partly because repair shops had difficulty getting vital information quickly from the corporation's central mainframe. But Caterpillar improved its engine division's repair efficiency in

1992 by implementing a round-the-clock computer system. This system linked the Caterpillar service shops around the country to the central mainframe, which stored critical technical information required to repair engines, including warranty reports and factory specifications. Operating 24 hours a day, seven days a week, the system speeded repairs, better satisfied customers, and enhanced Caterpillar's reputation.

General Electric's Advantage program provides dealers with such services as business revitalization loans, software to help manage the business, a store remodeling kit, and a customer education program. GE's consumer service division has an army of 1,500 service technicians who do in-home appliance repairs. They also set up an answer center; besides answering consumer telephone calls, the staff gathers information about products from callers, and this information may be taken into account in new product design.

Even small stores can develop a reputation for service, like Mitchells of Westport, a $15 million, upscale, family-owned-and-operated store in Connecticut. Mitchells employees call customers when new shipments arrive, set up appointments with customers, and have wardrobes ready and waiting when they arrive. Employees periodically check—on computer—their clients' purchase histories in order to anticipate their needs.

Jack Mitchell, the co-owner of Mitchells of Westport, is well aware of the value of customer service. "Without the total focus on extraordinary customer service, which has been the foundation of our business from the beginning, combined with the technology to track the spending patterns of our customers, our business may not have survived and subsequently thrived in this retail environment," he says.

There may not be anything terribly new in customer service, but the more you attend to the customer, the greater the chance this person becomes a repeat customer and spreads the word about a pleasant and productive shopping experience. Keep in mind that it is one-third as expensive to retain a customer as it is to attract a new one. The more you know about your customer, the better you can stock your stores. The more you know about your competition, the more you'll be equipped with the right stock and services.

Nordstrom is legendary for having smiling, knowledgeable, and independent-minded associates who go to great lengths to please. When Nordstrom moves into town, the competition trembles, reorganizes the sales staff, boosts advertising, and beefs up assortments.

When Wal-Mart moves in, small retailers are often driven out of business, but they can survive if they find something different to offer. It's not easy.

FIND POINTS OF DEPARTURE
TO BEAT THE COMPETITION

One discounter, Jamesway, planned to play up both its smaller stores (as more accessible and convenient for older customers) and its soft goods orientation (to combat the bigger and more hard goods–driven Wal-Mart). It wasn't enough; other problems such as lagging merchandising systems also dogged the business. Credit problems set in, and the chain was liquidated.

When Nordstrom opened in the Westchester Mall in White Plains, New York, it moved into Neiman Marcus and Saks Fifth Avenue country. Knowing the strength in designer merchandise that these other stores maintained, Nordstrom entered the market with unusual strength in children's wear, shoes, and menswear.

Consumer Research: The Door to New Opportunities

By examining point-of-sale purchasing data, you can learn what your customer is buying and trigger automatic stock replenishment. But these statistics don't necessarily tell you what the customer is buying elsewhere. That's why you have to talk to the customer directly and query suppliers to gather competitive information.

After Macy's went bankrupt, it did consumer and manufacturer surveys to see where the merchandising fell short. The research was something Macy's hadn't thought of doing in decades. The company learned it was missing a major opportunity in the moderate-priced apparel market, an area dominated by May Department Stores, JCPenney, Dillard Department Stores, and other competitors. Macy's proceeded to renew ties to important moderate vendors, such as Levi Strauss, and dropped expensive designer lines, which did more for window dressing than for generating sales.

Go beyond the Necessities: Entertain the Consumer

Retailers today regard a visit to the store more like entertainment such as going to the movies or theme restaurants. It's an experience that goes beyond just buying some necessities. In the past few years, retailers have incorporated into their stores a range of services to energize the atmosphere and put the fun back into retailing, such as espresso bars, beauty salons, and restaurants; appearances by designers, models, and celebrities; and private shopping nights, book signings, and interactive games.

Meanwhile, mall operators are enhancing their properties by renovating and expanding to attract the latest retail concepts and jazzing up the common areas with marble floors, Italian fountains, and a better breed of restaurant. Some even serve wine. Major regional malls across the country, including the two biggest in the East, King of Prussia, outside Philadelphia, and the Roosevelt Field Shopping Center in Garden City, Long Island, are leading the transformation.

Retailers and developers are seeking to lure a nation not particularly keen on letting go of its disposable dollars and are trying harder to be regarded as a form of recreation much like a social event or a family outing.

Again, Look to the Research

It's necessary to learn how consumers are spending so you can concentrate on redirecting those activities or feeding off them by offering displays, product concentrations, and special events. To help you get a handle on what the public is up to, information is available—and not just from consultants and market research firms that sell information, or consumer groups. And it's not the kind you necessarily have to dig for.

A journal called *American Demographics* offers reams of information about the population's behavior and habits. The Simmons Market Study examines portions of America's population and provides information about product preferences, demographics, and media preferences. Trade associations offer seminars and materials about consumer patterns, and the U.S. Commerce Department conducts research on consumer buying. Knowing how the wants and needs of the customer base are changing is critical to the development of a solid marketing plan.

The American Driver Shifts Gears

One of the keys to a successful marketing campaign is knowing your audience and finding the best way to appeal to its needs. But even after you have successfully reached that target audience, there is no guarantee that it will remain the same. Demographics and psychographics are in flux. Research needs to be reviewed constantly to evaluate—and perhaps redefine—your perception of the consumer's needs.

Look at the ways auto manufacturers have approached advertising since the beginning of the television age. TV has been the medium of choice for carmakers, who sponsored many of the first shows. The reasons are obvious—before consumers even consider such a large purchase, they want to take a good long look at it. That good look at the car itself has been the mainstay of most car commercials.

Until the 1980s, most car commercials looked essentially the same. They appealed to the man of the house (the one who traditionally decided on large purchases) and focused primarily on the year-to-year design changes. Notable exceptions to this were Volkswagen and Volvo, who recognized an opportunity to get into the American market by being different. At the time, American manufacturers snubbed their noses at these attempts, taking the position that Americans would always buy American cars. The lesson would soon come.

In the late 1970s, America changed dramatically. Gas became expensive, so the consumers' priorities shifted to fuel economy. As inflation, which drastically affected the price of a new car, spun out of control, the focus turned to quality and durability. Sharp rises in highway fatalities made safety an issue and so the attention shifted again. And finally, the demographics of the country were going through a radical transformation: The baby-boomer generation now represented the largest segment of car purchasers, and the American family no longer resembled the Donna Reed household. Women were fast becoming a large buying segment. The target audience no longer consisted only of married men; single people and single parents of both sexes were included as well.

American carmakers were slow to respond to these changes in their consumers' needs, while foreign carmakers—the Japanese, in particular—made major gains by being in sync with what the American buyer wanted in an automobile. Toyota burst on the scene by making a car that got great gas mileage; Subaru focused on durability, Volvo on safety. But American manufacturers maintained their strategy of selling cars on design alone and soon found themselves in the unenviable position of losing huge market share and having to play catch-up.

It wasn't until the 1980s, after doing extensive customer research and awakening to the realities of the times, that American carmakers really began to focus on what was important to the consumer. They had to convince the buying public that American cars were well made, economical, safe, and durable. "Made in America" had to take on a new meaning—one incorporating everything that mattered to its audience. And American automakers had an advantage: The foreign makers would never be able to use this strategy. Once the product was redesigned, "made in America" began to work for American carmakers.

Chevrolet's "Heartbeat of America" campaign exemplified this new strategy. It took a strong stance against imports by appealing to the great American ideal, showing automobile designs that catered to a broad range of American lifestyles. The campaign stressed that there was a Chevrolet for every American car buyer. Oldsmobile used a bold strategy that stated that this generation of Oldsmobile was a totally different car than the one you grew up with. Their campaign, "A New Generation of Olds," began with the line "This is not your father's Oldsmobile," making a reference to the new demographics of car buyers as well. The campaign used celebrities and their real-life children to illustrate this point.

American carmakers learned a tough lesson: Keeping track of your target market's changes through research is very important and must be an ongoing process.

Consider How the Company Is Managed

Is the company led by an entrepreneur who detects consumer trends and sets the direction for the company? Does it do things by the book, with decisions made from the top and handed down to be executed? Is top management open to suggestions from middle- and lower-level management or from customers? How well does management communicate internally and with the public? How well does the firm target market?

JCPenney gives its store managers some independence in ordering products, but the items are still chosen from the established master list. Macy's and Saks use the buyer-planner system: Buyers shop and determine the buy, while planners shape how the products get distributed to the stores by interpreting sales data and communicating with store and regional managers. Nordstrom has a regional buying network to help cater more completely to local tastes.

When Philip Miller became the chairman of Saks Fifth Avenue, Saks sources said he was involved in everything from buying decisions to advertising. He was all over the place, working harder than anyone. But Saks floundered. New strategies flopped. There were rumors, denied by Miller, that he was looking for a new job. As the company shifted priorities, with a goal to go public and improve the bottom line, Miller fought hard to make things work. He recruited, among others, a new president, Rose Marie Bravo, who had strong relationships in the market and an aggressive approach to making Saks the launchpad for new products. Soon, weak strategies were eliminated and Miller seemed to gain a grip on the management, by delegating more responsibility, and forged a clearer path for the company.

David Farrell, the chairman and CEO of May Department Stores, has always held a tight grip on management. He is said to rule with an iron fist and marinelike efficiency and maintain conservative, highly centralized merchandise strategies, all of which keeps costs low.

Indeed, management needs to blend its corporate policy with an effort at "thinking small," or considering what's really happening at the store level. No company is too big for that. Thinking small has been a concept espoused by Leslie H. Wexner, chairman and CEO of The Limited, who has boasted that his $8 billion company maintains a small corporate staff and a policy of encouraging divisions to act independently, without sharing information. However, that Chinese Wall has broken down on occasion when a division became troubled and Wexner and other corporate officials stepped in to correct problems.

Debt Can Be Death

Finally, the marketing plan should include an evaluation of the company's financial condition. The level of cash and credit available will dictate how quickly the company can react to external conditions, such as new strategies by competitors or a sudden turn in the economy, and whether it can quickly tap into the latest products on the market. Are you able to pay your suppliers on time? Can you meet your debt payments, or are your interest payments or payments on loans cutting into your ability to be responsive to customers? A burdensome debt position can be a fatal distraction in the life of a business. Olympia & York, a developer with a vision to create new financial centers, fell into bankruptcy after being drained by its Canary Wharf project in London and Britain's financial problems in the late 1980s. The company failed to correctly read the market.

Broadway Stores, once California's dominant department store chain, collapsed under the weight of debt stemming from takeover battles and the state's prolonged recession. It could never come up with the money to revitalize its tired, aging stores. In 1995, Federated Department Stores, seeking a vehicle to expand its Macy's and Bloomingdale's chains, smelled blood at The Broadway and took it over.

Ironically, four years before, Federated had plunged into its own bankruptcy after Robert Campeau, the Canadian developer, took over the chain in a highly leveraged buyout. Federated emerged from Chapter 11 bankruptcy in 1992.

Enormous interest payments can result in a highly leveraged company sinking under the weight of its debt. With $250 million in debt, Furr's/Bishops, a cafeteria chain, had to give up 97.5 percent of the company to its creditors to avoid going into bankruptcy in 1995 after defaulting on payments. Its $23 million annual interest payment chewed up the company's cash flow and the ability to expand or renovate its restaurants.

Remember, the financial condition is but one important element in the business summary. An enormous debt load can sidetrack a company from the right path set by the marketing plan.

2 | Positioning the Company

"I just love these executive committee meetings."

◆ ◆

NO MATTER HOW GOOD YOU THINK YOU ARE and no matter how well you think you know what's good for your company, there will come a time when you experience a rude awakening. And while you may come away from it feeling like you've just been fed to the lions, always view it as a learning experience.

I experienced this firsthand in 1979 when I was the vice president of marketing for Macy's New York. Direct mail and direct marketing were taking off in a big way around the country, and I was assigned to develop a master plan for breaking out a separate mail-order business and getting Macy's into the act. I was young, eager, and ambitious and I knew this was my chance to make my mark. Unfortunately, in my enthusiasm, I failed to do my homework. I came up with a pie-in-the-sky proposal with unrealistic goals and a major advertising and marketing strategy based on little research.

So when I delivered my proposal to Art Reiner, then Macy's New York CEO, he quickly set me straight—in front of the entire executive committee. He told me I wasn't prepared. He was right. I failed to address the current state of the merchandise, stocking appropriate inventory, servicing the mail and phone customer, and discovering what the competition was doing. He said to start all over.

Beaten and bruised, I returned to the drawing board. But this time, I started by doing my homework. I spoke with buyers, department heads, vendors, experts in mail and phone ordering, companies that were successful in these areas, and companies that flopped. Now I had the hard facts and figures and was ready to re-present to Reiner. My rude awakening became a valuable lesson.

In this chapter, you'll learn about the value of assembling information to assess the state of your company and conducting that so-called "situational analysis." It sets a foundation for change to propel your company in the marketplace.

◆ ◆

IS IT THE MESSAGE OR THE MESSENGER?

Call it a case of advertising agita. The message is dull, lacks impact, and does not generate incremental business. No one takes notice. The same lackluster sketches appear week after week, month after month, accompanied by mundane, ledgerlike lists of prices and items. The image sinks into the morass of competitive advertising clutter. Business is slow and something must be done.

Now consider this: These faceless, lifeless media messages may be the least of your worries for the moment. Before doctoring the ads, more comprehensive surgery may be required. A complete diagnosis must come first. Digging right into the advertising would be satisfying, but that's like applying a tourniquet to an external wound when there's internal bleeding. It's a common trap.

Businesses can retool only after conducting a situational analysis—a thorough examination of strengths, weaknesses, opportunities, and threats, known as the SWOT evaluation. It aids in determining how to accomplish your marketing, advertising, and financial objectives in your current competitive surroundings.

Examine the Company's Condition

A detailed examination of your company—its past and present status and goals and an environmental scanning for opportunities and competitive threats—will provide an understanding of the business from an insider's point of view and that of customers and competitors. It's like taking stock of what you have currently and assessing what you could have. This means more than just counting the stock keeping units (skus) and adding up the assets. It means thoroughly examining what it's all worth and what it stands for. What about intangibles, such as goodwill and public image? Is the company community-conscious, concerned about the environment, the handicapped, the future of education? Or are profits the only concern?

Frederick's of Hollywood: The Show Must Go On

From fiscal year 1993 to 1994, retail store sales at Frederick's of Hollywood declined 1.1 percent to $72.4 million from $73.2 million. After examining the disappointing numbers, the consulting firm of Levy, Kerson, Aronson & Associates undertook research on behalf of Frederick's to learn why the stores were slipping.

The major objectives were to determine whether Frederick's stores had reached maturity, whether shopper attitudes had shifted and consumers were less interested in Frederick's lingerie, whether the competition had intensified, and whether there were weaknesses and opportunities at Frederick's.

The Big Survey

Levy developed a seven-page questionnaire that took about a half hour to fill out. A professional field service team intercepting shoppers in 16 Frederick's stores in malls around the country distributed 4,600 questionnaires. Of those, 1,239 usable questionnaires, or 27 percent, were returned. As an inducement, each survey included a dollar bill. Levy also sent follow-up postcards reminding people to return the questionnaires, which helped in getting the high response.

Many questions were asked to measure perceptions of merchandise, quality, and prices (among other issues) at Frederick's stores and those of the competition. Levy also conducted interviews with top Frederick's merchants, including the chairperson, the head of stores, senior buyers, and suppliers. Consultants worked under cover in the stores, watching how customers were serviced and seeing how merchandise was displayed.

All the Results: The Good, the Bad, and the Sexy

The following positive conclusions were drawn: Frederick's was not a mature business and still had room to grow, and Frederick's of Hollywood was still the best place for sexy, fun, lacy, and revealing lingerie with a distinctive, racy point of view.

However, it was also learned that Frederick's was not well merchandised. Frederick's viewpoint was being co-opted by the competition, including JCPenney, May Department Stores, and Victoria's Secret. In response, Frederick's worked up even more extreme merchandise looks. Levy also discovered that Frederick's got a lot of browsers who weren't converted to shoppers and that Frederick's needed larger stores to sell lingerie-influenced sportswear, large sizes, and mainstream looks, including bra and panty sets.

Frederick's needed to seize upon trends. It covered the trends but didn't capitalize on them. For example, it sold push-up bras long before the competition but didn't promote them enough and didn't make the category into an everyday business. The research indicated that the chain needed to consider more advertising to bolster categories with greater volume potential. Frederick's was overlooking margin and sales opportunities and, too often, "The company was more reactive than proactive," says Marian Henneman, a senior consultant at Levy. "It recycled old looks."

Frederick's Future

Based on these conclusions, Frederick's embarked on some new strategies. It started seeking stores with more space than the existing 1,200-square-foot units and created a plan to get most units to include more than 2,000 square feet by the year 2000. That would enable the chain to make stronger fashion statements and project the trends.

In addition, Frederick's hired a director of design, strengthened the merchandising staff, and subscribed to a trend service. As the survey concluded, "Despite heavy competitive pressures, external trends are basically favorable to Frederick's. . . . Over the past decade, society as a whole became more receptive to sexy lingerie and in that sense Frederick's market potential has expanded. . . . The business is mature only from the standpoint of the limitations imposed by the retail space and merchandising approach."

DON'T LET PROBLEMS FESTER

Typically, such assessments aren't made, or are made too late, in the heat of a corporate crisis. Today, corporations operate in an era of accountability, heightening the need for self-evaluation. Shareholder groups are active, Wall Street demands short-term gains or downgrades the stock, and consumer groups boycott companies that violate their ethical concerns. These groups have the power to send your company into a tailspin. Businesses turn on perceptions. Credit lines can quickly dry up. Merchandise can go stale in a matter of weeks.

CEOs Driven out of Office

Often, companies bite the bullet under intense outside pressures and after problems fester for too long. In August of 1994, Connor, Clark & Co., a Canadian investment house holding a major stake in Greyhound, publicly called for the ouster of Frank J. Schneider, the CEO of the bus service. In less than a week, he was out. His management was criticized for having too little experience and doing little for the stock. He cut costs but could not get the buses to arrive on time or enough people to ride them. Stockholders and passengers were also upset that many routes and destinations had been dropped.

In February 1995, the board at Morrison Knudsen Corporation, the construction and engineering firm, finally tossed out chairperson, CEO, and president William Agee after years of lackluster results and a catastrophic $300 million loss in 1994 stemming from cost overruns on railcar contracts. Agee had been accused of corporate excesses and pressure was mounting from both lenders (threatening not to renew credit agreements) and shareholders (threatening lawsuits).

It's Never Too Late for a Comeback

Union Carbide is an example of another company that had to bite the bullet but managed to pull off a dramatic long-term comeback. A methyl isocyanate leak in one of its plants led to the 1984 disaster in Bhopal, India, which killed 3,000 people. After accumulating a mountain of insurance and legal problems and costs, the company was threatened by takeovers and was forced to buy its own stock to avoid getting gobbled up. That increased the debt beyond manageability, so the company sold off some of its best products, including Eveready batteries and Prestone antifreeze, cutting the company's sales nearly in half. It spun off what it considered all noncore businesses, drastically cut employment, and focused on becoming strictly a low-cost chemical and polymer producer.

Wang Laboratories was a giant in the computer industry throughout much of the 1970s and early 1980s. The company, however, overlooked the rising use of personal computers, stubbornly refused to have its hardware and software made compatible with those of its competitors, and lagged in an industry changing at an accelerating pace. As a result, revenues plummeted, cash flow deteriorated, and new management was brought in to reinvent the company. The ax fell on thousands of employees, pieces of the business were sold off to reduce debt, and strategic changes were implemented. Most notably, a plan was implemented to market IBM hardware and concentrate on software and integrating capability—major changes from the past. A trimmed company with new directions resulted in better financial results, and bankruptcy was averted.

Survival of the Nimble

Corporate survival hinges on determining strengths, playing them to the maximum, and responding to the competition's strengths and weaknesses. A differential advantage or competitive advantage is the "distinct competency" of a business over its competitors. A company can distinguish itself in delivery and home installation; train customers to operate computers, power tools, or VCRs; teach customers how to build wardrobes; and show unique product usages and other services that cater to the target market. In the near future, customers will flock to a sporting goods center that sells running shoes, provides a schedule of local races, and gives tips on interesting running routes. Companies that go beyond just selling a product—those that sell a lifestyle—win out in the long run.

The cable TV industry has attempted to portray itself as a lifestyle choice with an advertising campaign touting the benefits of cable, the future of cable technology, and the potential of interactive cable TV. The campaign used the tag line, "Cable TV. More than a wire." Rayovac, the battery company, has used lifestyle advertising by depicting real family situations, such as children wearing in-line skates using the batteries to recharge their boom boxes. And Motorola has used the lifestyle theme to pitch its computer chips with the tag line, "Products powered by Motorola are fast becoming a way of life."

In discounting, several regional chains, even those with $1 billion or more in annual sales, have crumbled under the clout of Wal-Mart and Target. Chains such as Venture, Caldor, and Bradlees have scrambled for new strategies to offer customers a reason to shop them rather than the national giants, and in several cases, they have chosen apparel as the answer. Wal-Mart, aware of the competition, responded in spring 1995 by launching its own Kathie Lee line of sportswear. The line is positioned prominently, near the entrances, with big photos of Kathie Lee Gifford flagging the goods.

What is so unique about a company that it seduces customers off their armchairs and into the aisles? It's a matter of providing entertainment; filling needs; and offering value, service, and fast and efficient checkout lines. The three busiest stores in Manhattan in 1995 were Warner Brothers Studio, Century 21, and Old Navy. Warner Brothers keeps the entertainment level high with bold visuals, fun items, and interactive elements, appealing to both kids and parents. Century 21 consistently offers deep discounts on designer goods and the thrill of a bargain. People don't mind braving the crowded aisles if they can unearth a real bargain. Old Navy opened in early November, and was superhyped by its parent corporation, The Gap. Lots of curious shoppers were anxious to check its low prices, warehouse-style trappings, and clever displays.

Sears Solves Its Problems: Showing Its Softer Side

Sears, after years of complacency, finally took stock of itself and devised a sweeping plan of action, probably averting a financial crisis. Once the nation's largest and most dominant retailer, Sears found itself in the 1980s in third position behind Wal-Mart and Kmart, lacking identity and languishing in poor profits and sales. Other chains were more aggressive in seeking identity and expanding profits.

A Changing of the Board

It's 1992. Sears's board decides changes are overdue and hires Arthur Martinez, a Saks Fifth Avenue vice chairman, as chief executive to overhaul the business. The choice is considered surprising since Martinez is a financial executive, not a merchant (although creativity is often more about intellectual innovation than artistic flair). He considers the assignment "the opportunity of a lifetime." While he doesn't pick the products, he confidently sets the new strategy.

Says Martinez:

> When I became chairman and CEO of the Sears Merchandise Group in 1992, we quickly examined every facet of our operations and developed five strategic initiatives:

- To focus on our core businesses—apparel, home, and auto-motive—where a winning strategy was already in place or where such an advantage could be developed. These three core businesses were found in department stores located in many of the best malls throughout the country.

- To make our stores attractive and a more compelling place to shop. To accomplish this, we allocated $4 billion over five years to renovate our mall-based stores.

- To become more locally market-focused in terms of our product and service mix. When customers walked into Sears, we wanted each of them to feel that the store was "built just for me."

- To reduce our overall costs at every level throughout the orga-nization.

- And, finally, to create a new culture and set of values to lead us into the future. This meant an environment entirely focused on and driven to serve the customer.

Along with these initiatives, we closely examined our target customer. To the surprise of many, it was not a 45-year-old man shopping in our hardware department. It was a woman of the American family. She more than likely has children and owns a house. The family's annual income ranges from $25,000 to $60,000. As the financial gatekeeper of the family, *she* serves as its chief financial officer and primary purchasing agent.

She was responsible for 96 percent of the purchases of women's apparel, 94 percent of children's apparel, and 65 per-cent of men's wear. She was the primary influence in 88 percent of home fashion purchases, 70 percent of appliances, and even 38 percent and 36 percent of home improvement and automo-tive products, respectively.

Martinez promises that this woman will soon shop for herself at Sears, as well as for her family. The next step: Martinez announces the shutdown of the 105-year-old Sears catalog, figuring a turnaround of the "big book" is impossible. Sears also sheds disparate businesses including Coldwell Banker real estate and Dean Witter financial, since Sears stores are bringing down the value of these other businesses. Scores of weak Sears stores are closed and 49,900 jobs cut, while 10,000 full-timers are put on the selling floors. Morale at Sears increases as things change, and public perception of a once-lumbering chain improves.

Martinez recruits Robert Mettler, a former May Company executive and solid moderate merchant, to be president, and John Costello, former president of Nielsen Marketing Research, to be senior executive vice president and general manager of marketing. By the time the dust settles, 44 percent of management at the executive level is new. District offices and regional offices are also greatly changed.

A Changing of the Merchandise

The company moves beyond basic commodity items—the predictable polyester pull-on pants and drab housedresses—and shifts into well-priced knockoffs. As part of its new fashion appeal, Sears creates $26 acrylic sweaters actually copied from $300 European cable knits. Trading up also means putting linings in $30 linen jackets, which a year before would have been $20 and unlined. The linoleum is ripped off from the selling floors and carpeting is laid down; better goods should be displayed in a more flattering environment.

Furniture is removed from core stores and sold through separate specialty chains, opening space to reintroduce cosmetics and expand women's apparel and accessories. Career wear rises from 25 percent of the sportswear total to 40 percent, petite sizes are rolled out aggressively, and more brands are sought. There are difficulties landing new labels; however, Sears carries Lee, Dockers, Levi Strauss, and Gloria Vanderbilt, among others. The strategy: Those who shopped Sears for hard goods should also shop Sears for soft goods. At the time the new strategy was adopted, only 18 percent of Sears's customers were purchasing in more than one department.

A Changing of the Image

By making the hard choices, Sears is poised in September 1993 to launch its "softer side" advertising, a $40 million campaign emphasizing the new Sears and beginning a four-year effort to boost apparel sales to 40 percent of total volume. Sears puts the apparel account up for review in January of that year and Wells Rich Green, Hal Riney & Partners,

Saatchi & Saatchi, and Ogilvy & Mather, which had been doing the Sears merchandise campaign, vie for it.

Martinez, Mettler, and Costello select Young & Rubicam to launch the campaign, based on Young & Rubicam's strength in research and media planning. The campaign breaks in fall 1993 and hits TV in September 1994. Sears decides to increase the apparel ad budget by 20 percent and shift a bigger proportion to TV and radio and away from print. TV ads kick off during an Emmy Awards telecast on ABC and coincide with two-page ads in Sunday magazine sections of major newspapers, including the *New York Times,* the *Chicago Tribune,* and the *Los Angeles Times.* TV spots show women in Sears outfits and play a jingle with the "come see the softer side" message.

The print ads, which appear in about 15 women's fashion and decorating magazines, take a similar tack, pitching Sears as a store that sells more than hard goods. One page shows a car battery and reads "I came for a Diehard"; the facing page displays a model in an alluring black evening dress, saying, "And left with something drop dead." Another two-page truck, or spread, reads, "I found something to help my 2-year-old go to sleep," and on the next page a model in a silky chemise and robe, saying, "And something to keep my 40-year-old awake."

Martinez says,

> The campaign was an immediate success. It was arresting, inviting, and compelling, but it also was a risk for Sears. While we had made significant improvements in our apparel assortments, quality, price, and fashion levels, we had just begun our store renovation program. The key question was whether to start the campaign as early as possible—while most stores had yet to be remodeled—or wait until our new apparel presentations were in place. To move our transformation forward in the eyes of our customer, the campaign was launched.
>
> We believe that the image campaign is continuing to change consumer perceptions. This is evidenced by our apparel's 6.8 percent comparable store sales growth in 1995, for example, versus about half of that for a peer group of apparel retailers.
>
> Not only did it create a positive impression among our target customers; it also was quickly adopted by the entire Sears or-

ganization as the anthem for the company's transformation. So successful was the "soft side" campaign, that we borrowed the upbeat feel and tempo of the television spots to develop our whole-house campaign highlighting the "many sides of Sears."

BLUNDERS BY THE BIG BOYS

Once you have identified your strengths, you need to face your weaknesses. Your customers know what your weaknesses are, but they'll shop your business despite them. The weaknesses are well-known by your competitors because they use your weaknesses to sell against you. Once you have identified your trouble spots, you can work at improvements. Strengths will keep some customers returning, but a combination of improving strengths and diminishing weaknesses is a significant proactive position.

The fashion and retail industries play up their strengths and positive sides—store openings, new collections, product launches. Then they try to sweep under the rug the dark sides—store closings, layoffs, discontinued merchandise, and poor quality. Misfires in the 1980s and 1990s have become commonplace, and mistakes are becoming less transparent.

A Macy's Mess

For decades, the strength of Macy's Herald Square was in being all things for all people, attracting wide audiences with big inventories. In the late 1980s after expansions and debt concerns, however, Macy's selling floors became confusing and unproductive, and you had to cover a lot of ground to find what you wanted. Sensing a store in disarray, management in 1995 took the first steps in reorganizing the store and decided to put weight behind some key areas and drop others. Out went pricey designer merchandise and in came a new beefed-up contemporary department with 15,000 square feet. It included several lines from the West Coast at better and upper-moderate prices. The idea was to tell shoppers that Macy's stood for something, and the message was supported through new advertising in the *New York Times, New York* magazine, fashion shows on the floor, and direct mail. They're trying to make it work.

The French Faux Pas

Galeries Lafayette, the Paris-based department store chain, flopped when it opened its first and only store in the United States, moving into Trump Tower and trying to compete with Bergdorf's, Henri Bendel, Bloomingdale's, and Saks Fifth Avenue. It never delivered the excitement of its Paris emporium nor could it find a niche in New York's fashion circle. It scored best on opening day with its free croissants and subsequently by selling cappuccino and T-shirts to tourists, while the unique French secondary designer lines languished on the racks. Corporate losses were blamed on the New York store, marking a setback for Galeries's overseas ambitions.

Penney's Pulls the Plug

JCPenney was ahead of the game when it developed a home shopping channel on cable TV in the early 1980s, but the company invested millions more than it had expected, experienced technology problems, and got a poor response from the test market in Chicago. It eventually pulled the plug on the project.

Herald Center Heralded

New York City's Herald Center was hailed by city officials as the multi-level mall of the future when it opened in the 1980s on the site of a former Korvette's store with a flashy assortment of unique better specialty shops. The mall missed its market. Shoppers were looking for something more moderate and more familiar, like The Gap. The mall was also poorly designed in a city where vertical retailing has never caught on.

Proact, Don't React

When Bloomingdale's opened a store in the Roosevelt Field Shopping Center in Garden City, New York, in 1995 to replace one that had closed nearby, the new unit had about 40 percent more sales staff. The strategy was to win over customers right from the outset, though some thought the move was a preemptive strike against Nordstrom, which was soon to become Bloomingdale's neighbor in Roosevelt Field. Bloomingdale's denied the beefed-up service was a response to Nordstrom and claimed they would have done it anyway.

In the nineties, a wave of new discounters including Bradlees and Filene's Basement moved into New York City. Kmart is also planning to open on 34th Street. Conway, a local discounter with a strong presence in the 34th Street midtown area, responded by remodeling sites, stepping out with new ads on buses and in the stores featuring model Veronica Webb, and taking a higher profile after years of anonymity amid the budget market.

Thus, a company's strengths and weaknesses seem to rise to the surface when competition appears on the horizon. Then it's time to pose the question, What can be done to meet the new challenge?

Don't Overlook the Obvious

Don't minimize the power of observation. To learn more about your company, pick out some items and stand in a checkout line. Ask a sales associate about a sale, a discount, an item, fabric content, or perhaps a service—such as a refund or home delivery—and observe the reactions of your staff. This is market research.

Other forms of observation can be mechanical. These include video cameras that record shopping and service behavior and the flow of traffic. Note which areas draw shoppers and which are overlooked.

You can also tape-record your operators to evaluate their selling style and shop by catalog to see how operators at your competitors handle an order. Lands' End, the catalog company, gets kudos from customers for its helpful order takers. If a customer calls to order an item and it is no longer available or is only available in other sizes, the telemarketer often goes the extra yard. The telemarketer might know or find out about upcoming catalogs that could feature the same merchandise.

When surveying by mail or in person, customers should be queried on the strengths and weaknesses of your business.

ANALYSIS OF PRESENT ADVERTISING

Just as there were several preliminary steps to follow in producing a marketing strategy, there are several preparatory actions that must be performed to develop a clear, concise, well-defined, and focused advertising strategy that is part of the total marketing program. The first step is to conduct a situational analysis of present advertising. At a minimum, this should be done annually, but it can be conducted as frequently as once a month to understand where money is spent and how wisely it is being used. Certainly, internal accounting records will indicate the amount of money spent on each type of advertising.

Don't ignore outside support such as clipping services and market research firms. They can provide copies of your ads and those of the competition and help in defining and evaluating the competitive differences. The goal is to reach your target market through the selected media with coordinated, powerful messages that create and build an image and induce the customer to buy your products or services.

Review previous advertising campaigns to understand how target markets have responded to a variety of ads in the past. Often the best predictor of future behavior is recent past behavior. The recent responses of customers to advertising messages and images will serve as effective guides to the new or updated focus of your advertising campaign.

BEYOND THE THREATS: OPPORTUNITIES

Once you have a clear picture of the company's strengths and weaknesses, consider the competitive environment. What threats do you see on the horizon? Now is the time to scan the competitive environment for actions that could be harmful to your firm. What is happening to your competitors? What does McDonald's notice about Burger King? That their smaller rival has been grabbing a lot of the youth market by tying in with Disney animated movies, including *Toy Story, Pocahontas,* and *Beauty and the Beast.* Burger King restaurants sell dolls and puppets of characters from the movies, thereby promoting the Disney projects and ringing up more burger sales. Previously, McDonald's worked with Disney on rereleases of old classic animation features, and it's expected that McDonald's, with its heavier marketing budget, may lay down some big McBucks to realign with Disney on future releases.

Malls also fight for market share and must be aware of what's happening in the market. That landscape is rarely stable. Turnover is steady and there's always one company ready to move into someone's turf or fill the space vacated by another company. Until the late 1980s, Long Island was dominated by a handful of malls including Roosevelt Field, Green Acres, the Americana, Walt Whitman, Sunrise Mall, and the Miracle Mile shopping strip. Since then, the scene has become crowded. Roosevelt Field Shopping Center, the second largest mall in the East, is renovating and expanding to become a destination much like King of Prussia, the largest mall in the East.

The mall's redevelopment was sparked by the area's explosion in discount shopping in just about all product categories. Roosevelt Field saw the threat to its business and had three choices: do nothing and hope for the best, lease space to discounters to complement its array of regular-priced stores and compete head-to-head with nearby discounters, or go upscale, which they did. So far the decision has paid off: Roosevelt has successfully attracted new anchor stores and boutiques for its added shopping levels.

Banana Republic grew big by promoting the safari look for urban customers seeking casual clothes, but the khaki look became ubiquitous, was widely knocked off, and eventually played itself out. Banana then began marketing suits, soaps, shoes, and career clothes, along with its original casual line, all at better prices. Hess's Department Stores, which started as a concession in the lobby of the Black Bear Hotel in Allentown, Pennsylvania, developed into a department store that converted the hotel to selling space, was taken over by a real estate developer, and grew into a major mid-Atlantic chain. In the end, overexpansion and recessionary times drove it out of business.

Seize the Moment

Now is the time to define what situations to respond to easily and quickly by constantly scanning the environment, looking for information about technology, culture, society, government, the economy, and customers. Watch for news about these topics in newspapers, magazines, and trade journals; on television; by listening to employees; through accounting and financial reports; and by keeping abreast of what's happening around the world and where the opportunities lie. Construct and maintain a daily information-gathering program.

MASTERMINDING THE STORE

Donna Karan: Crossing New Borders

It's 1994, and the U.S. market is turning its nose up at designer clothes. Donna Karan is ready for greener pastures. Tensions are growing with her partners, Tomio Taki and Frank Mori; reports from U.S. department stores are proliferating about late deliveries and weak sell-throughs (sales results); an initial public offering never gets off the ground.

On October 6, Donna Karan enters the DKNY flagship on Old Bond Street in London. The grand opening is tomorrow, but it's a soft opening: no big bash is planned. However, there is still enormous press, since the opening coincides with fashion-show week in London.

"This is Donna's vision," says Stephan Weiss, her husband and partner, business adviser, and asset protector. "It's always been, from before we even opened the doors in the U.S. in 1985; growing internationally has been a strategic goal."

"It's a straight extension of our U.S. strategy," adds Stephen Ruzow, president of Donna Karan. "We see it as a major opportunity."

Though it is heavily U.S.-oriented, the goal of the company is to have a third of its volume in Europe, a third in North and South America, and a third in Asia. DKNY's competition seems less fierce in Europe.

For 1995, the company sees $150 million in overseas volume out of $500 million in total wholesale sales, of which 71 percent is from the United States. Eleven percent is done in Japan, 4 percent elsewhere in the Far East, 10 percent in Europe, and 3 percent in other countries. The Karan team believes the European market has more designer growth potential than the United States does.

Karan's approach to overseas marketing is different from that of most other apparel firms. Though the company's retail stores are licensed, its merchandise is not. "The industry approach is mainly through licensing," Ruzow says. "We chose not to do that. We have a very tight distribution philosophy which keeps the product in demand. DKJapan has now made us the single largest American vendor there that is not licensed or done through joint ventures."

The organization continues to aggressively pursue growth opportunities abroad, undaunted by its 1994 problems. In April 1995, the company announces a joint venture with Hotel Properties Ltd., a billion-dollar holding company headquartered in Singapore, which invests $21 million in Donna Karan Japan, a subsidiary formed in 1992. The

36

purpose is to accelerate growth in Asia from China to South Korea and to establish a network of 29 freestanding Donna Karan and DKNY shops.

"Account executives are constantly traveling between internal markets, throughout Europe and Asia. We are determined to seize this international opportunity," Ruzow says.

THE RIGHT CORPORATE CULTURE TO MOVE AHEAD

Innovation or Status Quo

A business is more than just sales and profits, products and personnel. There is a certain mood, management style, set of standards, and manner of communicating among employees, which collectively form the corporate culture.

At one end of the culture spectrum is the May Department Stores, which is ruled by organizational flow charts, bureaucracy, and adherence to the dictates of the CEO. Its department stores are run by the numbers and the matrix system, where the display and distribution of a brand are determined by rigid sell-through, margin, and turnover targets. It's never fashion first.

At the other end of the spectrum is Ben & Jerry's, a company known for encouraging risk taking, employee empowerment, an open-door policy of communication between upper and lower tiers, goal setting, creativity, and the establishment of a set of values.

Ben Cohen and Jerry Greenfield, founders of Ben & Jerry's ice-cream company, have developed a reputation for listening to employees. When owners of franchise shops told them how yogurt shops were stealing their customers, Ben and Jerry added yogurt to the menu and retained many customers.

Ben & Jerry's also listens to customers to determine what flavors they want and whether they like the new flavors being tested. In addition, the company has encouraged customers to support causes and charities that the company donates to. For example, Ben & Jerry's prints on the ice-cream containers the 800 numbers of organizations that help children in trouble or give information on how to help save the rain forests.

The company's philosophy is to build a charitable, capitalist organization that supports environmental and social causes and to gain a lot of media attention and goodwill along the way. Getting customers involved with the company makes them feel good about buying the product.

Another great example of how corporate culture allows ideas to flow from the bottom up (from employees to management) exists in Phoenix at the Childress Buick auto dealership. It was an employee's idea to hook up nine-volt batteries to dashboard cigarette lighters so that when the engine battery has to be replaced, programmed radio stations aren't lost. This saves the car owners a lot of frustration when they get their cars back and turn on the radio. Another idea that sprang from an employee suggestion was to have a video player and popcorn in the dealership's customer lounge.

At Childress, employees are encouraged—through an employee manual on "quality customer care"—to come up with ideas and to exchange them in a monthly newsletter, in e-mail to colleagues, by contributing to suggestion boxes (the ideas are stored on computer and a team acts on them), and at town hall meetings held four times a year.

Employees get to know each other and learn about each other's needs on the job. For example, the body shop crew knows the sales reps and tells them about potential customers for new cars.

IBM is another company that's known for encouraging employee ideas that improve service and, ultimately, the bottom line. The company has given out cash awards ranging from $50 to $150,000, depending on how valuable the idea was. The goal is to improve customer satisfaction by giving all employees incentive to find ways to improve the business. In 1990, IBM reportedly paid out $20 million for suggestions that led to more than eight times that amount in savings.

Lexmark, a laser printer manufacturer that spun off from IBM, took the suggestion-box concept in a different direction. Rather than paying employees for ideas, it solicited ideas from workers at team meetings. If those ideas translated into better company performance, workers received stock options and bonuses.

Successful companies with a healthy culture often bear rich histories and stories about great leaders and people who made a difference. There's a mystique or unusual quality about the company leaders.

Stories abound about the late Frieda Loehmann, founder of Loehmann's, who pioneered the off-price business by going door to door making deals with Seventh Avenue designers and manufacturers to sell the best labels at a discount to the masses. Allen I. Questrom, the magnetic and sociable CEO of Federated, has re-created the company from a grouping of independent-minded store divisions to a centralized retail machine to establish Macy's and Bloomingdale's as national department store chains and has recruited several colleagues from his past to build a new team for the mission.

Says Robert Kerson, the executive search consultant, "Corporate culture really reflects the attitude and will of the chief executive officer." These are people on a mission that goes beyond just delivering profits. It's a mission that sets a tone to a company, brings something new into the world, and grabs market share from others. At the same time, it unites the organization and stimulates creativity. There's a spirit that permeates. Workers who are proud of their jobs buy into the corporate culture, deliver a better product, and are more productive. Your corporate culture will flow down to your employees, who need to be considered as part of the response to customers and the threats of competitors or idiosyncrasies.

Exxon found out about corporate culture the hard way, after a catastrophic tanker spill in Prince William Sound. The oil company did plenty to clean up the mess, but its employees didn't project to the public a perception that Exxon sincerely cared about the environment. The right employee culture and camaraderie were not in place. The result: thousands of credit card customers cut up their cards in disgust.

Use good intuition to determine the best corporate culture for you, your team, your customers, and your product. Rely on your own sound instincts and judgment. You don't need a management consultant to tell time with your own watch.

3 | Know Your Consumer and Competitor before Writing the Game Plan

"That's <u>not</u> what I meant by getting to know your customers better!"

◆ ◆

OKAY, YOU'VE THOROUGHLY RESEARCHED and reacquainted yourself with your company. Now it's time to make that top-to-bottom examination of the customer and the competition. Meet them head-on, face to face, to move beyond your four walls.

Nine times out of ten, when I analyze the customer and the competition, I learn something I didn't know before—something that proves crucial in the planning. When my agency worked for Seaman's Furniture, our task was to develop marketing plans and a new image for television advertising. The chain was in Chapter 11 bankruptcy and an image overhaul was desperately needed as part of the recovery. We (and Seaman's) were positive that Levitz was the biggest competitor. However, when we conducted exit surveys—at five key stores on two occasions—we discovered that Huffman Koos and numerous local specialty furniture stores ranked much higher among consumers than any of us had thought. We were also surprised that customers were driven much more by style and quality than by price alone.

These findings led us to significantly upscale our creative approach. Quality and style became larger components of our advertising story. As a result, Seaman's image changed and customers viewed the store in a different light. Sales recovered, Seaman's emerged from Chapter 11 and went public, and we were gratified that in our planning, we revisited a landscape that we thought we knew. We started all over again, threw out our misconceptions, and came up with a fresh approach.

As this chapter delineates, there's more to just meeting and greeting customers, sizing them up, and suggesting a few colors and styles. Your mission is to discern their spirit and mind-set, to learn what items they buy from you and the competition, and to discover the essence of the competition. Your goal? To develop a new perspective on customers.

◆ ◆

BABY BOOMERS AND THEIR NEW VALUES

How fast time travels. Baby boomers, those born between 1946 and 1964, have begun to turn 50. This has profound implications for marketers of all types. First, this country is aging as a whole, but it's a more educated, more activist, more active, healthier, more cynical, and more selfish population—the "me" generation of ex-hippies with shorter hair and families to take care of—that's creeping up on the nation. Marketers had better reach out beyond the youth culture.

"Future shock" is upon us, technology keeps accelerating, and life revolves around the home: working there, at the home computer, and entertaining there, in front of the home entertainment center. Family relationships are being altered, as more time is spent together. Those who survived the drug- and love-happy 1960s are protective of their families and are instilling more traditional values. Lives are more intertwined as family comes first, jobs come second. Careers are important, but as a means to provide for the family rather than for self-gratification and aggrandizement.

The New Family Spirit

Companies are tapping into the new family spirit with advertising spots depicting sentimental moments at home. Cotton Inc., for example, depicts the special dinner—with Dad putting on a tuxedo, presumably for a wedding, and the kids watching in awe. Then comes the voice-over: "Life moves too fast. Sometimes you have to tell yourself to stop, look around. This is the good stuff. This is the fabric of our lives. This is cotton." Cotton Inc.'s ads, created by Ogilvy & Mather, were shown during the '96 Summer Olympics in Atlanta and at major movie premieres and TV concerts such as Barbra Streisand's—all programs potentially drawing full family viewing.

Goody's, the Knoxville, Tennessee–based chain, also tapped into the family spirit with a new advertising campaign in 1995 that stressed Goody's as a family store, offering name-brand assortments and everyday low prices. TV ads featured a country-style jingle, "Feels good, feels true, Goody's feels like you."

It's big in the fragrance industry, too. Markets are selling memory lane, not sex. The Fragrance Foundation sponsored an ad campaign for the industry that, like Cotton Inc.'s, was built on wholesome, nostalgia-filled scenes at home.

People are looking for stability, something to hang onto, and are tired of "trend overload," the blitz of styles saturating the marketplace and stores, coming and going at warp speed. Casual for the workplace, Friday wear, streetwear, pouf skirts, the sixties look, the Jackie O. look. Pick a decade, it's in the stores, and in a couple of months, it's nowhere to be found. The consumer is understandably confused.

Talbots: In Touch with Tradition

"Focus," says Arnold Zetcher. That's the word he's been repeating since he became Talbots chairman and CEO in 1988, and it is his mantra for success in retailing—and for not confusing customers. "At Talbots, being focused and staying focused is the core of our management approach," Zetcher says. "First, we work very hard at knowing who our customer is and what she expects from us, and then we channel all our efforts into meeting her expectations. That intense focus on the customer is what makes a specialty store special.

"To stay focused, a company has to be able to answer two questions: who are you and who is your customer," Zetcher explains. "At Talbots, we know we are the headquarters for classic women's apparel and that our customer is an educated, affluent, and typically a professional woman over the age of 25. Therefore, every decision we make, in every area of our company, is based on those facts. If you can't clearly answer those two questions, you have no context to evaluate your decisions and goals."

At the opening of Manhattan's first Talbots Kids & Babies store, on the northwest corner of Second Avenue and 79th Street, on a torrid August day in 1995, Zetcher described the chain's latest concept as an extension of the Talbots formula, which stays clear of whirlwind fashion trends. Just like Talbots women's stores, the kids' stores focus on the classics: enduring, traditional looks that don't play off fads. Talbots, the Hingham, Massachusetts–based specialty chain, remains in its own world of classic wool blazers, blue suits, long pleated skirts, long floral dresses, turtlenecks, and white cardigans, never straying from its conservative, New England roots.

The new kids' stores follow the tradition. It's the kind of store that excites parents more than children. There's no Mickey Mouse, Power Ranger, or Pocahontas clothes, no licensed clothes, no sports logos, nothing hip-hop or Tommy Hilfiger. Even the colorful geometric fixturing, the powder blue and soft yellow walls, the yellow columns and curved archway leading to the baby department, and the confetti-patterned carpeting are done in-house, tastefully, by Talbots. There's playwear, toddler sizes, a layette program for newborns, and all-occasion clothes for boys and girls in sizes 4 to 16. There are also gifts, such as white knits with trimming for $55. Overall, it's an assortment of safe, salable clothes, detached from the fashion fast track. It's the Talbots tradition capturing the nation's return to traditional values.

The strategy has been working. Talbots continues to fire out strong profits and sales, surpassing $1 billion in sales in 1994, as other specialty chains foundered. Its performance is bewildering to other companies that persist in grasping for the right look of the moment or the hot item of the season. Lacking that, they seek high-profile strategies that gear advertising for impact or controversy and create sizzle but lack the steak.

The clothes adults buy at Talbots—perhaps not the most exciting in the market—reflect family values and a desire to instill those values in their children. Just as baby boomers are more tightly regulating what their children watch on TV and what hour they should go to sleep, they're formulating tighter dress codes. Their values convey that the world is filled with minefields, so step lightly—and dress tastefully.

These values are altering consumption and clothing requirements. The lifestyles and behavior patterns of customers are changing rapidly and, consequently, detailed descriptions of them must be compiled. That includes the demographics, the objective and quantifiable population statistics that are easily identifiable and measurable of the best customers. Demographics that must be considered are age, race, gender, ethnicity, income, education, occupation, family size, family life cycle, religion, and social class. Demographics are very closely linked to and may often determine the needs of the customer. By being able to describe these, an understanding of the customer will arise.

THE CUSTOMER WISH LIST

Consider creating a black book for preferred customers. Using the database of credit card users, list the names and addresses of your best customers. This will help target direct-mail advertising and promotions. The next step is to determine the age, gender, race, ethnicity, income, education, and occupation of the best customers. These characteristics can combine to indicate the needs and desires of the consumer as an individual with special interests such as physical fitness, advanced education, or personal development.

Customers want clothes to fit their active, health-conscious lifestyles. Companies such as Speedo, Sports Authority, and Nike are capitalizing on the fitness boom. In 1995, The Limited made its first move into the arena by purchasing Galyan's, a small Midwestern sporting goods and apparel retailer. Consider new concepts in your business that address these desires.

Customers also want clothes that stay in style for more than one season. In 1984, Saks Fifth Avenue discovered through market research and merchandise reviews that its customers wanted more than designer, contemporary, better office and party clothes and accessories in the areas where Saks scores. Research found that customers wanted "real quality, real value, classic traditional style and timelessness and continuity of selection every month" and found it at other stores, but Saks was determined to get business out of its existing base. According to Paul Leblang, Saks's senior vice president and marketing director in the 1970s and 1980s, Saks had a big hole in its merchandising and couldn't get it plugged by shopping the marketplace. The question became where to find classic, quality casual clothes.

Real Clothes, a private label line, was a solution, but initially it had to be considered an experiment rather than a full-blown launch. A catalog was deemed proper, because it would reach the Saks customer base and there would be no risk devoting selling space in the stores to a new line. There would be reduced inventory risk as well. The chain, with 40 stores at the time, estimated a $20 million inventory investment to launch the line in all stores, and there was a further risk considering that a launch would require 400-square-foot in-store shops. Instead, Saks went with distributing a 36-page catalog to 600,000 households and figured roughly a $1.6 million inventory risk. However, advertising costs are not considered risky. In the catalogs, the clothes were surrounded by "symbols of tradition—the class ring, teddy bears, a Hershey kiss," Leblang notes.

The copy stated: "Uncluttered. That's the way I'd like my life to be. I know it's the way I want my clothes to be. That's why I feel so comfortable in Saks Fifth Avenue's Real Clothes. They're not overcomplicated; not forced. They don't try too hard to make a statement. They let me do that."

Real Clothes eventually got included in the regular Saks catalog and supported by magazine and newspaper ads. Leblang credits the Real Clothes success to market research, knowing the target audience, and good execution.

TODAY'S TRENDS AND SHOPPING HABITS

Carol Farmer, the futurist, calls the 1990s "the less decade." With some categories nose-diving, new products and methods of selling must be devised. Open a spa to encourage physical fitness but also sell the exercise equipment that's in the spa; offer cosmetic makeovers and massages in conjunction with the exercising.

After sprucing up the customer's exterior, focus on the inner self by selling self-help books, psychology books, or even best-selling novels. Perhaps cross over to electronic media by offering computer software and electronic books. These adjunct categories could be right for the business, depending on your target market. It's working at Bergdorf Goodman, traditionally a store for fine apparel, which is moving more into gifts and home products, even vintage silver, wicker pet furniture, and celebrity books. It's a move to capture more gift-giving business around Christmas and other holidays and be less dependent on fashion. As lifestyles center more and more on the home, there could be growing opportunities for marketing gardening tools and lawn products, supplies for hobbies enjoyed at home, or home protection devices such as burglar and fire alarms and carbon monoxide detectors.

The trick is to maintain a consistency of price, quality, and style as you broaden merchandise offerings, so you harmonize and don't send mixed messages to customers. The offerings must strike a chord with them, encourage multiple sales, and maintain a taste level.

People are shopping more at home, through catalogs and infomercials, TV shopping channels, and the Internet. Marketers need to know who is clicking onto the Internet and when and what other new selling channels are being turned on. (So far, the Internet on-line venue has not been a profit center.)

Look at the Demographics

In formulating new marketing strategies, study the target market's occupations, disposable and discretionary incomes, family size, and the customer's place in the family life cycle. Disposable income is what is left after paying taxes; discretionary income is the money left after paying for necessities. The larger the family, the more necessities it requires and the less discretionary income it has. That is terrific if your store provides the necessities.

Include the psychographics of the target market. They will serve as a valuable guide for you in understanding what makes your customer tick. Attitudes toward fitness and family values, perceptions of quality and self-esteem, target market trends, and leisure activities all play a part in your audience's ultimate response.

The Tourist Market

If you are in a city or location that draws tourists, focus on catering to them. Manhattan has seen a boom in tourists in the 1990s, fueling strong gains at the flagship stores of Saks Fifth Avenue, Bloomingdale's, Henri Bendel, and Warner Brothers, affecting both retailers and manufacturers. That could imply concierge services, hotel deliveries so tourists don't have to drag their shopping bags around town, co-op advertising with hotels and airlines, joint discount programs, directories in multiple languages, and bilingual sales help.

In Las Vegas, developers are increasing nongambling options to attract more tourists and all members of the family, not just mom and dad.

Hotels are offering group incentives, and casinos are going way beyond the usual gambling facilities, featuring themed amusement parks with rides and shows and glitzy attractions, such as the Mirage Hotel's dolphin pool and erupting volcano and the Luxor Hotel's Egyptian museum. Tourists are fueling other kinds of development, including the transition of Times Square, Manhattan, from a seedy enclave of XXX-rated movie houses to legitimate theaters and stores, including projects by The Disney Company, Madame Tussaud's wax museum, and AMC Entertainment, a movie theater chain.

FORCES IN YOUR FAVOR AND HABITS HARD TO BREAK

Follow Trends in Disposable Income

With the 1990s stock market surging to new records, disposable income among investors increased and even if investors didn't cash in the stocks, they felt they had more money. As the market climbed, so did the propensity to shop, particularly at the designer shops on 57th Street and Rodeo Drive. Such labels as Tiffany, Chanel, Prada, and Armani soared, as moderate sportswear sank. Yet it wasn't the return of the conspicuous consumption of the 1980s; people weren't so interested in the designer label or stockpiling status clothes. It's more a case of seeking something that bears lasting quality, spending extra for it, and believing there is nothing wrong with a little self-indulgence. Perhaps the children are grown, away at college, or married now, and it's okay again to treat yourself to a little luxury.

Follow Your Customers through Their Family Cycles

The family life cycle concept suggests that as people age and their families grow or shrink, shopping habits change. Differences in buying habits exist between singles and married people of the same age. Material needs and desires change, depending on whether there are children in the family and how old they are. The arrival of the firstborn sends family spending spinning. Baby bottles, diapers, baby furniture, and teddy bears take priority. From then on, there is a focus on age-appropriate toys and children's clothing, which will be affected by peers. When children reach the age of eight or nine, brands become important. Through media and advertising, children became more aware of the brands and what other children are wearing.

Family spending shifts again when children leave for college. Perhaps there is less discretionary income, but what is left may be spent on adult recreation such as dinner and theater, pleasures postponed when the children were small. Products bought during this time reflect less influence of the children and a return to how the customers perceive themselves. This is a time when physical fitness and good appearance once again become the focus. If the business already focuses on physical appearance, consider sponsoring events with clothing and beauty consultants to attract these parents and help them redefine themselves.

Religion and Culture: They're Part of Shopping

Religion plays an enormous part in shopping decisions. Stores generally reap as much as 50 percent or more of their annual profits during Chanukah and Christmas seasons because of the surge in gift shopping. However, as the baby boomers reject the commercialization of Christmas, fewer gifts and less elaborate ones are being exchanged and traditional gifts are being replaced by a donation to charity in someone's name. Or perhaps there's a cash gift this year that could be used for something practical, instead of a bottle of perfume. Christmas 1995 was a season when all the negative forces of retailing—the "overstoring" of America, product duplication, price resistance, and shopper lethargy—seemed to converge, driving sales downward. Its impact may be felt for many years to come.

Consider a trend toward other religions and ethnic holidays where gift giving plays a role. African-Americans are increasingly focusing on Kwanza, just after Christmas, as a celebration entailing gift giving. Many who celebrate this new holiday also celebrate Christmas.

At the ShopRite supermarket in Cheltenham, Pennsylvania, a special effort is made to cater to the primary customers, who are African-American, Jewish, and Korean. Since many of the African-Americans are Muslims with dietary rules similar to those of kosher Jews, the store includes a deli and frozen food section with special kosher areas. In the international food section, which Koreans frequent, the store also provides a broad assortment of oriental foods.

America is a culturally diverse country, and businesses should reflect it. Determine the predominant ethnic groups in your area and take note of the religious and semireligious holidays celebrated and the traditions upheld. Then adjust your marketing messages accordingly.

Study the Sociographics of Your Customer

Social mores are often brushed aside, while income levels are used to indicate the interests of the customer. However, income alone doesn't suggest what will appeal to customers. Social class can signify product preferences, whether in furniture, books, or newspapers. Society plays a major role in consumer decision making.

Sony failed to realize that concept in the early 1980s. The company had developed the technically superior Betamax video recorders to compete with Matsushita Electric Co.'s VHS format and JVC, a leading VHS video recorder brand. Sony figured that consumers would go for the smaller and better-quality Beta format and relied on technological superiority and development but fell short on the marketing side. Sony didn't latch on to what people really wanted, which was to bring the cinema experience home and have a broad selection of movies to choose from for their home entertainment. Sensing this, JVC wisely concentrated on ensuring that a wider range of movies in the VHS format were available in video rental shops, which helped it sell many more VCRs than Sony. Consumers largely disregarded Sony's technical superiority and the Betamax format was wiped out.

Philips Electronics fell into the same trap with its versatile interactive compact discs, a digital entertainment format that plays into a television. The product never gained market acceptance. Philips failed to take into account the popularity of CD-ROM, which is similar to the Philips Compact Disc Interactive but plays into a computer.

In Europe, the new media (including on-line services and CD-ROM) may have a difficult time taking off for a variety of sociographic reasons. Most significantly, the telecommunications industry is tightly regulated, and telephone calls are expensive. Also, children surf the Internet while older people generally do not, and compared with the United States, a much smaller percentage of homes have computers.

Gauge the Potential of Your Customer Base

What is the potential of the customer base? Has the target market been saturated or has it barely been scratched? What is the growth potential locally, regionally, nationally, or internationally? Are they mutually exclusive? Is each target market large enough to pay attention to? Is the segment shrinking or growing? Questions about target markets need to be answered. Anticipate the changes that will occur for planning ahead.

If the target market is shrinking, consider how fast it is disappearing. If the market is getting smaller, marketing efforts should be redirected to lump that group along with another. Perhaps the focus on that segment should be dropped for the business to remain profitable. Some market segments are growing at a slow rate, yet it still makes sense to target them. Neiman Marcus acknowledges that the market for luxury goods is not growing, but in the past couple of years Neiman's has targeted the segment more intensely than ever, waging a war to steal share from its competitors as well. And foreign manufacturers of luxury products are looking to the United States for additional opportunities.

Understanding the Target Market

What do your best customers do for recreation and how do they spend their leisure time? Can a link be forged between businesses and what consumers do for fun? Galyan's, the sporting goods store purchased by The Limited last year, has a climbing wall for those who scale cliffs and rock climb and want to test out some equipment. NikeTown has mini-basketball courts so the Air Jordans can be tested for grip. It's all a matter of getting a grip on your customers.

New York Newsday provides a valuable lesson about what happens when you fail to understand the demographics of the target market. If you obtain and then properly use information on the sociographics of your customer and the potential of your customer base, you can avoid costly mistakes such as those made by *Newsday*.

The *Newsday* Experience

It's the mid-1980s. *Newsday* on Long Island is highly profitable. There's little competition for retail ad dollars: *Penny Saver* is the big competitor, and *Newsday* charges advertisers what it wants and steadily increases rates. The paper has an incredible 75 percent penetration of the Long Island market and becomes the glue that unifies the Island's string of independent towns, providing local coverage of business and schools, as well as national and international news and investigative reporting. The paper had invested heavily in editorial staffing to create a strong product.

The decision is made to start the New York edition, moving into Brooklyn, then Manhattan, coming off the stronghold in Queens and Long Island. Initially, costs are seen as low: adding a few more delivery trucks, running more papers off the press. And those expenses would be offset by getting more ads from retailers. In addition, the *Daily News* and the *New York Post* are financially shaky from strikes and relying heavily on small local advertisers paying low rates. Speculation about one or the other tabloid folding is rampant.

"*Newsday* smelled blood," recalls Chris Miller, a former *Newsday* vice president of marketing. And expanding into the city could create "a great power base" for Times Mirror, parent of *Newsday,* the *Los Angeles Times,* and other major papers. But things go wrong. The other papers don't die and *Newsday*'s circulation in Brooklyn flops.

"We did marketing research. We found that each borough was a separate market in terms of demographics and psychographics," Miller recalls. "Newspapers are a habit. Most have been reading their newspapers forever. It reflects who they are and if they buy it every day, it's because they like it."

Newsday's strategy to offer a hybrid product, a more comprehensive tabloid, gets rejected by tabloid readers who find *Newsday*'s 256-page edition, on average, too lengthy, and *Times* readers are too entrenched. *Newsday* fights harder with TV advertising, an unusual strategy for a newspaper. The most celebrated writers, Jimmy Breslin and Liz Smith, get on the tube plugging the paper. In the TV spots, each writer plays to his or her unique style: Breslin on a dark street getting the gritty details, Smith at a fancy restaurant whispering with those in the know.

The *Times* responds by beefing up sports and style sections and local news coverage. It becomes a battle at every corner newsstand. After a 10-year struggle and about $100 million in losses, *New York Newsday* calls it quits and shuts down. The lesson of *New York Newsday* is to understand the needs, wants, and desires of target markets.

COMPETITOR ANALYSIS

The Shadowy Side

Everybody gets into everybody else's business through the discreet networking that occurs in the corridors of industry conferences, at the lunches downtown, during cocktails after work. Executives of rival companies surreptitiously learn about who can be bought, what's for sale, who's antsy, and who's on the move. In 1994, behind-the-scenes merger talks were held between powerhouse May Department Stores and the weaker Mercantile Stores. Word got around, and Mercantile was obligated to disclose to shareholders that it was considering a merger but would not disclose with whom. Several weeks later, Mercantile said the talks were off, but wouldn't say why. The mystery loomed, and rumors spread that Mercantile, controlled by textile magnate Roger Milliken, couldn't get its price. The truth may be that the talks went further and that price wasn't the issue in the end. According to one source, the deal was close to acceptance, but Mercantile wanted more of its own members on the new board, which would be formed through the merger, than May would permit.

Every profession has its clandestine wheeling and dealing, yet the activity churns with greater turbulence in fashion retail circles. There's a unique seasonal nature to most businesses, and an incredible number of companies go in and out of business in just a few months' time. Mergers, consolidations, and bankruptcies proliferate. Job dissatisfaction is high, while the corporate family spirit is at an all-time low.

Defections from the Corporate State

Turnover persists, most noticeably in the lower rungs of employment. Typically younger executives, more idealistic and willing to uproot until they find a suitable career direction, jump ship with surprising frequency. Yet it happens too often on the middle and senior management levels as well. People don't stick with companies as long as they used to. Everybody and everything has a price, so it seems, and that's put another layer of uncertainty and cynicism on retailers and product manufacturers, on top of all the day-in, day-out strains of running a business and trying to make money. Bankruptcies and liquidations are bad, but they are often foreseen as business turns sour, credit dries up, and bill-paying slows. The writing is on the wall.

There's nothing quite as shocking and irksome as when a key executive jumps ship to the competition and takes the intimate knowledge of competitive positioning. It's almost like the minutes of executive committee meetings and planning sessions are being FedExed to the competition. Federated's top brass panicked when Roger Farah left to join archrival Macy's. The man orchestrating Federated's new central merchandising efforts for its divisions was branded a corporate traitor. So angered was Federated that it sued to prevent Farah from becoming Macy's president, and Farah was legally blocked from working for Macy's for a year and put on paid leave of absence on the basis of a no-compete clause in his old contract.

Loyalties are built up, then busted. For years Gabriella Forte was Giorgio Armani's president, with a reputation for pistol-whipping retailers into acquiescing to the designer's demands for precision presentation in the stores. Armani shops must be perfect, spacious, and well-positioned. In 1995, Forte signed a multimillion-dollar contract with none other than Calvin Klein, whose clean style and design flair competes with Armani for the designer customer dollar.

Silver King Communications honcho Barry Diller abandoned QVC, the nation's top home shopping network, in the fall of 1994. He joined QVC's archrival, the Home Shopping Network, as chairperson, in the fall of 1995. Diller brought along a former executive vice president of QVC, Jim Held. The pair took with them a wealth of experience that could bolster HSN, which had been a second-rate performer compared with QVC. And just a few months after Bloomingdale's announced in 1995 that it would be opening its first five stores in California in the fall of 1996, the chain swiped a top executive from the West Coast ranks of

May Department Stores, a fierce competitor, to be its California regional vice president.

The dearth of talent and the inability of the many industries to attract fresh blood has executive pirates on the prowl. The best defense is to know your competition and do what it takes to get the goods on him or her. The message is out: As industries contract and one company knocks off another, everybody and every idea are up for grabs.

INTELLIGENCE GATHERING: KNOW THE COMPETITION

The first step is to know your competition. Know who and what is out there. Consider at least the five or six companies that target the same market as your firm, the same five or six stores that carry similar merchandise for the same crowd.

Elements that need to be examined include your competitors' primary and secondary target customers and their market share and sales, both recent and current. Additionally, consider their positioning and marketing objectives; their product, branding, and packaging; and their distribution, store penetration, and market coverage strategy. Take a close look at their pricing policies, geographic dominance, and type of shops (locations and descriptions of locations). Personal selling policies, promotions, advertising platforms, and publicity programs also need to be analyzed. Give some thought to their media thinking and expenditures in TV, radio, newspaper, outdoor, direct mail, and other outlets. Finally, look at their customer service approaches and merchandising strategies. In doing this analysis, take into account your broad business definition and consider all of the firms your target market could patronize as an alternative to your company.

Talk to the Competitor's Troops

If a position opens up in the company, consider people within the ranks of the organization, of course. Also interview candidates from the competition. Their knowledge could be inordinately valuable and lead to major strategy revisions. It doesn't hurt Neiman Marcus to have Burt Tansky, a former Saks Fifth Avenue president, as its CEO. It doesn't hurt

Sears, a company repositioning into a moderate department store, to have Robert Mettler, a former May Department Stores merchant, as its top merchandiser.

Often, the initial stages of the search are done by a third party, such as a headhunter. It's more discreet this way and it could be awkward meeting the competition right off the bat, though some CEOs have been known to handle executive searches personally.

A Second Course of Action: Enter Enemy Territory

Take a field day to the mall, armed with notepads and a keen sense of observation. Examine inventories, prices, customers, signage, point-of-sale displays, housekeeping, and merchandise adjacencies. Use employees to shop the competition. Assign categories of products and services to individual employees and compare their findings to your own standards. Pick up another catalog and review the presentation. Determine whether the competition is drawing customers from a trading area that's as wide as your own. Learn where customers are from and why they chose this product or store. Go to the parking lot and list the states and counties indicated on the license plates. That will provide a ballpark idea of where people are coming from. If you manufacture a product and don't have a retail distribution site, go directly to small stores and interview the customers shopping in the departments where your product is sold.

Army versus Navy

It's commonplace for retailers to shop the competition and try to match or exceed what's offered elsewhere. When Old Navy opened its flagship last fall on Sixth Avenue and 18th Street in Manhattan, Federated Merchandising dispatched an army to investigate what all the hoopla was about. Old Navy, a division of The Gap, had introduced a new lower-priced concept housed in a lively setting reminiscent of the old-fashioned, almost nonexistent army/navy store format. And, of course, Old Navy was hyped with a barrage of preopening TV, radio, and outdoor advertising and promotion; fireworks; bus-shelter posters with maps pinpointing the location; and refurbished Chevy pickup trucks driving around town announcing the opening and distributing premiums.

A party the night before the official opening was highlighted by a Chris Isaak concert and refreshments: mini-hamburgers, ice-cream sandwiches, and drinks. The house was so packed that no one knew whether a few participants from the Federated Merchandising army ever attended.

Location, Location, Location

Be prepared for the competition to enter the market. How would the competition feel if you moved next door? It's an issue that arises all the time. In New York, Nordstrom executives have checked out sites in Manhattan, among them the former B. Altman location on Fifth Avenue and 34th Street and the former Alexander's building on Lexington and 58th Street. Given its strong reputation for service and fine fashion, a Nordstrom in Manhattan would rock the entire retail scene, though the Seattle-based chain has yet to announce plans to move in. To paraphrase the late cochairperson Jim Nordstrom, "I wouldn't want to subject my people to Manhattan." However, the speculation persists, giving Manhattan retail executives something to ponder.

"I'd rather see them move to 58th Street than 34th Street," says one Bloomingdale's executive, who believes it's better to have a competitor next door so you can feed off the traffic, rather than somewhat at a distance, where traffic would be siphoned. When there's a variety of stores adjacent to each other, there's more competition but also a bigger audience for capturing business. Don't fear the competition: take advantage of it. This is the age of cross-shopping. American consumers are smarter, doing more comparison shopping, and holding back on their purchasing. There's less loyalty to brands or stores. Target, the nation's second-largest discounter, invades markets already served by other discounters, with a strategy of rimming an area with a cluster of stores. Consumers will go where the prices are the lowest and will wait and wait until the prices drop, taking the risk that something won't get sold out.

It's the district or mall with the full array of bustling retail that attracts shoppers, particularly families. They prefer the one-stop shopping experience, removing the hassle of getting back into the car to drive elsewhere to shop, and the opportunity for cross-shopping. Price comparisons can be made more easily. Those are among the appeals and strengths of a mall.

Know Your Competitor by Asking the Consumer

Multidimensional scaling is a marketing research tool that helps judge how stores and products are perceived. Consumers are asked to rate stores or products on several attributes, among them, depth of assortment, ambiance, and level of excitement. All of this information is then entered into a computer to form a map depicting spatially how one store or product compares with another.

This information helps assess whether positioning strategies are effective and whether consumers perceive the product as management intends. This information can also be used to pinpoint the most direct competitors and determine their strengths and advantages. Knowing where the competition excels or falls short provides a jump start to initiating strategies for improved performance and enhancing the image of the company while reacting to the actions of competitors.

There are many marketing research firms that specialize in this type of analysis and have developed computer programs to massage the data and help reach conclusions. The American Marketing Association publishes a list of its membership of market research firms. Bear in mind that just as you probe the marketplace for trends in products, merchandising, and customers' needs, so does the competition. They have their strategic plans, goals, tactics, and objectives. The competition is looking over its shoulder and searching for the other guy's Achilles' heel. It's a matter of getting there first. Discovering the right resource. The right merchandise strategy. The hot item of the season.

Examine the Competitor's Ads

Competitors' ads usually focus on attracting your target market, so it is important to consider the effective techniques that they use. As previously discussed, there are three important aspects of your competitors' ads to judge: first the message, then the media, and, finally, how well either or both of those attract your target market. Just as there are many formatted television shows that succeed, a great ad, message, piece of artwork, or artwork format considered current and trendy can be used as a guide for your advertising campaign. The already-accepted, timely advertising direction clues you in to the type of situation, message, vocabulary, and artwork your customers prefer. It can also give you insight into the kind of information your customers want and how they would like this information presented.

One-Upmanship in the Competitive Landscape

If you hold a one-day sale, will *they* also set up a one-day sale? If you, as a theater manager, arrange for actors dressed up as the characters from *Toy Story* to appear from noon to 3:00 P.M. at your theater, will the theater down the street arrange for *Pocahontas* characters to make an appearance at the same time?

Breaking price is a hot issue. If Neiman's breaks price on fall designer goods before Saks, who do you think will get the customers first? One company might risk breaking price on a product, even though it's before the date when the supplier has said it's okay to mark down.

What is the lag time between an action that you take in pricing and the competition's response? If you raise your prices, will competitors lower or raise their prices? Anticipate the responses by reviewing past reactions. Take a look back as far as five years at changes made in products, decor, and promotion and how long it took for others to formulate responses. If the lag time is long, it's a competitive advantage using those parts of the marketing plan that can be controlled.

Can You Compete by Price Alone?

Price is a matter of perception. Abraham & Straus was perceived as less expensive than Macy's, even though there was tremendous overlap in merchandise and matching price promotions. That was because Macy's dabbled in designer merchandise and created an impressive main floor with chandeliers for its cosmetics department and a tone that spelled upscale. Price credibility was missing. Abraham & Straus kept things moderate and developed a perception that it had more reasonable prices. One product priced at $100 may appear too expensive for words. Another product at $100 may seem like an incredible buy. Remember, value, the catchword of the 1990s, is a consumer's perception of both quality and price.

A winning formula includes offering products with value in a setting that provides service, comfort, and ambiance consistent with the products offered. Recognize where the business fits on the luxury ladder. At the lowest rung, products compete on price. Ascending the ladder, customer services become more personalized and differentiated. The more customers are pampered with service and the more luxurious the ambiance, the more likely customers will perceive the store as expensive. Burlington Coat, an off-price, no-frills rack operation, experimented in the 1980s by opening stores with greater fixturing, bearing a more finished look. The change scared customers away. They sensed if the interior standards were rising, so must prices.

Price is the most basic way to compete. It's more difficult to one-up the competition on nonprice issues, which are not advertised as much, such as valet parking for ease and safety, automatic extended warranties, free delivery, or free assembly of products at home. Some firms decide to climb the ladder of luxury to offer more services as part of a strategy to beat price-based competitors.

Stocking Up Better and Faster

In the late 1990s, after decades of taking aggressive stock positions in anticipation of robust selling, most of the retail world has been cutting back on inventory. This paring down may be sound business strategy for fashion companies but not necessarily for other industries. Consider Julius Blum & Co., a Carlstadt, New Jersey–based supplier of handrail components, which takes an unorthodox approach. It keeps inventory levels way above what's necessary to meet the demand for the product. This service feature provides customers with immediate orders, and sales staff never have to check whether an item is in stock. While keeping inventories high can be costly, the company claims it costs the company more when orders are lost because of insufficient inventory. The company should know—it has been operating like this for decades and continues to thrive.

In the retail arena, the mix and depth of assortments provide another opportunity for competing. The wider the mix, the more assortments and categories of goods are carried. The deeper the assortments, the more styles in a line and the more sizes and colors in each style are carried. Obviously, wider and deeper assortments involve greater risk in inventory investment, management, and servicing the customer to prevent empty inventories. However, a store or manufacturer that carries everything and swings from one fashion look to the next can lose focus and confuse the customers. A narrower assortment can send a clearer message to the customer.

4 | The Marketing Plan

"He keeps telling me that
it's not that complicated."

BY NOW, YOU SHOULD BE NEARLY OVERDOSED ON INFORMATION. But hang tough because it's time to put it all to good use. That mountain of data is not as overwhelming as it might seem. In fact, it's become the foundation for formulating the marketing plan.

Ziccardi & Partners built a marketing plan based on gathering extensive data for Mamma Leone's, the famous Italian restaurant in New York's theater district. Around 1991, Mamma's was losing market share and no longer living up to its reputation as a festive Italian eatery for the entire family. The consortium that owned Mamma's—Restaurant Associates, owners of more than 100 other high-profile eating establishments—came to us seeking an ad plan to rescue the restaurant.

We began by doing our homework, which included consumer surveys and a number of visits to the restaurant. Then we came up with a comprehensive marketing plan for Mamma's. Our research showed that unless the product itself and the service were improved drastically, there was little that advertising alone—ours or anybody else's—could do to salvage the franchise. But the owners insisted they just wanted to change the advertising. So we bowed out of the competition for the account, even though it felt like we were taking *panne* out of our mouths. We didn't want to be onboard a sinking ship. Another agency took on the task, but one year later, it was *arriverderci* Mamma. The restaurant shut its doors for good. As we suspected, the business was too far gone. Even the best ad campaign in the world would not have saved it. A sophisticated, total plan was needed.

This chapter provides the guidelines for creating such a plan—one that will be more potent and sophisticated than the competition's. It tells how to construct a marketing map that covers all the bases—from product needs to cost analysis, from developing a consumer profile to creating the advertising, sales promotion, and public relations strategies—so you're ready to walk the walk.

OBJECTIVES AND STRATEGIES

In writing a marketing plan, the first item on the agenda is setting the sales objectives. The more thoroughly you understand the process of arriving at a sales objective, the easier to write a plan that will be realistic. Once formulated, the marketing objectives and strategies become the foundation of the marketing plan. The objectives describe what needs to be done to achieve the sales goals, and the marketing strategies delineate how the objectives will be accomplished. Keep in mind that developing strategies requires a great deal of thought. Balance is important: Make sure that the direction you map out is firmly rooted in logic, but be innovative.

Planning the Sales Targets

Establishing a planned sales volume is critical because it determines the pace of the marketing plan. Everything that follows in the plan is designed to meet the sales goal—from determining the size of the target market and establishing marketing objectives, to budgeting advertising and promotion dollars, to the hiring of marketing and sales personnel, to the number and kinds of distribution channels, and to the amount of product manufactured or inventoried.

Because sales plans have substantial impact on a business, they must be simultaneously challenging and attainable. If you plan for big sales gains, you have to plan a more ambitious marketing program and spend more than before. But if you plan sales too high and unrealistically, you'll waste the money spent on marketing, upset the expense-to-sales ratio, and probably cause profits to plummet.

You must set parameters for time-specific sales targets by scheduling start and end dates for executing the program. It is also important to determine both short- and long-term sales. Short-term sales plans generally are for one year or less, while longer ones are usually for a minimum of three years.

Setting measurable sales targets helps in determining what to include in your marketing plan and how to evaluate its success. Sales targets are quantified in terms of dollars and units for manufacturing firms; dollars and transactions (and occasionally units) for retail firms; and dollars and customers served for service firms.

MARKETING OBJECTIVES VERSUS MARKETING STRATEGIES

What is the difference between a marketing objective and a marketing strategy? A marketing objective is a statement of what needs to be done. A marketing strategy is a statement that details how a marketing objective will be achieved; it describes the method for accomplishing the objective. Don't worry if you don't understand the distinction at first. Distinguishing between the two can be a source of confusion and frustration, even for seasoned marketing professionals.

How to Write a Marketing Objective

Clearly, the marketing objective must be specific, with each objective focusing on a single goal. The objectives should be quantifiable in results and measurable within specific time periods.

The level of achievement earmarked for each objective should be tied to the overall desired sales goals for the coming year. For example, if you have planned an aggressive sales growth of 30 percent, then each marketing objective that will support that growth needs to be quantified accordingly. Unless you come up with a creative idea that performs magic, don't plan on building hefty sales increases with marginal increases in marketing expenditures.

How to Write a Marketing Strategy

Marketing strategies come in all different sizes, shapes, and colors. The most common are strategies that relate to seasonality, competitive issues, the target market, products, packaging, pricing, distribution, personal selling, and promotions. These strategies take into account advertising, merchandising, publicity, and sales promotion.

In addition, the marketing budget needs its own strategy. Once the total marketing budget is cast, an intricate strategy must be developed to know how many support dollars to allocate to each element of the marketing plan.

THE MARKETING PLAN CHECKPOINTS

Start off with a review of problems and opportunities that have been identified. Review the marketing objectives that you have formulated. Make certain that you have developed strategies for each category necessary to fulfill your marketing objectives. Use the following checklist to develop a comprehensive strategy to-do list.

Business Summary

___ Create the company black book. Include the names, addresses, and phone numbers of principals and senior officials.

___ Paint a business portrait that is accurate and not too narrow in scope. Use broad strokes to give definition to your company.

___ Make a comprehensive and specific list of products and services. Discuss the environment. Are you selling atmosphere? Is your business an interactive retail fun house or a place where people go to be pampered and to buy luxurious and pricey products?

___ Choose your customers. It's a big universe. Whom do you want— busy, working-class moms, suburban housewives with leisure time, or career chasers on the go?

___ Know the direct and indirect competition. Who are they? Filene's or the neighborhood flea market? Examine the landscape.

___ Describe the corporate culture and management style. Is it autocratic or democratic, top down or bottom up, executive committee or committee of one? Is there succession planning? Do you designate a second in command or would that create jealousies and deflate ambitions? If you choose to designate a second in command, when is the right time to do it?

___ Keep an eye on the coffers. Develop realistic financial projections and goals. Examine long- and short-term debt. Consider the performance of the competition. Money talks when it's spent on marketing. It takes money to make money, even if it's borrowed. A business can turn sour quickly, in a season or a calendar quarter. Learn the warning signs. List reserves and contingencies.

The State of the Company

___ List the company's strengths and weaknesses. Does the company have perceived value, fair prices, exclusive products and services, convenient locations, a loyal staff?

___ Write down what you need. Outline threats and opportunities. Is Kmart closing and Wal-Mart moving into your territory? Find some fashion. List new resources. Replenish quicker. Don't play catch-up. While people, places, values, technology, economies, governments, and competitors tend to change, business tends to resist. Are you limber or a Johnny-come-lately?

___ Record the skills of management and staff. Include the nature and composition of the team. Do you have market-driven merchants, bean counters, or both? Long-range planners or short-term gainers? Nurture key people. Talent is tough to hold. Offer a piece of the action to those you want to retain: stock bonus plans, equity, incentives. Offer involvement. It takes more than just a paycheck.

___ Does the shoe fit? The product mix must match the company's strengths and overall profile. Hermés won't sell health aids, just as Stride Rite won't sell silk scarves. Furniture is fine if you have the floor space for slow turners. Examine strategies. Which ones are working, which are flopping? Does the corporate culture fit the product mix? Consider private label versus brands. Find the right balance. Decide who should design private labels: in-house staff or suppliers?

___ Look at cost analysis: What's moving, what's getting stale? Set markdown standards. Clear bathing suits when it's time to move in back-to-school goods. Consider a different balance of home and apparel. Examine the potential. Don't shock your customers with an overnight overhaul.

Customer Analysis

___ Develop a customer profile using segmentation analysis (based on neighborhoods, lifestyles, education, and income). Is your customer the Wal-Mart woman; Kathie Lee or Katharine Hepburn? Hip

67

dresser or fashion victim? High school dropout or Ph.D.? Selling to a customer you don't understand is like trying to use a computer when you have no knowledge of its operating system.

___ Gather information on the segment's market history, trends, and seasonal shopping habits. What's changing? What's predictable?

Product Evaluation

___ Provide products that are consistent with the target market and its image of your company. Identify products by their labels, packaging, and positioning. Display them front and center on the main floor.

___ Identify product development needs to fill a void, strengthen a category, get wider margins, and achieve exclusivity.

Packaging

___ For manufacturers, make certain beauty is more than skin deep. Does the package match what's inside the box? For retailers, does the look of your store reflect your intended image? Do you need to use contemporary industrial lighting or Waterford chandeliers?

___ Provide a creative package that's unique. Is the look simple or functional? Does it stand out on a shelf or disappear in the crowd?

___ Make sure the package quickly communicates the name, benefits, and nature of the product. Does it catch people's attention or is it just another name?

Pricing Evaluation

___ Set the strategy. Everyday low prices or one-day sales; printed or negotiated prices?

___ Determine objectives. Do you want to increase volume, turn a profit, or both? Do you want to project value or project an image? Is your company a deep discounter or a full-price operation? What methods do you use to lure customers to the channel of distribution or to establish barriers of entry against the competition?

___ Determine your price markups. Customers are price-sensitive, savvy, and strange. Mark up too high and you'll insult them. Price too low and they'll be suspicious of the quality. They'll pay $40 for Levi's and hundreds for a Chanel and walk out the door wearing both.

___ Comb the competition's racks. How do prices compare with yours? When is it time to break with a sale? (Before they do!)

Distribution

____ Discover the competition's distribution patterns. Learn from their mistakes and repeat their successes.

____ Consider all regional differences. Is there enough penetration of product in any one given market? Remember, out of stock could mean out of business.

____ Decide whether you want to sell to the consumer, the trade, or both. Armani, Calvin Klein, and others sell both to consumers and Barneys on Madison Avenue.

Personal Selling

____ Do your customer's shopping habits and product information needs match the selling methods in your store?

____ Is the sales force marching to the advertising drummer? Does the positioning strategy say service while salespeople are saying "Help yourself"?

____ If you're a manufacturer, make sure outside sales representatives are presenting to decision makers and not just information takers.

____ Are you giving your sales staff pats on the back along with their commission checks? Salespeople need to be rewarded both emotionally and financially.

Advertising Media

____ Take the journalistic approach to media planning. Know who, what, when, where, and why before signing the media confirmation order.

____ Make sure there's enough spent in each medium to be seen and heard with adequate frequency. If not, it is better to limit the media choices. Consider dropping that costly spot during the *Good Morning America* TV show. It might be better to go with several spots during the less expensive *Imus in the Morning* radio show to increase frequency.

____ Are promotions short enough to provide enough frequency? Consider that 3-day events done 15 times a year have more impact than 15-day events done 3 times a year.

____ Choose your advertising weapons. Will you use the *Daily News* or the *New York Times*? What does your target market read or listen to? Do they watch PBS or prime-time game shows? Charlie Rose or Vanna White?

___ Set the ad budget and plan weekly tactics. What's right for you: Sunday newspaper ads, midweek circulars, or radio spots? What's affordable? What's already working? Which tactic produces sales?

___ Consider the competition's strategy. What is your competitor's response to your strategy?

Advertising Message

___ Does the advertising have a focus or is it trying to be all things to all people? If it's trying to be all things to all people, try again. Develop a specific, targeted message.

___ Does it make sense to do a single advertisement or create a campaign? Ads can get lost in the media clutter; campaigns tend to make waves and get noticed.

___ What's the right type of message: facts, sentiments, monologues, dialogues, diatribes, poetry, or vibes? Are you touching the fabric of their lives (so to speak) or a raw nerve?

Promotional Strategy

___ Are extraordinary measures required to grab the audience? Coupons, three-hour sales, early-bird specials, gifts with purchases, and free coffee: Are they gimmicks or real incentives?

___ Will you use promotions as a powerful short-term marketing tool or a long-term advertising strategy? Think short term and use advertising to sustain brand identity and position for the long term.

Publicity

___ Plan the publicity effort. Be proactive, not reactive. Don't lose patience if the key media people aren't listening. Publicity requires perseverance and persistence.

___ Develop positive relations with key media people. Celebrate Christmas with a basket of fruit. Show the media people that you care, are thinking of them, and can be helpful with stories.

Stand Ready

You control product, price, promotion, and distribution—the kind of settings in which the products are sold and the ways they are displayed. Understand the environment and be prepared to constantly react to changes.

THE MARKETING PLAN FOR THE LUXURY GOODS MARKET

In 1995, Ziccardi & Partners was commissioned by a group of investment bankers to conduct a comprehensive analysis of the international luxury goods markets and the players in the field. We isolated five brands we believed were fertile for growth and development in the United States and prepared a summary marketing plan for each brand.

One of those high-priced players is Céline, which was launched in Paris in 1946 as a children's shoe store. In 1966, Céline moved into the women's ready-to-wear market, and, 20 years later, was acquired by LVMH, a French luxury goods conglomerate controlling such prestigious brands as Louis Vuitton, Moet-Hennessey, Christian Dior, Kenzo, Christian Lacroix, Givenchy, and Guerlain.

For most of the time that Céline has been under the LVMH umbrella, it has offered a stodgy collection of classic ready-to-wear, leather goods, and accessories. Finally, around 1995, Céline took a new approach, revamping its classics with chic styling to appeal to a broad age range. Its rich assortment has included such items as pistachio-colored leather jackets, priced around $2,500, tote bags and backpacks ranging from $400 to $900, and knit jumpsuits at the high end of that scale. In April 1996, the company announced plans to develop a signature fragrance and opened a new Beverly Hills shop, complete with marble floor, a large skylight, and a video wall display, in keeping with the collection's contemporary approach.

As the line was updated, reviews of the collection by the fashion press grew more favorable. The positive reception has done little to generate brand awareness and sales, however. In 1995, Céline posted $194.1 million in worldwide volume, a small amount in comparison to Dior or Gucci. Céline is hardly a household name. Yet it is a potentially hot label that could ride the multibillion-dollar luxury goods boom in the United States, Europe, and Asia and experience enormous growth. We have included the Ziccardi marketing plan for Céline in Exhibit 4–1 because it provides a clear picture of a marketing strategy designed for explosive growth.

The plan contains an overview of the competitive environment in which Céline operates, along with a discussion of Céline's strengths,

Exhibit 4–1
CÉLINE MARKETING PLAN

Céline Marketing Plan

The luxury goods market is continuing to grow into a multibillion-dollar business. Regardless of their socioeconomic level, people want to enjoy products that enhance the quality of their lives.

A review of the recent literature about the luxury goods market in the United States indicates a very optimistic point of view.

The three major luxury conglomerates today are Vendome, Investcorp, and LVMH.

Vendome, part of the Richemont group, which controls Rothmans cigarettes, embraces Cartier, Dunhill, Piaget, Baume et Mercier, Chloe, Lagerfeld, Hackett, Seeger, and Mont Blanc. Investcorp groups together Chaumet, Breguet, Ebel, Gucci, Riva Yachts, Tiffany, and Saks Fifth Avenue. The French LVMH group controls luxury brands such as Louis Vuitton, Moet-Hennessy, Dior, Kenzo, Céline, Lacroix, Givenchy, and Guerlain.

Céline, with 94 percent of its volume concentrated in Asia and Europe, relies heavily on these economies as a source of volume and growth. The development of a significant U.S. presence would provide Céline a better distribution of its risks, volume, and growth. Although substantial opportunities to build a significant business in the United States exist, there are inherent limitations currently facing Céline.

The problems, hence opportunities, that Céline faces are as follows:

Target Markets — An underdeveloped secondary market exists that represents millions of potential Céline customers.

Competition — Current competitors offer more American-styled goods. Louis Vuitton and Gucci both have designer and non-designer merchandise, enabling them to market to wider consumer segments, but are vulnerable to a "new star in town."

New Products — Céline, whose product mix does not include fragrance, home, or men's products, can successfully build additional classifications.

Product Design — While maintaining the well-established European and Asian product, a modified, contemporary, American point of view would be better received by the U.S. market.

Pricing — Price levels are too high to appeal to a secondary, less affluent market. Maintaining current "status" price levels, while creating a tier of lower priced merchandise, would provide an opportunity to move into secondary markets and a better competitive position (i.e., similar to Gucci).

New Areas of Distribution — Key geographic areas (where Céline customers live and work in dense numbers) currently have no Céline presence. Upscale specialty stores are currently resistant to the product. Direct-mail opportunities have not yet been explored. The development of these outlets provides fertile grounds for growth.

Branding — The Céline brand is perceived as dated; the updating of an already high-quality product would provide an exciting spark to the Céline line.

1

Exhibit 4–1
CÉLINE MARKETING PLAN *(CONTINUED)*

Advertising — An effective media and creative strategy to communicate the Céline message to current and new customers will provide the necessary information network to "sing loud" the new praises of Céline.

Sales Promotion — Promotions have not been used to activate sales. Céline needs to run the right kind of high-profile, upscale promotional events that would appeal to the target market.

Merchandising and Stores — Heightening visual excitement in stores, married with the appropriate fixtures, store layouts, and seasonally correct merchandise, would generate greater impulse buying at the store level.

Publicity — With its marginal visibility in the press, Céline would benefit strongly from a well-planned PR program that included aggressive press networking and the development of a designer personality.

MARKETING OBJECTIVES

- Create an advertising media strategy to increase exposure efficiencies by 35 percent.
- Reposition Céline as a contemporary U.S. luxury player by doubling the appeal to a younger secondary market.
- Change perception of Céline in the American marketplace and build consumer business by 43 percent.
- Increase point-of-purchase sales productivity by 25 percent.
- Maintain price levels on current merchandise to reinforce Céline's quality position and status.
- Create a secondary tier of merchandise with 30 percent lower price points to expand into secondary markets, with preemptive competitive strategies, such as those of Gucci.
- Increase Céline's brand awareness level by 20 percent with strategies geared toward packaging, store layouts, and rebranding efforts.
- Open new segments of customer markets. Increase these markets 10 percent the first year.
- Develop new business classifications to account for 20 percent of total volume in 1997.

Build sales as follows:

Year	MM
1995	$ 14.5
1996	28.9
1997	66.5
1998	75.3

Allocate a $3.25 million marketing effort to support the sales objective.

Exhibit 4–1
CÉLINE MARKETING PLAN *(CONTINUED)*

MARKETING STRATEGIES

• Demographics

1995

Primary

Mostly female, 35+, Household Income (HHI) $150,000, professional, mostly affluent urban and suburban

1996

Primary

Mostly female, 30+, HHI $100,000, professional, socialite, upwardly mobile

Secondary

Mostly female, 25+, HHI $50,000+, aspirational

1997

Primary

25+, HHI $100,000, professional or "soon-to-be" socialite

Secondary

Mostly female, 25+, HHI $50,000+, aspirational. Include male gift-purchasers, 25+

1998

Expand menswear business. Include men in primary target market

• Product and Pricing

Product

Modify product in United States to a more forward, contemporary, and American point of view while maintaining the already well-established European and Asian product and customer loyalty.

Develop a fragrance, as well as home and men's product classifications.

Pricing

Maintain price levels on current merchandise to substantiate Céline's quality image positioning (status).

Create a tier of lower-price merchandise to expand into secondary markets, preempting competitive strategies, such as those of Gucci.

3

Exhibit 4–1
CÉLINE MARKETING PLAN *(CONTINUED)*

MARKETING STRATEGIES *(continued)*

• Positioning

Differences from Competitor

- Larger selection of unusual fabrications and unique fabric designs
- Better, French quality
- Favorite luxury accessories of top 100 fashion trendsetters
- Constant influx of new merchandise
- Create new-star-in-town syndrome

New Products

Greater expansion into secondary markets

- Fragrance and home
- Menswear

• Packaging/Store Appearance

- Create more appropriate store layouts to enhance specific merchandise classifications
- Create more effective visual presentations with a cohesive point of view

• Branding/Name/Reputation

- Update an already quality-perceived brand

• Advertising

Creative

- Develop the BIG idea on the following premise: Convince the markets that the Céline product is the best in value and quality and that new directions bring the product to a much more contemporary point of view

- Support the conviction

- Set the tone of the advertising, i.e., upscale, innovative, prestigious, luxurious

- Redefine the creative elements for a new format

4

Exhibit 4–1
CÉLINE MARKETING PLAN *(CONTINUED)*

MARKETING STRATEGIES *(continued)*

• Media

Develop an effective multimedia platform that reflects more frequency in the initial three years of the new marketing plan, because:

- A revamped product will appear in the marketplace
- New products will be developed
- Complicated messages need to be segmented and simplified
- New secondary markets must be reached
- Current primary market will be maintained

• Merchandising

- Create visual excitement in stores with a more forward, contemporary point of view. Be "fashion right"
- Create exciting point-of-purchase visuals to spark impulse buying
- Design the appropriate fixturing, by classification, to enhance sales through stronger impulse purchases
- Create and direct major events at the store level

• Personal Selling

Select and develop strong, effective store managers who will:

- Better understand the Céline customer
- Develop outstanding customer service programs, associate incentive programs, seminars, and so forth
- Develop sales incentive programs for sales force

• Publicity

- Communicate constantly with the press to develop a larger-than-life designer persona
- Communicate various forms of the new marketing and advertising program to members of the press

• Testing

Confirm and modify the series of strategies recommended in this marketing plan by conducting focus groups in current and proposed major cities where Céline does and will do significant volume.

5

Exhibit 4–1
CÉLINE MARKETING PLAN *(CONTINUED)*

MARKETING STRATEGIES *(continued)*

• Expenditures

Marketing Mix Element	$M	Estimated Percentage of Total Budget
Media		
NATIONAL MAGAZINES	1,170.0	36%
(25 Insertions; 1-pg, 4C ad)		
Vogue, Harper's Bazaar, W, Vanity Fair, Elle		
TELEVISION (:30 spots)	1,200.0	37%
(75 TRPs/week for 9 weeks)		
Chicago, Dallas, Washington, New York		
DIRECT MAIL	200.0	6%
(4 markets; 3 drops/year)		
100,000 pieces per market, postage		
Media Total:	**2,570.0**	**79%**
Production		
MAGAZINE	45.0	2%
1-pg, 4C ad		
TELEVISION	100.0	3%
1:30 spot		
DIRECT MAIL	75.0	2%
Photography, Type, Printing		
Production Total:	**220.0**	**7%**
Sales Promotion	120.0	4%
Publicity	200.0	6%
Merchandising		
Store Signage	30.0	1%
POP Displays	10.0	0%
Research	100.0	3%
Total Marketing Budget:	**3,250.0**	**100%**
Total Sales Estimate:	**28,900.0**	
Marketing Budget as percentage of sales:	**11.2**	

weaknesses, and potential. Targets are established for sales, advertising, and publicity, and innovative strategies are presented that could accelerate the growth of Céline and transform the brand into a recognizable label with a designer personality.

A FLEXIBLE MODEL FOR GROWTH AND CHANGE

The marketing plan provides a battery of strategies to maximize growth and profitability. Charting such a course can provide the framework for enlivening any type of company, whether it's an haute couture house such as Céline, a budget brand such as Old Navy, or a brand unrelated to fashion.

Marketing plans are guides to prosperous futures. They need not be rigid. To gauge progress, they should be reviewed periodically, through focus groups or other research methods, as the final stage of the Céline plan suggests. Objectives should then be adjusted accordingly.

The Céline plan is more than a model for survival. It's a model for staging a repositioning, establishing new goals in sales and profits, changing the corporate culture, charging up the workforce, instilling pride in the organization and its products, focusing the products, targeting an audience, and beating the competition. In short, it's a model for creativity and marketing success.

ADVERTISING, SALES PROMOTION, AND THE NEW MARKETING REALITY

5 | Creating and Developing the Brand Image

"Image problems?
Let's start with the doorman."

WHETHER IT'S THE UNKEMPT DOORMAN or the lazy salesperson asleep on the job, at almost every company, there's room to improve the image. It may be a matter of sprucing up the staff, improving the quality of the service, or renovating stores. Or perhaps it means overhauling the advertising.

From Macy's to the May Company, from publishers to hotels, Ziccardi & Partners has developed marketing strategies that attack and rebuild advertising programs so they have a comprehensive perspective—catapulting new products into a brand status or aggressive sales results.

We faced this challenge when we were asked to create the first television spot for Brain Quest, the children's learning game. The game was already on the market for many years and sold more than 10 million copies. It was time to celebrate the milestone and boost sales to reach the next 10-million mark. We had to convey lots of information: new versions of the game are available, it can be played alone or with friends or parents, it has questions based on school curricula, and Brain Quest makes learning fun.

We packed all that and more into a commercial that spoofed the spaghetti western *The Good, the Bad, and the Ugly,* broadened the game's image to appeal to a larger audience, and achieved strong sales results. In the commercial, the hero was "The Kid," the smartest dude on the block, who challenges four other kids to a game of Brain Quest. They're tough competition because they play Brain Quest, too. As he rides off into the sunset (on his bike), he asks, "So what have we learned today?" They respond with the positioning line, "It's okay to be smart!"

Giving the product a unique appeal is what this chapter is all about. The essential message is that there are many ways through advertising to position products—even those similar to the competition's and those that have been on the market for ages—with a new image and a mark of distinction.

STRETCHING THE BOUNDS OF ADVERTISING

Ads are getting bigger and bolder, bulging with daring images and messages that often cross the threshold of popular acceptance, fire up controversy, promise the moon, and denigrate the competition. They're molded by new competitive challenges, by companies desperate to survive and recapture customers, by the political tide, by rapidly changing lifestyles, and by suddenly emerging technologies.

Is Slicker Advertising Better Advertising?

Special effects in photography and film have made advertisements slicker, costlier, more entertaining, and more Hollywood. Witness the Chanel No. 5 perfume ad in 1995 with model Carole Bouquet, androgynously decked out in a dowdy shirtdress and moussed hair, in which she's transformed, through the process known as morphing, into a buxom Marilyn Monroe cooing "I want to be loved by you." Look at Louis Armstrong and Humphrey Bogart superimposed in a nightclub scene for diet Coke, in a format mixing old movie footage with new film.

Think of those fantasy ads by Jean-Paul Goude, the French director and ad creator who gave Grace Jones her severe, flattop look for her music videos. Writing, editing, shooting, and creating special effects for surreal Egoiste and Coco ads, he, in effect, reinvents dreams. "My commercials are my vehicles to express myself artistically," Goude says. "They reflect my inner feelings. Usually, I do my best work when my work reflects my personality. I'm a gentle person, thinking like an artist in a world that is commercial. I consider my commercials to be fables, jewels." His ads create excitement and dialogue and have sexual overtones, yet are without the questionable taste or hard edge of some Calvin Klein jeans ads that have depicted teenagers in suggestive poses.

WHAT'S WRONG WITH IMAGE ADVERTISING?

Price-Driven Advertising's Not the Answer

Too often advertising is driven by price, price, price: the one-day only, never-again blockbuster sale, which seems to happen every week. It's 50 percent, 60 percent, 70 percent off. It's about cut-out coupons that offer another 10 percent off. That tactic has long been used by supermarkets and drug chains, but it's spread to department stores and better chains. Lord & Taylor will run four, five, or six big ads in the *New York Times* with coupons offering additional reductions on merchandise already marked down. It's time to turn it off, rethink the strategy, and strike the right chord.

Recycling Old Ad Themes Doesn't Work

The recycling of old ads and themes—McDonald's replaying its "All-Beef Patty" theme, Ace Hardware replaying its "Ace is the Place" theme, and Bradlees, the regional discounter, bringing back its "Mrs. B" personality as part of a renewed marketing effort to pitch store openings and some remerchandising efforts—just never ceases. The lack of fresh creative ideas and the reliance on tried-and-true methods may be safe, but that certainly doesn't mean they're successful.

Sex: Does It Sell?

The vast majority of advertisements still fall into the same formats and themes. There are bare-chested men, busty women, supermodels, and rock stars pitching products and bargains and signing multimillion-dollar contracts as spokespersons. There's a half-naked hunk lugging a Samsung microwave oven, with copy that says "cook with a microwave, it's healthier." Imagery that suggests far more than flying features an exotic, lush, tropical rain forest with a native in a grass skirt to pitch an airline package.

One of the hottest products in retail in the mid-1990s was the push-up bra. Wonderbra spurred sales through ads where the message was sexy. It showed a woman in the bra with a sly expression and the tag line, "Winner, Best Special Effects."

Fashion advertising is often tied to sexually suggestive messages to convince consumers that wearing the clothes will make them more sexy. That doesn't mean it would work in all situations. It would be the wrong message for a store like Wal-Mart, for example. The chain has been increasing its fashion merchandising and in 1995 rolled out the Kathie

Lee line, an exclusive sportswear and accessory collection for Wal-Mart, modeled after the enduring Jaclyn Smith collection for Kmart. To successfully sell more fashion, Wal-Mart must consider developing more advertising to project a fashion image. It won't be easy. It has to show fashion that looks good, looks wearable, and is not overly polyestered, while projecting a low price and mass appeal. The selection must be tasteful, casual, maybe updated a bit, but not anywhere near trendy or too sexy, and not even a penny above the working-class woman's budget.

Too often, ads seem like just another hard body or pretty face shot by a flamboyant photographer, rather than thoughtful messages or images that suggest reaching for a higher standard, raising one's self-confidence, or remaking oneself. One example is Nike's "Just Do It" campaign, which inspires youth, senior citizens, and the handicapped to participate in sports.

MORE THAN ONE WAY TO POSITION THE SAME PRODUCT

The Menswear Business: Two Approaches

Cambridge Members, a menswear chain, drew upon its strengths to convey an image that it is different from other menswear chains in its area. For example, after a spate of chic men's store openings in the heart of Manhattan's luxury goods district—Brooks Brothers, Barneys, and Bergdorf Goodman Men, among others—in 1995, Cambridge Members opened a unit on Broadway and 33rd Street, a not-so-chic part of New York. Cambridge decided it wanted to project a more down-to-earth image that would be appropriate for its location and distinguish it from the competition. It decided to portray itself as less trendy and less expensive than the East Side men's stores, while also offering high-quality goods at prices that suggested value. As part of a campaign to project this image, Cambridge ran a funny ad ribbing the competition, with a photo of a man in a suit climbing a Madison Avenue street pole, looking lost, and asking, "Where did your favorite store go?" The ad urged shoppers to discover "exceptional quality, classic good taste and prices far, far less than other luxury men's stores," such as those on Madison Avenue.

Another menswear chain, Today's Man, took a cooler approach in an attempt to convey a sexy, cutting-edge image. When it hyped the opening of its store on Fifth Avenue and 44th Street in April 1995, it ran ads on city buses that showed a shadowy photo of a well-proportioned, naked man in a reclining pose (reminiscent of the mood of Calvin Klein's Obsession ads) and the word *patience* in the top left side of the ad. The message: Here's a guy who's got it all—handsome, cool, and in control; he's Today's Man. In retrospect, the ad was misleading because the company never had the right merchandise for customers who might have responded to the ads by visiting the store. The store carried more moderate goods at a time when the market for these clothes was actually shrinking. People seeing the ads may have checked out the store but not found the sophisticated merchandise they expected, based on the ads. Sales fell off plan and the chain went bankrupt in early 1996.

The Health Club Business:
A Cerebral Approach to the Body

The Equinox health center took a cool approach, projecting a serious, cerebral, and upscale image with its message, "where body, mind and spirit are created equal." The message was laid across a close-up photo of an intense woman in a ninja outfit, readied, with her hands up, as if defending herself. The mood is vastly different from the ads of a competitor, the Pier 60 Sports Center, which decided not to use image advertising when it opened on Manhattan's West Side in February 1996. It took a straightforward approach by providing information to the public about facilities and unique features, such as the mile-long indoor track, an amenity that few health clubs or gyms offer—especially in Manhattan.

HIP OR NOT HIP? THAT IS OFTEN THE QUESTION

It's possible to cast a business as fun and hip, as a place where the shopper comes to be entertained, to learn about new trends, to see new products, to see other people, and to be seen. Stores with this focus trumpet designer appearances, informal modeling sessions, opportunities to get autographs from supermodels endorsing products, food tastings, and product demonstrations.

It's Hip to Be at Bloomie's

Bloomingdale's, for example, highlights certain departments or new shops in its weekly "Diary" full-page ads in the New York Times. Just like any diary, Bloomingdale's records the special or unusual products or events of the day. A January 1996 Bloomingdale's ad mentioned a new Louis Vuitton shop in the Arcade, a new sleepwear department on the fourth floor, the Le Train Bleu restaurant on the seventh floor, and free beauty advice offered in Cosmetics. Underneath the diary portion of the ad, Bloomingdale's reinforces its image as a happening kind of store with unique products, such as Estée Lauder "FastTrack Skincare," offering free consultations from Lauder experts about how you can see improvement in your skin in a day. The ad showed five big alarm clocks and said, "Don't wait a second longer . . . Start today. See Better Skin Tomorrow. First at Bloomingdale's."

These diary ads portray Bloomingdale's as a place where there's plenty of action and constant additions to the merchandising, a one-stop shopping experience but more upscale and exciting than most department stores. Some department stores might take the one-stop shopping approach without projecting an image and simply list the food, clothes, recreational items, books, plants, pharmaceuticals, parking facilities, credit arrangements, delivery services, and return and warranty-repair policies that they offer. That's fine for the time-pressed shopper who's not interested in "the shopping experience."

It's Hip Not to Be Hip

Many companies try to project a hip image to appeal to younger markets and generate excitement, glamour, and interest in their products. Others take an antihip position. That's why Coke shows an 80-year-old Italian woman dressed in black, drinking Coke, because "it's been around for a long, long, long, long time." After dismissing Pepsi as being only for kids, she turns to her window, where just outside is a younger group—in their sixties—blasting a radio and, of course, drinking Pepsi. She yells at them to lower the volume, and the "kids" turn it up, displaying their own brand of youthful defiance.

In an effort to target a younger audience that fancied itself as getting out of the hip genre, Dewar's Scotch ran a campaign that included an ad showing several young men with goatees and a caption that read, "OK, so you've done the goatee thing . . . now we can just move on."

Sometimes, a company can present an image that's offbeat or eccentric and goes out of its way not to be hip, thereby becoming different and entertaining. Tanqueray Gin created a spokesperson who might be considered a kind of antihero. He's Mr. Jenkins, a refined but wisecracking, sixtyish, roguish aristocrat who always has a martini in his hand and uses one occasion to toast the macramé bikini. He's hip in an unorthodox way.

CREATE AN IMAGE WITH A SINGLE PRODUCT

Another way stores can present a distinct image is by focusing their ads on a single product classification carried in great variety and depth. Nordstrom, which was founded as a shoe store and progressed into selling clothes and accessories for the entire family, soft home goods, and some gifts and cosmetics, seeks an image as a store with great depth in merchandise. In one case, Nordstrom used full-page newspaper ads that read RANGE across the middle and showed shoes in a variety of shades by Hush Puppies, a line that became trendy again in the mid-1990s. Few stores stock as heavily across several categories as Nordstrom, particularly in shoes, and the ads strengthened that reputation.

Similarly, when Easy Spirit opened its first store in Manhattan in early 1996, it sought to present an image as a store with an enormous variety of shoes for different lifestyles and activities. Some of the company's ads conveyed this message by saying it had 80 sizes and widths "for women, men, shoes for every part of your life. Career, fitness, and fun . . ."

SUCCESSFUL POSITIONING

Positioning is merely the creation of an image in the minds of customers, establishing the perception of the product and store *relative* to the competition. To be successful in the long term, positioning considers the attributes of the products or services you're selling, the needs and wants of the customer, and the characteristics of the competition. This is already established through the business review, which is a good place to start garnering the necessary information.

How Your Imagery Can Keep Going and Going

The Energizer battery has done a good job positioning itself as a product with longevity. It uses irony and wit in its ads. Some ads are photos of people in their nineties, with weather-beaten faces, wearing what you would least expect—Walkmans. The copy, sandwiched between two small batteries, reads, "The longest lasting battery in the world."

Levi Strauss also plays the longevity theme in some ads by casting its image as a product that can take a lot of abuse and last for years. In one ad without any Levi product, there's just an old leather punching bag, as a metaphor for time. The leather on the bag is cracking—a sign of age and of having taken a lot of punches over the years. Way in the top left corner is the message, "Levi's 501. Born to resist."

Volvo has also done a good job of steering its image as a product that outlasts the competition. In one of its ads, there's an old, almost antique-looking Volvo parked next to two auto wrecks that have been compressed into scrap metal boxes. The ad has a huge headline driving home the point: "An 18-year-old Volvo and two of its contemporaries." In other ads, Volvo's theme of being a superior product is perpetuated. One unusual ad gets across the message that Volvo is a very safe car—without even including a car in the ad. Instead, it cleverly shows a diver submerged in a metal cage threatened by a huge shark with its teeth showing—like *Jaws*. It tells a dramatic story: The diver seems too wobbly on his feet in the cage, and you can't help gazing at the danger. In tiny print in the corner of the photo is the simple message "Cages save lives. Volvo."

Creating a Position for a Basic Commodity

A more mundane but nevertheless effective approach to advertising product was done by the California Milk Processor Board. The similarity with Volvo is that in some of the board's ads, the product is never shown. That was a smart decision, considering milk in itself isn't particularly exciting to look at or especially interesting in the scheme of culinary choices. It's an everyday staple that people take for granted. Yet the board wisely chose to emphasize that it's a product we shouldn't take too lightly and to remind us to replenish regularly. It did this by depicting the frustrating occasions when there's no milk in the refrigerator, but there's a hot cup of fresh brewed coffee waiting or a tray of chocolate brownies fresh from the oven. In each case, the question "Got Milk?" is posed.

Updating an Image to Reposition a Product

The strategy for repositioning Coach—from a quality yet dated accessory line to one with a focus fitting the 1990s—involved portraying Coach's market as contemporary, upscale women who are part of a long line of traditional, centuries-old American families. In effect, the advertising campaign branded Coach as an updated classic for the modern woman. A good example of one ad in this campaign showed the great-granddaughter of F. Scott and Zelda Fitzgerald reclining comfortably in an outdoor setting, her Coach bag by her side.

THE ALL-IMPORTANT POSITIONING STRATEGY

Positioning is how your product is perceived in the marketplace relative to the competitor. Whatever is being advertised, it is crucial, before creating the advertising, to examine the competition's strengths and weaknesses in appearance, design, name and reputation, geographic position, prices, advertising, promotion, merchandising, selling, and publicity. Once this is done, it's time to write the positioning strategy, a statement that should be succinct and provide clear and specific information for the advertising and all of the other tools in the marketing mix.

Execute the Strategy Companywide

In 1994, Haggar put together a positioning statement to create a store that appealed to men who hate to shop. It did this, not so much through advertising, but rather through visual merchandising. Haggar created a store in the spring of 1995 that might be considered the antitrendy store for the man who has little interest in fashion but could be feeling pressure from friends or family to work on his wardrobe. Inspired by the hit TV show *Home Improvement,* Haggar, working with FRCH Design World-wide, created unglamorous, unpretentious 4,000-square-foot stores for men's casual and dress clothing targeted for those ages 25 to 49. Haggar used plenty of props that men traditionally relate to, like bowling balls, license plates, cue sticks, and an overall innovative retail decor with exposed studs, wooden closet doors doubling as endcaps, and exposed ceilings. There were also couches and music videos interspersed with Haggar commercials for those who just wanted to sit and rest—shopping is more exhausting for those who hate it. Also setting the scene were in-store poster ads supporting the lighthearted tone, such as "100 percent wool. The sheep would be proud" and "Great Stuff. Clearance specials at extra low prices."

Positioning Prerequisites: Advance Thought and Planning

Macy's learned about planning a positioning strategy the hard way. Its $150 million ambitious but ill-fated image campaign on TV, launched in the spring of 1991, contributed to R.H. Macy & Company's financial collapse. Few retailers have developed a sustained TV strategy that's image-oriented, entertaining, and impressionable. Macy's objectives were to convey an image of itself as the family store, to reposition out of its incessant price promoting, and to recapture lost market share.

At the time, Macy's had a large advertising department, as big as many agencies, with a $200 million to $300 million budget annually, or about 6 percent of sales. The campaign would begin in New York, New Jersey, and Connecticut, and Macy's would be the single largest local advertiser on ABC, NBC, and CBS stations. The campaign would get rolled out to other markets in 1992, when TV spending, including airtime and production costs, would hit the $150 million mark, or roughly five times what Macy's spent on TV advertising in the previous year.

"What became apparent as we began to study advertising was that if you wanted to talk to an audience, you'd better think about TV," said Edward Finkelstein, then chairperson and CEO of Macy's. "McDonald's impressed me the most. It's got great institutional advertising, very active price promotions, movie tie-ins, where you could get a video for a low price, with your food order, or get mugs. I always admired McDonald's." Finkelstein also concluded that Macy's one-day sale ads were not increasing market share and that Macy's approach to advertising was off balance.

Four advertising agencies made presentations on how to position Macy's. Lintas won with the tag line, "The Magic of Macy's," which reflected Macy's magically grand special events such as the Thanksgiving Parade, the Fourth of July fireworks, Santa Land, and the Flower Show.

A series of commercials was created for prime time: for menswear and the Thornton Bay private label, china, glass and silver, children's wear, ready-to-wear, housewares, and domestics. There were also institutional commercials touting national brands, private labels, excitement, fashion, friendly service, newness, and Macy's as the family store.

The campaign was kicked off at a huge party at Macy's Herald Square for 400 vendors, where the carpet department was turned into a theater to preview the ads. Finkelstein told the crowd, "We're going to make it happen." But it didn't happen. As the campaign progressed, sales continued to slide and losses continued to mount. Macy's filed bankruptcy in January 1992, and the campaign never got into full swing, never hit $150 million in expenditures. Macy's didn't pull the plug on it but phased it out slowly.

As one former Macy's executive recalls, "You can look at it two ways. It was a bold, creative step, unique for the times. But you can also say, since the company went bankrupt, it was wasteful. For it to be meaningful, for it to have an effect, you have to stay with it for a long time. We didn't. We needed to start this earlier."

BRANDING: THE NAME OF THE GAME

A brand or name should help communicate the product's positioning and its inherent qualities and advantages. When establishing branding parameters, keep in mind that the name—and how it appears in the advertising—reflects the right positioning of the product and contributes to awareness and knowledge of the product and its purpose. The advertising should also be memorable and project a positive visual concept that sticks in the minds of the public when the product is mentioned, seen, or read. A brand should have a personality of its own and should lend itself to creative usage in the advertising. Many companies and brands fail to project a personality that the market responds to. Advertising can be structured for a new product or store to give it a personality or to educate consumers on its benefits.

To successfully brand a product, certain questions need to be answered. Does the brand name have attention value and will it make its mark in a low-interest category? Does the name provide a competitive difference? Does it help to truly differentiate the product from its competition? Does the name have relevance? Will the name help to communicate values the target audience cares about? How about the competitive position of the product or store? How does the name—and the concept and positioning behind it—stand up against the positionings of the competition? Is the branding believable? Will the audience question the concept behind the name, even if it proves to be true? And, finally, does the brand name have the potential to extend to new products being created under the corporate umbrella?

Branding with Private Label Merchandise

One counterstrategy is to increase the breadth of product and services through a private label program. This strategy is on the rise in the 1990s, though that seems to be cyclical, with retailers over the course of years raising and lowering their level of private label merchandising.

The strategy offers no direct competition, since it's your own product, designed to your specifications by either an in-house design team or a manufacturer. It is the chance to provide something unique to the marketplace and also attain wider gross margins. However, just like any brand, it can be knocked off. JCPenney's Arizona denim-based jeans and sportswear line is getting copied left and right. Other retailers, noticing the success of Arizona, have countered with their own introductions, such as Sears's Canyon River Blues line, which debuted in 1995.

Beginning in the late 1970s, Bloomingdale's had many successful import promotions, including items from France, China, and Italy. They were major differentiators and flashy, festive vehicles for kicking off the fall season. Over time, however, they ran out of steam and shoppers tired of them. When new management arrived in 1991, the concept was shelved and another concept for exclusivity was introduced, the Only at Bloomingdale's campaign. It is part private label products bearing the Bloomingdale's label and part packages of products from designers and brands sold only at Bloomingdale's. Sometimes it includes merchandise that Bloomingdale's launches a season ahead of other stores.

Is a Great Name Enough to Make a Successful Brand?

In the spring of 1988, when Paloma Picasso launched her line of designer accessories starting at $500 for a handbag and up to a few thousand for an alligator bag, "No thought had gone into the marketing," recalls Victor Lipko, president of the company at that time. "A lot had gone into Paloma Picasso as a brand. She was married to an Argentine playwright (they met in Paris) who pushed her to develop her name as a brand. She was in every ad. The ads were about Paloma. Not about the product."

The company spent about $350,000 on ads in *Vogue, Town and Country, W, Elle,* and *Harper's Bazaar.* The business peaked in spring of 1989 with $4.8 million at wholesale or roughly $10 million at retail, but eventually reality set in and things turned bad. Stores cut back on orders after having to heavily mark down goods to sell them and getting clobbered on gross margins.

There is a long list of products and stores that stand for nothing in the minds of customers. Unfortunately, the people behind these products or running the stores don't know it. Consumers aren't fooled. Eventually these products and even the stores disappear.

South Sea Pearls: Branding for an Upscale Client

When our agency was given the advertising assignment for the South Sea Pearl Consortium, the challenge was twofold: to position South Sea Pearls in the marketplace, creating a strong product awareness, and to create a unique brand image, positioning South Sea Pearls as the best of all pearls and as a gem of equal or better value than diamonds and other precious jewels. Our presentation to the consortium was concise and targeted. It went straight to the heart of the assignment and provided the solution.

Background

After extensive research and meetings with the client—including a trip to Australia to see where the pearls were cultivated—we started by reviewing the assignment. First, we looked at the reasons why South Sea Pearls are so special. Using the research information provided by the clients, it was easy to see that South Sea Pearls are the world's finest pearls because of their luster, color, shape, size, and complexion. We then reviewed the marketing challenges of the assignment, which included overcoming low brand awareness and position.

Objectives

We presented an overview of what we were going to do, which included creating a unique global brand image and developing a powerful brand awareness.

Strategy

Again, the strategy was brief but to the point. Our plan was to develop an advertising/promotional program targeting individuals who were aware of the product as well as unaware buyers and retailers.

Program Elements

An outline of the vehicles we intended to use to accomplish the assignment included consumer print advertising, retail cooperative efforts, joint promotions with other high-end products (i.e., Cristal and Ferrari), a consumer/retailer educational brochure, and point-of-purchase materials.

Tone of the Advertising

These four words would immediately set the style and delivery of the campaign:

- Sophisticated.
- Intelligent.
- Elegant.
- Global.

Positioning

Next we addressed how we would position the product. The positioning mind-set was that the South Sea Pearl is a unique and precious gem that is, at once, rare, romantic, enduring, prestigious, magical, pristine, and of heirloom quality.

Execution

It was now time to reveal the creative. In Exhibit 5–1 (a, b, c), the creative execution of the campaign, we addressed everything in the objectives, strategy, and positioning. The copy platform positioned South Sea Pearls as being better than the competition:

a. *There are mountains and there are the Himalayas.*
There are pearls and there are South Sea Pearls.
b. *There are chapels and there is the Sistine Chapel.*
There are pearls and there are South Sea Pearls.
c. *There are coral reefs and there is the Great Barrier Reef.*
There are pearls and there are South Sea Pearls.

Theme Integration

The positioning line of the campaign situates South Sea Pearls as a gem superior in quality to other gems and also as a long-term, lifetime investment.

South Sea Pearls

Gem of a Lifetime

The campaign turned South Sea Pearls into a highly recognized brand that meant something to consumers and also boosted sales to a new

Exhibit 5–1a
SOUTH SEA PEARL CONSORTIUM/HIMALAYAS AD

There are mountains.
And there are
the Himalayas.
There are pearls.

And there are
South Sea Pearls.

South Sea Pearl – Gem of a Lifetime.™

THE PEARLS FEATURED ARE CULTIVATED SOUTH SEA PEARLS OF AUSTRALIAN ORIGIN.
FOR ALL INQUIRIES, CALL 1-800-441-SSPC.

South Sea Pearl Consortium™

Exhibit 5–1b
SOUTH SEA PEARL CONSORTIUM/SISTINE CHAPEL AD

Exhibit 5–1c
SOUTH SEA PEARL CONSORTIUM/GREAT BARRIER REEF AD

plateau. Perhaps even more noteworthy, the campaign was orchestrated without resorting to any of the common methods of marketing: sexual innuendoes, price promoting, or special effects. It didn't break any rules, but it didn't play by the old set of rules either. If it had, South Sea Pearls would have been just another also-ran.

6 Formulating the Creative

"Don't you think that slogan
sounds a little desperate?"

WHEN COMPANIES ARE GROPING FOR NEW BUSINESS, they often rush to the advertising team and demand a new strategy. A new slogan. A new message, and they want it yesterday. It's a sign of desperation. Developing advertising is a complex and lengthy, sometimes wrenching, creative process that should be dealt with methodically and calmly. Yet sometimes it turns into an adventure that starts with a 36-hour deadline on a proposal to pitch a major account.

When Ziccardi & Partners was just one month old and eager to grab accounts, it heard that the Trump Regency Hotel in Atlantic City (one of the few noncasino hotels there) was developing a new campaign to draw more business. While it had already begun the agency review process, we thought we could nudge our way into the competition. I hastily drafted a letter to Donald Trump, telling him that I had just purchased the agency that promoted his two books; he forwarded the letter to the Regency's general manager and we were in. But we had less than two days to present the creative.

We needed a big idea. We took the Regency's weakness—no casino—and turned it into a strength. To the businessperson, we touted the extensive conference facilities, lavish catering, and business atmosphere with no distractions—not even a one-armed bandit. "Your Business is Our Pleasure" was the positioning line.

To the consumer, we positioned the Regency as the perfect family getaway, with a great beach, spacious rooms where kids stay for free, fun dining, and a rooftop health spa. "Your Pleasure is Our Business" was the positioning line.

The finishing touches were added to the plan in a car on the way to Atlantic City. We were the dark horse that won the account. We had the big idea, the right idea, which unfolded after a complex yet disciplined creative process. We didn't have much time, but we worked and reworked everything. We hit the right formula, and it seemed to come out of the blue. Of course, it never really does. It's guided by a marketing plan, your own creative juices that result from your experiences, lifestyle, business sense, common sense, and emotions.

In this chapter, you'll learn that formulating the creative advertising is a crucial, time-consuming team process that involves examining all elements and themes in the ads, from headlines to copy to art and the fine print at the bottom. Since you've already learned about the power of advertising and where the trends in the industry are headed, you're ready to delve into the creative process and discover its mysteries as part of the marketing adventure.

DEVELOPING THE MESSAGE

Bright ideas and beautiful photographs aren't enough. Creating advertising is a lengthy, often agonizing, yet rewarding team process that involves learning about the product, assessing its attributes, conveying its essence, and establishing a tone. Then the creative process intensifies. The team creates and re-creates the copy and the visuals, puts it together, and then rips it all apart until the elements work in tandem to communicate a powerful message, one that leaps out and demands a response. Remember, the team is not just developing ads. It is formulating a campaign that speaks out to the world.

There is flexibility in the process. For example, the ad copy (the written words in an ad) can be short or long. A few words might suffice. There are occasions, though, when verbosity is appropriate, particularly with new products such as computers and electronics geared to the more technical consumer. Simpler products may need some explaining, such as Fisher-Price toys, where ads under the headline, "Fisher-Price toys don't bite back," explain in about a dozen paragraphs how the toys don't have rough edges and don't pull apart when a baby chews on them. That's what parents need and want to know.

Ads can show the product, as Fisher-Price's do, but they don't have to, as witnessed by Volvo's ad showing the shark menacing the diver in the cage. An ad can have a headline or no headline. Calvin Klein underwear ads are visually striking. They show the perfect male or female form and the brand name. But in Calvin's underwear ads, there are no flourishes and no headlines.

THE BIG IDEA

The format depends on the "big idea," a concept coined by David Ogilvy. The big idea can be expressed in five words or five paragraphs, through a giant photo, a montage, or an illustration. Calvin Klein's big idea in his CK One fragrance ads revolves around attitude and sex. He shows swaggering bare-chested young men and women touching each other. For CK Jeans, he shows teenagers lasciviously posed in underwear, but in the underwear ads, he emphasizes the body form and body consciousness, for a more aesthetic approach. Ralph Lauren's big idea is to project the American dream, posterity in the Hamptons, a romantic lifestyle of horseback riding, tall blond women, health, and fitness. The message is bucolic and classic and emphasizes that Polo products— whether pinpoint oxfords or fall evening gowns—stand for quality, Americana, and "tradition that looks modern."

Benetton's big idea has been to promote insight and indignation by running controversial photos, such as a young Croatian killed in Bosnia, condoms in different colors, an AIDS victim on his deathbed. Some think it's a bad idea for Benetton to capitalize on the plight of others for its own gain. Oliveri Toscani, creator of the ads, has been on the defensive. He once said, "I don't find my work so strange. It's natural for me. I'm not a salesman. Advertising is not just for selling. It can reach a nerve. There are other meanings, other reasons. What makes the difference is the communications. You don't remember a specific product, but you do remember the communication."

THE HEADLINE CAN BE KEY

Most advertisers would agree that effective communication through advertising can start by developing the headline. Decide whether or not to use one and whether it fits into the big idea. A headline can take various tones. It can issue a command that urges people to action. *Men's Journal,* an outdoor magazine, has run ads bearing quotes from famous people such as Nikita Khrushchev stating, "Life is Short. Live it Up" and Robert Redford's statement, "Other people have analysis. I have Utah." The ads inspire people to dive into life and to begin by reading the magazine.

The big idea shapes what the headline says and its appearance. A headline could pose a question or a challenge to the audience to pique interest in a new product. That's exactly what Milky Way does in its low-fat candy bar ads. Milky Way taunts consumers, "Bet You Can't Tell It's A Lite?" and then explains that the candy bar has 50 percent less fat. Other ad headlines ask questions, but they may be rhetorical. Perdue Chicken does that in some of its ads. In one, Frank Perdue, the chairperson, holds out a half-chewed chicken leg and defiantly asks, "Who cares where the beef is?"

In each ad, the headline must be provocative and arresting, like Health & Racquet Club's "Stress dissolves in water." That line puts the emphasis on the word *stress* and portrays the club as an elixir to the stresses and strains of life in the big city. Another example is Cave Creek's sardonic "Tastes like hell" headline. That headline positions its Chile Beer brand as a unique, dynamic beverage with a distinctive, fiery aftertaste. Underneath the headline, there's a dramatic picture of a man breathing fire.

APPEALING TO THE EMOTIONS

Advertising, like other media and art forms, reflects the human condition. Ads, through copy and visuals, can express fear, loss, sexuality, sadness, anger, irony, mirth, or humor and use these moods and emotions to connect with an audience and help sell products.

Sadness

Ads can be emotional, touching the reader by conveying feelings of nostalgia or loss. One such ad for *Time* magazine featured photos of the late Jacqueline Kennedy Onassis cavorting with her children. Ads can also evoke sadness and horror, as in another *Time* ad that showed a photo of a dead African child refugee left unattended.

Fear

Other emotions, such as fear, work in public service advertising. One ad geared to stem teenage pregnancy has a large photo of a young, clean-cut man, looking somewhat devious, and the quote, "Trust me. I won't get you pregnant." The message is: Don't let good looks and reassuring words confuse you or lead you astray; there are other people and hot lines that can help you avoid a mistake.

Appeals to fear emphasize the consequences of not buying the product or service. For example, an American Cancer Society ad shows it understands women and why they avoid mammograms, listing such reasons as "I'm embarrassed. I'm nervous. There's no history of breast cancer in my family." But it points out that those reasons are trivial, considering what is at stake. The ad bluntly concludes, "The only reason why you should. It may save your life."

The Downside of Overplaying Fear

The insurance industry has focused on the fear of dying and leaving loved ones emotionally and financially bereft. Sometimes, the industry has come on too strong, and ads have associated it with images of doom rather than hope, indicating that once death or disability strikes an individual, the situation for the rest of the family can be bleak. The intention, however, was to encourage buying insurance as a cushion against tragedy. Prudential ads have shown people in mourning or dying; these ads received notice in the industry but did little to boost sales. Prudential switched tactics and created ads that showed people in near-death experiences eager to get "a piece of the rock."

Vulnerability

Taking a more positive spin, the Allendale Insurance company also plays down catastrophes and plays up minimizing the risk of tragedies. In one ad, it has a big photo of a bottle of vegetable oil and the headline, "It's terrific on salads, great on pasta and makes one heck of a fire." Next to that is a small picture of a factory on fire, an explanation that vegetable oil is combustible, and a description of Allendale's efforts to reduce the risk by developing a better sprinkler system. Cigna Group Insurance also took a more positive approach to difficult situations. One Cigna ad shows a woman in a wheelchair bowling, suggesting that people with disabilities shouldn't give up on enjoying life. It says that "planning ahead" in the event of disabling accident or illness "can make an enormous difference."

Humor

Novelty ads use humor or suspense to grab attention and motivate purchasing and are highly effective when the competition hews to one format. Campari, an Italian liqueur, has a way of suggesting it's a welcome alternative to the standard drink served up at cocktail hour. In one wacky ad, there's a young ingenue type on the ledge of a building, exclaiming,

"If someone offers me another glass of white wine, I'll jump." The tag line at the bottom of the ad reads "Escape from beverage boredom."

Wendy's has used humor almost exclusively, relying on the remarkably successful "Where's the Beef?" campaign and more recently using Dave Thomas, the chair of the company, as the spokesperson, and a genuinely funny one at that. Recent spots underscore the power of humor, especially when it addresses the needs of its audience. One spot has Thomas in an elegant restaurant contemplating his meager plate of nouvelle cuisine. He shakes his head in dismay, knowing that for a truly filling meal at a much lower price, one should eat at Wendy's.

Among the advertisers during Super Bowl XXX, Pepsi was the hands-down winner in the humor category. The spot with the trained goldfish that plays dead to get a sip of Pepsi and ends up flushed down the toilet for its trouble and the one with the Coca-Cola deliveryman who tries to sneak a can of Pepsi only to have the entire shelf collapse were highly effective in using humor and strengthening Pepsi's brand image.

APPEALING TO THE EGO

Emotional appeals can also speak to ego. For example, a gold necklace can be described by detailing the length and carat weight of the piece, but a focus on the gold necklace as a reward for the buyer would be more effective. Showing gold as a gift expressing affection for a person would also be more productive. A Mayor's Jewelers ad, for example, shows how a piece of jewelry can enliven a business suit, with a woman raising her arm to show off an eye-catching wristwatch, thereby making a fashion statement. The ad also demonstrates that jewelry is a great gift that makes an impression; it says, "At Mayor's . . . a gift of gold is a gift of love."

APPEALING TO LOGIC

More straightforward ads that hype a competitive advantage such as price or quality, elements that are objectively quantified, are called logical ads. They generally lack emotion. For example, certain Toyota ads sought to stress the superior road performance and price of its Avalon model. Therefore, one ad reads, "Drive an Avalon, and even the road relaxes. After all, Avalon's refined driving performance and quiet, comfortable interior tend to bring on that state known as bliss." The ad also says the price of the car starts at around $23,900.

Wrangler has an ad that combines logic and humor to express the comfort of its jeans, as well as its reputation for performance. It shows a cowboy sleeping on the back of a bucking bull in a rodeo and reads, "Have We Made Our Relaxed Fit Jeans Too Comfortable?"

Some Campbell's Soup ads also use the logic format to attempt to overcome an image that canned foods aren't as nutritious as fresh foods. Campbell's, seeking to position its soup as a nutritious, healthy component to one's diet, has used an ad with the headline "Health Insurance." The ad copy points out that Campbell's Vegetable Beef "contains more than ⅓ of the day's allowance of vitamin A in a single serving" and that the soups are also easy to digest. Campbell's, of course, hopes the public swallows its health pitch.

CELEBRITY APPEALS

Ads can include celebrities, a common way to connect with audiences since these are people we know through the movies, TV, sports, or politics, and they are often seen as role models. Often, celebrities appear in public service advertising. Recording superstar Stevie Wonder is featured in an ad against drunk driving, saying, "Before I'll ride with a drunk, I'll drive myself." Celebrities are also used to push products. The Gap, for example, ran photos of Muhammad Ali, Steve McQueen, and Zsa Zsa Gabor in khakis, a best-seller at the chain, though it's not clear whether the khakis are actually Gap products. Tina Turner is used in an ad for *McCall's* to project a new image for the magazine and suggest that it has more to it than people might think. The ad is dominated by a photo of a beaming Turner and a sarcastic headline under her face, "One of the drab homebodies who reads *McCall's*."

PICK UP ON TRENDS—BUT BE UNIQUE

When a new advertising trend suddenly emerges, look immediately for similarities in competing advertising. But when following a new trend, be careful to find ways of standing out from the competition. An example of not standing out from the competition occurred when black-and-white photography reemerged as an advertising art form in the late 1980s. It quickly became the contemporary, hip direction—for fashion ads in particular. Many advertisers picked up on the trend, and inadvertently their ads began to look painfully similar.

The advertisers that succeeded in this trend took a unique approach in carefully planning the direction of their campaigns, as well as selectively choosing models and the style of their hair and makeup. The ads from this era that best illustrate this point came from designers Donna Karan, Calvin Klein, Giorgio Armani, and Ellen Tracy. While they are all done in black and white, they are completely individual in look and approach.

KNOW WHAT YOUR CUSTOMER WANTS TO SEE

There is as much to learn from poor ads that turn off customers or drive them away as there is from great ads that attract customers and lure them in. No matter how beautiful or innovative a campaign appears to be, it can fail miserably if it's not correctly targeted to the advertiser's core customer. An example of this was the Anne Klein campaign done in 1993 that used hard-edged, provocative models in stark, cold, metallic settings. Although this acute departure in style was a hot topic when the campaign broke, it failed to stimulate sales. The image portrayed was clearly one that the more conservative Anne Klein customer could not relate to.

Also, consider the effect of media noise from saturation. Are there so many competing ads in that medium that the consumer is ignoring all of them? If this is the case, think about using some novelty in the advertising presentation and choice of media.

EIGHT EASY PIECES: PUTTING IT TOGETHER

After thinking about all the various emotional appeals that could be telegraphed in an ad, it's time to decide on the form and content of an advertising campaign. There are steps to this process that, if followed sequentially, bring order and discipline without compromising creativity.

1. Developing the Creative Strategy Template

Exhibit 6–1 (a–g), is the creative strategy template we completed for one of our clients, Millennium Broadway (formerly called Hotel Macklowe). This template is Ziccardi & Partners's guide to finding solutions and focusing thoughts. It demonstrates how we organize our ideas before we begin our creative strategy sessions. The template forces us to think about what we want to say, rather than how to say it. The how part comes later, after isolating what the consumer really needs to know. Once this document is prepared, there's a ton of creative raw material from which to produce the final copy and get the big idea.

After doing this diligent homework for our client, we came up with the positioning line "Extraordinary Vision." The eight-page insert, as shown in Exhibit 6–2 (a–c), was the result of a well-thought-out creative strategy.

2. Creating the Copy Platform

The copy platform is simply a statement of the ad campaign's objectives with a summary of the target market, the product's benefits, its unique selling proposition, and its big idea. Include the nuts-and-bolts data, such as disclaimers, store hours, and locations, some of which is mundane but necessary to include in the ads. Then develop the positioning platform indicating how the campaign positions the product for consumers and whether it establishes, strengthens, or reshapes attitudes about the product.

The copy platform should be clever and memorable. It doesn't always have to be literal, and it should appeal to the imagination. Take the Howard & Phil's Western Wear campaign. The company wanted to include in its platform that the clothes were authentic Western wear, can stand up to a lot of wear and tear, are made with quality fabric, and appeal to men who are rugged, outdoor-oriented types, not Fifth Avenue shoppers. To convey a sense of independence and masculinity, the company devised an ad with a cowboy gritting his teeth and clutching his rope on a dusty plain, with the short, three-line copy platform, "HOWARD & PHIL'S—nowhere near—MILAN   PARIS   NEW YORK."

Exhibit 6–1a
MILLENNIUM BROADWAY/CREATIVE STRATEGY TEMPLATE

Creative Strategy Template
Client: Millennium Broadway

Client: *Millennium Broadway*

Job#: *MB 27865*

Job Description: *Image campaign / Print*

AE: *J. Friedman*

1. Product /Service

- *MB is a three-star New York City hotel consisting of five distinct segments:*
  - *Rooms and services catering to the business traveler*
  - *Rooms and services catering to the weekend guest*
  - *The Manhattan Conference Center*
  - *The Hudson Theatre—an authentic NY Broadway theater*
  - *Restaurant Charlotte—for breakfast, lunch, pre-theater dinner*

- *MB is located in the heart of Times Square*

- *MB is uniquely designed with art-deco decor throughout*

1

Exhibit 6–1b
MILLENNIUM BROADWAY/CREATIVE STRATEGY TEMPLATE
(CONTINUED)

Creative Strategy Template
Client: Millennium Broadway

2. Competitive Arena

- *All upscale midtown hotels that cater to business travelers and weekend guests*

- *All New York City conference facilities*

- *All New York City hotels that have ballroom facilities for special events*

- *All restaurants in the theater district*

3. Snapshot of Primary Prospect

- *The individual business traveler who comes to New York during the week*

- *The leisure guest and tourist who stays in New York on weekends*

- *Conference planners who site for their corporate conferences*

- *Individuals and businesses who plan large catered events*

- *Shoppers, tourists, local businesspeople, and theater-goers who dine in the area*

2

Exhibit 6–1c
MILLENNIUM BROADWAY/CREATIVE STRATEGY TEMPLATE
(CONTINUED)

Creative Strategy Template
Client: Millennium Broadway

4. Audience Lifestyle/Characteristics

- *Upscale professionals who either live in NY area or visit frequently for business or personal reasons*

- *Disposable income for shopping, theater, and other NY activities*

- *College educated, readers of the New York Times, Wall Street Journal, New Yorker, business publications, arts and leisure publications*

5. Audience Mind-set/Psychographic Info

- *These target audiences have certain things in common when they use hotel facilities. They tend to stay in more upscale hotels that offer a wide variety of services and amenities*

- *They do not usually select their hotel by price, but they expect great service in return*

- *They will return to hotels that they are happy with*

- *They appreciate the style of the hotel as well as its services*

3

Exhibit 6–1d
MILLENNIUM BROADWAY/CREATIVE STRATEGY TEMPLATE
(CONTINUED)

Creative Strategy Template
Client: Millennium Broadway

6. Problems / Opportunities

- <u>*Problem*</u>: Since its opening five years ago, MB has not yet had a coordinated approach to its advertising

- <u>*Problem*</u>: Advertising has been weak, not reaching deep into the market segments that MB should be reaching

- <u>*Problem*</u>: There is fierce competition in all areas— from other midtown hotels, catering facilities, conference centers, and restaurants

- <u>*Opportunity*</u>: Because current advertising does not have a strong presence, there is an opportunity to "launch" a new campaign with a big splash

- <u>*Opportunity*</u>: The design of MB is unique among New York hotels—there is a "feel" to this property that no other New York hotel has

- <u>*Opportunity*</u>: No other New York site has so many amenities under one roof

4

Exhibit 6–1e
MILLENNIUM BROADWAY/CREATIVE STRATEGY TEMPLATE
(CONTINUED)

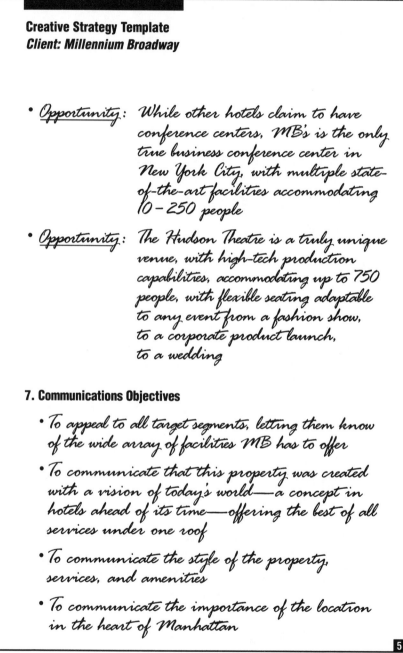

Creative Strategy Template
Client: Millennium Broadway

- *Opportunity:* While other hotels claim to have conference centers, MB's is the only true business conference center in New York City, with multiple state-of-the-art facilities accommodating 10 – 250 people

- *Opportunity:* The Hudson Theatre is a truly unique venue, with high-tech production capabilities, accommodating up to 750 people, with flexible seating adaptable to any event from a fashion show, to a corporate product launch, to a wedding

7. Communications Objectives

- To appeal to all target segments, letting them know of the wide array of facilities MB has to offer

- To communicate that this property was created with a vision of today's world—a concept in hotels ahead of its time—offering the best of all services under one roof

- To communicate the style of the property, services, and amenities

- To communicate the importance of the location in the heart of Manhattan

5

114

Exhibit 6–1f
MILLENNIUM BROADWAY/CREATIVE STRATEGY TEMPLATE
(CONTINUED)

Creative Strategy Template
Client: Millennium Broadway

8. Product / Service Position

- *In style and choice of facilities, MB's position in the marketplace is unique for all of the previously mentioned reasons*

9. Emotional Issues

- *This property offers the consumer the best that New York has to offer and appeals to people who have discriminating tastes and demand uncompromising service*

10. Key Points *(The advertising promise)*

- *Will provide you with the most enjoyable stay you have ever had in New York*
- *Will make your next business conference a successful and comfortable one—and one that will net results*
- *Will make your next big event one to remember*
- *Will provide you with all the services and amenities of the hotel that you demand*

Exhibit 6–1g
MILLENNIUM BROADWAY/CREATIVE STRATEGY TEMPLATE
(CONTINUED)

Creative Strategy Template
Client: Millennium Broadway

11. Copy Points *(Feature/Benefit—if collateral, attach copy outline)*

- *Sophistication, elegance, service, amenities, one-of-a-kind, state-of-the-art, a vision of the future*
- *List of all the hotel areas and their features*

12. Tone of Communication

- *Graphic approach should be fashionable and elegant, while conveying a seriousness about service to the customer*
- *Copy approach should have the same elegance and speak to an educated, knowledgeable consumer*

Platform Approved:

Account Services: _____ Date: 6/5·94

Creative Director: _____ Date: 6 -15-94

7

Exhibit 6–2a
MILLENNIUM BROADWAY/EIGHT-PAGE INSERT

WELCOME TO THE VISION
HOTEL MACKLOWE.

CONSTRUCTED IN 1990. CREATED FOR THE
FUTURE. DESIGNED FOR A NEW LEVEL OF PHYSICAL
AND PSYCHIC COMFORT. HOTEL MACKLOWE. A
PLACE WITH VISION. BUSINESS VISION. PEOPLE
VISION. EXTRAORDINARY VISION. BEGINNING IN
THE ELEGANTLY MURALED 44TH STREET LOBBY.
EXTENDING INTO EVERY SUPERB DETAIL IN
EVERY METICULOUS ROOM. AND CONTINUING
WITH A STAFF THAT ANTICIPATES DESIRES.
HOTEL MACKLOWE. AN EXCEPTIONAL MERGING OF
PURPOSE AND PLACE.

Hotel Macklowe

EXTRAORDINARY VISION.

Exhibit 6–2b
MILLENNIUM BROADWAY/EIGHT-PAGE INSERT *(CONTINUED)*

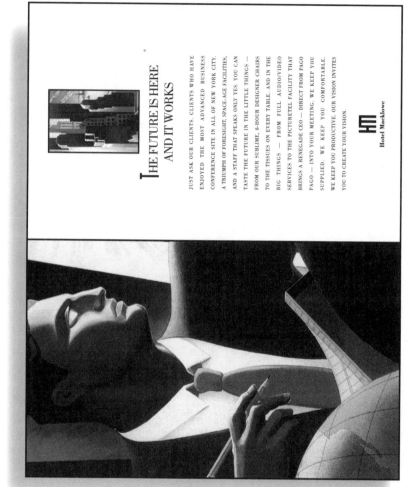

Exhibit 6–2c
MILLENNIUM BROADWAY/EIGHT-PAGE INSERT *(CONTINUED)*

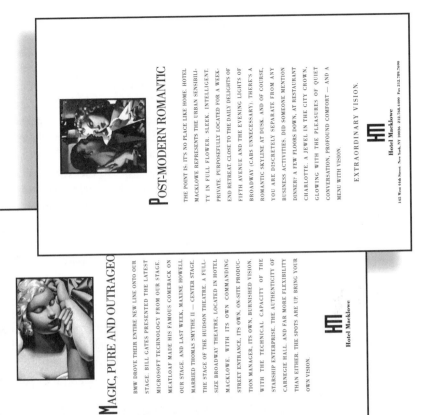

Pᴏst-Modern Romantic

THE POINT IS: IT'S NO PLACE LIKE HOME. HOTEL MACKLOWE REPRESENTS THE URBAN SENSIBILITY IN FULL FLOWER. SLEEK. INTELLIGENT. PRIVATE. PURPOSEFULLY LOCATED FOR A WEEKEND RETREAT CLOSE TO THE DAILY DELIGHTS OF FIFTH AVENUE AND THE EVENING LIGHTS OF BROADWAY (CABS UNNECESSARY). THERE'S A ROMANTIC SKYLINE AT DUSK. AND OF COURSE, YOU ARE DISCRETELY SEPARATE FROM ANY BUSINESS ACTIVITIES. DID SOMEONE MENTION DINNER? A FEW FLOORS DOWN, AT RESTAURANT CHARLOTTE, A JEWEL IN THE CITY CROWN, GLOWING WITH THE PLEASURES OF QUIET CONVERSATION, PROFOUND COMFORT — AND A MENU WITH VISION.

EXTRAORDINARY VISION.

Hotel Macklowe

145 West 44th Street. New York, NY 10036 212.768.4400 Fax 212.789.7690

Magic, Pure and Outrageous

BMW DROVE THEIR ENTIRE NEW LINE ONTO OUR STAGE. BILL GATES PRESENTED THE LATEST MICROSOFT TECHNOLOGY FROM OUR STAGE. MEATLOAF MADE HIS FAMOUS COMEBACK ON OUR STAGE. AND LAST WEEK, MAXINE HOWELL MARRIED THOMAS SMYTHE II — CENTER STAGE. THE STAGE OF THE HUDSON THEATRE. A FULL-SIZE BROADWAY THEATRE, LOCATED IN HOTEL MACKLOWE. WITH ITS OWN COMMANDING STREET ENTRANCE, ITS OWN, ON-SITE PRODUCTION MANAGER, ITS OWN, BURNISHED VISION. WITH THE TECHNICAL CAPACITY OF THE STARSHIP ENTERPRISE. THE AUTHENTICITY OF CARNEGIE HALL. AND FAR MORE FLEXIBILITY THAN EITHER. THE SPOTS ARE UP. BRING YOUR OWN VISION.

Hotel Macklowe

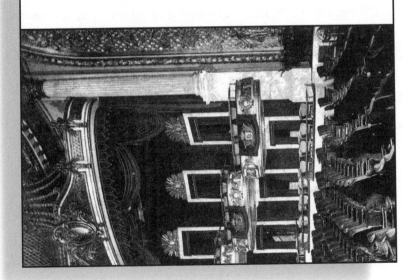

3. Brainstorming the Concept

The concept provides the basis for selecting and arranging all the elements that must be included in a successful campaign or ad. The concept is the basis and focus of the ads and is developed from the examination of the product or service to be advertised (i.e., its special characteristics and the feelings it gives people, such as a sense of freedom, power, or success). The concept is what unifies the ad and gives it a critical message or theme. The concept could be simple. For example, one Timex ad features a diver jumping off a cliff in Acapulco to prove that a Timex watch "takes a licking and keeps on ticking." In a John Smith's Bitters commercial, a dog performs amazing tricks after being promised just a drop; "He just needs the right motivation," explains the owner. In another ad, a beautiful woman urges a man to "take it off, take it all off" with Noxema shaving cream, while the "The Stripper" tune plays in the background.

The concept could be presented like a comic fantasy. Consider the spot that shows a monk who, overwhelmed by an order for 500 illuminated manuscripts, gets divine intervention in the form of a Xerox copier. One ad for Chanel No. 5 is centered around a mysterious swimming pool. Two for British Airways show Manhattan Island—descending from the sky like an airplane—coming in for a landing at Heathrow Airport, and thousands of people forming a human face.

The concept emerges after arduous brainstorming, and once it raises its head, it initiates an exciting new process of refining, strengthening, and simplifying the look and content of the ad. You'll know when it's right, if you let intuition guide you.

4. Defining the Tone and Style

The tone and style of an ad must now be determined. As previously stated, the ad can be factual, atmospheric, deeply emotional, or funny. The factual approach is appropriate when the message to convey is price, discounts, or special offers, such as a gift with purchase. For example, in mid-January 1996, after the retailing industry collectively experienced a poor Christmas, Computer City ran a full-page newspaper ad with a bold headline reading, "FREE MONITOR, with purchase of select computers." The ad listed the days the deal was valid and which computer purchases qualified.

Two competing companies can take completely different tones in their ads, and both can get good responses. Maytag has relied for decades on its amusing image of the lonely and bored Maytag repair technician. The message is an effective one because it underscores the dependability of the brand's washing machines in a comical way. Frigidaire has taken a different approach. While it has used the tag line "The Look of Better Performance" to promote its appliances, the central theme has been to pitch products with an upscale, stylish image to enhance the look of kitchens.

Humor can be used in factual ads to educate and entertain at the same time. Sony, in one of its more memorable print ads, showed some of the various products from its Walkman line wearing different hats to inform the consumer that they're available in different "personalities," for "all the sides of your personality."

Emotional approaches deal with matters of the heart and are used in most image advertising. They can be very effective when intertwined with factual elements but are extremely tough to do and require more space. In some Keds ads, an emotional appeal is created with the depiction of the bond between a mother and daughter. On the first of two pages, the mother and daughter—both wearing Keds—are hugging. The mother says she's proud of her daughter, who sometimes tells her more than she wants to know, but gives her more emotionally than she ever expected, and the daughter says warmly that her mom made her feel pretty when she had braces. The second page shows four different styles, with the message "Keds never stop growing."

Banana Republic ads seem more effective, combining both wit and the romantic lure of travel, as well as the practicality of wearing its clothes while traveling. One ad has the headline, "How to Stay Calm, Cool and Respected," and advises: "Plot a midsummer cruise to the polar icecap. Fold map into fan: use for ventilation and flirtation. Wear long, gauzy skirts that channel sultry breezes. Speak slowly. Cultivate languor." Included is an illustration of a ventilated cotton dress, priced at $32, with a woven belt, priced at $24.

Funny ads are difficult to write because what one person finds funny, another may not. The more viewers who react with a smile or a laugh, the better the ad. Everybody should at least get the joke. Prince created a successful humorous ad to sell its popular tomato sauce. It superimposed a bottle of the sauce on a photo of the Mona Lisa—one of the world's most famous and recognizable paintings—with the word "Original" underneath it. In a second shot, it superimposed a bottle of the chunky-style sauce on a photo that showed an overweight, fat-faced version of the Mona Lisa, with the word "Chunky" underneath it. Since most people in Western cultures are familiar with the Mona Lisa, they would get the joke. The copy said, "Whether you choose our original sauce with imported olive oil and Romano cheese, or our chunky homestyle with bits of tomato, herbs and spices, you'll get classic Italian taste."

5. Creating a Mood

Will it be nostalgic, like those mother-daughter Keds testimonials, or inspirational, like ads by designer Isaac Mizrahi to introduce his bridge collection called Isaac? A February 1996 Isaac ad suggests that women have dreams and should chase them and that Isaac is a more affordable collection geared for younger, idealistic women who want to fulfill their dreams. It says, "The typical American woman doesn't want to be typical . . . Inside every woman is a star." On the second page of the ad is a pensive teenager in a raincoat in a car, a metaphor for her drive to go places in life.

"The thing I was most interested in expressing," says Mizrahi, "was not necessarily an age thing, how old or young she is. What is more interesting is I am portraying this woman's life. She's a star. Not necessarily an actress. Maybe inside every woman, there is a star. Without that line, the ad doesn't mean as much.

"One thing I wanted to say in these ads, about women today, is that they have dreams and aspirations, and for these women, it's not just about the power office suit. Women have very dimensional lives. They need these clothes as solutions. The pictures in the ads are about being reflective, vulnerable. I just wanted to say that the best parts of life, the best parts of being a woman involve aspiration, wonder, and vulnerability.

"This campaign is something we are developing. There is a lot that is going to be said. It will broaden. It will get more product-specific and hopefully, still retain the mood and the message."

In an age where many fashion advertisers use sex, nudity, and controversy and try to shock the public, Mizrahi believes, "There is also something to be said about taste. I think the [Isaac] ads are effective, modern, without necessarily being controversial or distasteful or vulgar. There's so much vulgarity out there. It's about having a quality idea, before any application."

Ads can also show a slice of life, something Saks Fifth Avenue has done in men's and boys' wear ads depicting a father teaching his son to ride a bicycle. Martex shows another slice of life to communicate that its home products play an important part in relationships and add to bliss in the bedroom. One Martex sheet ad shows a very content, spent couple in bed lying on the wrinkle-free linens. The headline is "Martex. The Bare Necessities," and the copy reads, "Wrinkle-free 100% cotton sheets. Because you have better things to do with your time than iron." It's clear what the couple has been doing.

Ads can also be melancholic, such as those for Amnesty International. One shows a dark photo of a seated woman, her face not visible, holding a hairbrush. Her husband was abducted by government agents. Her words are poignant: "His hair is still in the hairbrush. I see it sometimes when I open the medicine cabinet and want to throw that hairbrush away. But I'm afraid to lose the only part of him I have left."

6. Setting the Stage

Is the ad going to be demonstrative, showing the purpose of a product or how it is used, such as the Nike one that emphasizes its products' durability and the performance of its outerwear in rough weather? In the ad, a man is shown hauling a boat out of the water in a storm, with bold lettering stating, "Neither Wind, nor Rain, nor Snow." Or is it going to be in the form of a minidrama, or a comedy, such as the slapstick ad for Avalon spring water? It's an action scene at an outdoor cafe, where a man has apparently said or done something out of line, and his girlfriend dumps ice in his lap. He's shocked. The copy reads, "Do What Comes Natural. Avalon. Imported Natural Spring Water. Refreshment. Pure and Simple."

7. Crafting the Headline

Since many people don't read the body copy, the headline contains the most important words in the ad. It must be memorable and compelling. A strong headline attracts attention, arouses curiosity, and lures the reader. It addresses the wants and needs of the primary prospects while summarizing the key selling proposition and identifying the product and its benefits.

The headline should talk the language of the shopper. Make it personal and strike a chord that resonates with the target market. The headline can help turn a good ad into a creative ad. "Does she or doesn't she? Only her hairdresser knows for sure" is one of those immortal headlines. For Clairol, it captured a dominant market share of women who color their hair. The double entendre—the question and the answer—and the benefit associated with the product were telegraphed in a clever, catchy, and provocative manner. It had it all.

Headlines can present news, make a claim, incite curiosity, give direction, challenge the reader, and offer advice. A personalized, brief message that grabs attention and stresses a consumer benefit is defined as a slogan. Here are some memorable ones from major brands:

- Just Do It.
- Always Coca Cola.
- The Heartbeat of America.
- The Choice of a New Generation.
- Have It Your Way.
- Bet You Can't Eat Just One.

8. Planning the Layout

After the copy is written and the space requirements are determined, you're ready for the blueprint, also known as the layout. The layout reflects the final size and shape of the ad and defines the spatial relationships of all the elements. There are five major elements in the layout: the headline, the illustration or photo, the body copy, the price, and the logo. Decisions will have to be made on arranging the major elements, as well as the typography, white space, and tag lines. Juxtaposing all these elements for maximum impact is an art.

Early in my advertising career, I was fortunate to attend a Newspaper Advertising Bureau seminar, where I learned a system of classifying layouts by the number of items per ad. I worked with these grids and discovered that the primary tenet of a good layout is creativity expressed in a well-organized manner. An overview of the Fundamentals of Layout (Exhibit 6–3) was an invaluable tool for creatively expressing my ideas within a technical frame of reference.

Principles of a Good Layout

In designing an ad, keep some fundamental principles in mind. The basic elements—the art, copy, white space, and logo—need to be kept in balance with each other. One element—usually the price, headline, or artwork—should be more dominant than the others. The ad should have a good flow, so that the reader's eye moves sequentially within the ad (from top to bottom and left to right). Also consider the proportions: The size of the elements must relate well to each other, as should the ad's width to its height.

Overall, there should be coherence and a harmony among the elements. The ad should look unified and hold itself together well. Borders, boxes, tints, and shapes are additional tools that can be used to achieve perfect unity.

THE BUSINESS OF BUSINESS-TO-BUSINESS

Should We Use Emotions in Business-to-Business Advertising?

Many advertisers feel that emotional messages should be used less often in business ads and that copy should be more serious and straightforward.

Exhibit 6–3
FUNDAMENTALS OF LAYOUT

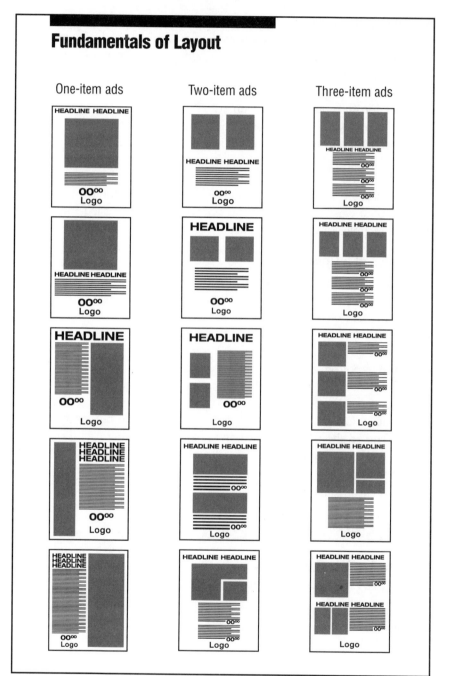

I believe that people respond to emotional appeals whether they're buying personal items or items for their business, and that although more facts are usually required in a business ad, it's generally advisable to add emotional impact wherever possible.

Pharmaceutical companies have been perceived as cold, calculating firms eager to develop and market massive amounts of drugs as quickly as possible, sometimes providing false hopes to the afflicted. Some say they are driven by profits rather than humanitarian reasons. Pfizer has sought to project a positive image through advertising. In one ad that appeared in *The Wall Street Journal,* there was a testimonial from Melinda Sheppard, a wholesome, outdoorsy woman from Nantucket Island in Massachusetts, who is pictured rowing a boat, wearing a big smile, and saying, "I remember thinking, I'm 25 and can barely move. What kind of life am I going to have?" The ad explains that pain started in her foot and spread through her body until she could barely walk, but through exercise and a medication developed by Pfizer, "Melinda's back to enjoying an active life." The tag line is "Pfizer. We're part of the cure." It brings a human dimension to a company more likely to have been associated with chemicals than cures.

Creativity in Business-to-Business

In addition to packing emotion, a good business ad can be developed with a great deal of creativity and fun. After a few misfires, in late 1990, Barclaycard was desperate to gain market share. Rather than cutting rates or fees, it embarked on a comical campaign depicting a bumbling spy, an English version of the old *Get Smart* TV series and a takeoff on James Bond, to appeal to a population in England that generally despised credit cards. In one commercial, the character Latham is asked what he needs for his assignment. He rattles off a strange list of items, including potatoes and dental floss, and what he gets instead is a Barclaycard, which Latham thinks is some sort of ingenious weapon. He unwittingly signs it with a pen that shoots fire. What the campaign did was create an amusing character to help make a product more palatable and personable and hold the audience's attention as its benefits were explained.

Viking and *The Stinky Cheese Man*

Another fun, creative approach was evident in our cover of *Publishers Weekly* for Viking Juvenile publishers. Children's authors John Scieszka and Lane Smith had turned the world of children's books upside down with their irreverent book, *The Stinky Cheese Man and Other Fairly Stupid Tales.* Their publisher challenged us to come up with a campaign that would create a new market for this title among college-age readers. Once we did, the question became how to announce it to the publishing trade in the same irreverent fashion.

Again, the creative direction had to be as nontraditional and outrageous as the book itself. The answer was in creating a radical, upside-down concept for the cover of *Publishers Weekly,* as seen in Exhibit 6–4. We even went so far as to turn the masthead of the magazine upside down, too—something that we anticipated might cause some problems from the publication's point of view. Much to our delight, *Publishers Weekly* thought the concept was wonderful and agreed to let it run. The impact of the cover to the trade was strong: It caught everyone's immediate attention and the calls started coming in, to *PW,* to Viking Juvenile, and to us. The reviews were unanimous—everyone loved it—and more importantly, it captured the imagination of the industry and created the big story that Viking wanted.

The consumer campaign for this book included an animated TV spot that used characters from the book. The spot was so unique that Ziccardi & Partners won a Telly Award for it in 1995.

Departures Magazine

A good business ad can appeal to a wish, while also being factual. Our trade ad for *Departures* magazine illustrates this concept. *Departures* is mailed only to holders of the American Express Platinum Card and is widely considered *the* book for people with very upscale lifestyles. Our challenge was to create an ad that would reach corporate executives and media planners, illustrating to them the effectiveness of advertising in *Departures* since purchases could be tracked via the American Express Platinum Card. The client had some strong success stories to illustrate this point, and we decided to use them in the series of ads we developed, one of which is shown in Exhibit 6–5. The headline read: "Don't you wish every reader response card worked . . . like ours."

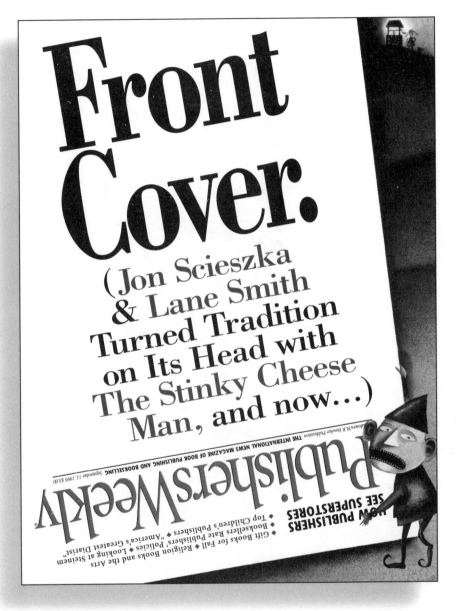

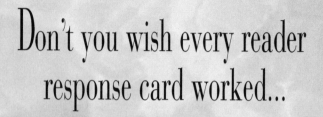

Don't you wish every reader response card worked...

like ours.

"At Seabourn we demand return on investment from our advertising, and *Departures* delivers. Seabourn is an eager partner with *Departures* Magazine because in the last two years Platinum Card charges have more than tripled.**"**

— LARRY PIMENTEL, CTC
PRESIDENT, SEABOURN CRUISE LINE

A success story like this can come only from *Departures* — the magazine created exclusively for Platinum Card® members.

Departures readers are the most affluent consumers in the country,* spending billions last year on their Platinum Cards — and over $2.7 billion in travel-related services alone!**

Generate a higher level of response and return on your advertising investment. Call *Departures* magazine publisher Jack Laschever at 212-382-5755.

DEPARTURES MAGAZINE. LIFE AT ITS BEST.

*1996 MMR ranks Platinum Card members #1 in median household income and net worth. **American Express Database 1995

Accompanied by one strong graphic, the body copy reflected the success stories for Seabourn Cruise Line, BMW, North America Switzerland Tourism, and Sulka Watches. The message was clear: The American Express Platinum Card tracks purchases better than any reader response card.

News America—Wish

Another example of a good business ad appealing to a wish while being factual is our ad for News FSI Canada, a division of News America FSI, as referenced in Exhibit 6–6.

TEAMWORK IS ESSENTIAL IN THE CREATIVE PROCESS

In creating good advertising, the one thing that matters greatly is how well your creative team works together. This is no small task when it comes to the direction and execution of a concept. Communication within the team is essential in making everything come together. You can do the homework, the legwork, and the artwork, but in the end, if the concept doesn't gel, you're back to the drawing board. Part of the challenge here is learning to see things from another's perspective—an interpersonal communication process. (This point is not only helpful within your team but can be a great advantage when presenting creative to a client, too.)

Lifelong conditioning affects our responses to everything. Get to know others' points of view. Be open to their perceptions and make them aware of yours to get to the larger picture and the objective viewpoint. Remember, we see the world—and everything in it—not as *it is,* but as *we are.*

HOW TO TURN ON THE CREATIVE LIGHTBULB

A great idea doesn't come through divine revelation. Seasoned creative minds go through a thought process that is developed through years of experience. Fortunately for those who need to study the process and

Exhibit 6–6
NEWS FSI CANADA/TRADE AD

If you're not in here...

you're not in here...

...or in 4.7 million Canadian homes.

Generate sales now and in the future with:

Two high-impact inserts—and twice the options. We're the only company that publishes *two* high-performance vehicles at *two* different times during the week. On the weekend, there's the magazine-quality *Coupon Clipper.* And, for exclusive weekday delivery, we offer the super-sized *Plan & Save.*

The greatest reach at the lowest cost. With a national household penetration of 45%, and a combined circulation of 4.7 million, there's just no other way to deliver your message to a larger audience at a lower CPM.

Lasting impact. Your advertisement in one of our high-quality, four-color inserts does more than boost sales for the life of your promotion. It builds consumer brand awareness for the life of your product.

The greatest efficiency. We offer the two most comprehensive and efficient newspaper market lists in the nation. Whether you choose to run in *Coupon Clipper, Plan & Save,* or both, you get a fantastic value—delivery to over 120 markets in one media buy, with minimal duplication.

Call the office nearest you to start boosting sales now.

Toronto	Montreal	Vancouver
Tel: 416-681-6740	Tel: 514-939-0887	Tel: 604-943-6177
Fax: 416-364-9879	Fax: 514-939-9577	Fax: 604-943-0991

develop classic creative thinking, there is a technique available to aid in successfully crafting a big idea. Although some people are more naturally innovative than others, the following principles can help most of us to develop various levels of creativity and imagination.

First, gather materials. Research the product, the company, and the problem. Equally important, become an astute observer of the world. Get interested in everything from skydiving to ancient Egyptian rituals. Whenever reading or observing, jot down and file facts that strike you as particularly interesting, sexy, riveting, or funny. Although this is a lifelong job, you will eventually build an inventory of material that might be an important source of inspiration for one of your big ideas.

Remember, new ideas are nothing more than a combination of existing elements coming together in a specific, newly discovered way. For example, when the copywriter on the Nike account couldn't come up with anything dynamic to say and pondered it for too long a time, his or her boss could very well have said, "You're taking too much time. . . . Just do it. . . . Just get it done."

As a next step, once you have developed what you feel is the right research material, look at everything upside down, inside out. Take all of the pieces of the jigsaw puzzle and start putting them together. If you were the marketing director for a major bank and learned that your target market prefers jeeps to sedans, rent a jeep for the weekend and drive through city streets and country roads to feel what it's like to be driving that jeep. Literally put yourself in the shoes of a jeep junkie. As you think of the tangible things you like about the experience, become insightful and try to define whether any of those conscious thoughts evoke emotional reactions. Does sitting higher than most other drivers on the road give you a sense of power? Does driving a trucklike vehicle make you feel more forceful? If the answer is yes, maybe the big idea for your banking customers centers around the power that comes along with building a large investment portfolio. Think of it as *listening* for the big idea, rather than *looking* for it.

As bits and pieces of thoughts come to you, write them down. Although they may at first seem less than dynamic, remember the new idea theory that says brilliant ideas are really a sum of existing notions reordered in the creative universe.

The third stage is what I refer to as the Freudian stage. Let the whole notion of what it is you're trying to discover just drop. Forget about the challenge; don't even think about it. Your subconscious needs to take over and absorb the information. Turn to your day-to-day tasks, go to a movie, and take a lot of time for recreation.

The fourth step happens when you say, "That's it, that's the answer." Out of nowhere, without warning, bingo, you have it. It's similar to what happens when you go to sleep at night with a problem and wake up in the morning and out of the blue a solution pops into your mind before your first cup of coffee. That's precisely how good ideas happen. Remember the kid who, after intensely studying for a test, felt he couldn't remember a thing. But since he's adequately prepared, when the proctor says to begin, he aces the essay questions, not only remembering what he studied, but reinforcing his book knowledge with previous life experience.

The final stage is the morning after. In this step, you take a cold shower, get over the initial euphoria, and face the fact that, well, it just doesn't feel as good as it did the day before. Here's where hard work and patience pay off. Submit the idea to criticism, keep an open mind, don't be proprietary, and be agreeable to all modifications that will make your original idea work. A good creative idea is always subject to refinement. That's part of what makes it good.

DETERMINING WHO DOES THE CREATIVE WORK

In-House or Out-of-House?

For almost as long as there has been advertising, retailers and manufacturers alike have wrestled with the best way to execute their advertising. Do you build an in-house ad shop or do you go to an outside advertising agency? There are two schools of thought on this issue with many pros and cons on both sides.

Deborah Aiges, vice president of marketing at Random House, considered five major factors—clout, quality, control, convenience, and cost—before deciding to use an outside agency to handle all of her advertising needs.

Clout

Media clout refers to the ability to negotiate media placement and rates. To successfully negotiate, the buyer (whether agency, media buying service, or retailer) needs to have clout with the media vendor. This clout is based on quantity of spending and the buyer's relationships with key players within the vendor's organization. These relationships are developed over time. "There's something to be said for agencies who buy a lot of print and/or broadcast media" and their ability to "develop relationships with newspapers and magazines," says Aiges.

Quality

The quality issue can be a touchy one when making the comparison between using in-house services and outside agencies. Many people, such as Aiges, feel that it's best to "leave the job where the job should be, with the professionals. Agencies, being in the business of advertising first and foremost, stake their reputation on the quality of their creative staff and their work."

Control and Convenience

An in-house agency is at an advantage because it has no learning curve. There is an instant understanding of your product or business because the staff know your business as well as you do and their creative work can reflect it. But with in-house convenience comes aggravation. According to Aiges, "supervising the in-house agency has a big aggravation factor. When you turn your account over to an agency, they inherit the aggravation."

Cost

Cost-effectiveness is also a highly contentious issue when choosing between in-house and out-of-house agencies. A well-designed in-house agency has its own production facilities and negotiates directly on the company's behalf with media and other outside suppliers. However, there are some substantial disadvantages that can undermine the benefits of having an in-house agency. Going in-house means staffing up: hiring creative, media, and production people, just for starters. And the costs for salaries, benefits, space, computers, and myriad other necessities add up quickly. Determining the right number of people to keep on staff or to have as freelance staff is also a balancing act. "When we were in-house, we were never able to staff up enough to keep the work going," says Aiges. "And when we thought we could save on potential media commissions, we took another hard look."

An agency with at least $40 million in billing can muster up a lot more muscle in negotiating rates and position than any in-house shop can. They also make more efficient and better-timed buys because they are in the marketplace daily, representing a wide variety of clients. In-house buys are limited both by the number of purchases and the dollar volume. The buyers rely on the stations themselves to supply information on spot costs. This is a limiting factor in understanding the pricing levels in the marketplace. The result is that the in-house buyer may end up paying a higher unit cost for each spot aired.

Obviously, there are many factors to consider before choosing to either go in-house or hire an advertising agency for your marketing needs. Each case is different, but keep in mind the most important dimension of all—creativity. More than anything else in its marketing arsenal, a powerful creative idea gives an advertiser the leverage to make dramatic market changes. And outside agencies tend to have a full staff of creative people who bring a wide variety of product experience to the table.

We've all witnessed great advertising ideas that have revolutionized the market in the areas of package goods, automobiles, soft drinks, and computer technology. Recently, a handful of retailers have benefited greatly by using outside agencies to develop strong image campaigns (which they were unable to do in-house) while the competition chose instead to remain price oriented in its advertising approach. These include Target, which has managed to create the image of an upscale discounter with fashion ads that still contain a price element, and Sears, which, through its "softer side of Sears" campaign, awoke the country to the fact that it sells more than hardware and washing machines.

The Sears campaign has the requisite elements: It is catchy, sets a tone, offers an opportunity for discovery, and inspires consumers to react. It also provides a platform that Sears could run with in future ads using different elements but still maintaining the same "softer side" theme. It has what all great campaigns have—that big idea.

7 | Media Planning

"The media plan is late.
To begin with, the Super Bowl was yesterday."

WHETHER AN AD HAS IMPACT depends as much on where it's placed and when it runs as on its quality. Sure, there's no better mass exposure than the Super Bowl—it's watched by millions. But it's still no panacea. Broadcasting ads during the Super Bowl amounts to big bucks, and it's very risky, particularly when the Dallas Cowboys trounce the opposition in the first quarter and the audience tunes out. If the ad doesn't penetrate that day, you're finished. Your money may be better spent by scheduling well-targeted, less-expensive time slots and running ads more frequently.

When it comes to placing media, there are always a multitude of options. However, the biggest challenges come when working with small budgets and advertisers who still want as much impact as possible. Here's where the real talent of an experienced media planner comes into play.

Ziccardi & Partners once developed an ad campaign for Villard Books, which published *Closer to the Light,* a book about children's near-death experiences. The media budget was very small, yet Villard felt the book had potential and wanted to create a stir. We looked at the most impactful ways of allocating this small media budget. If we had gone with a standard book approach and placed ads in the *New York Times Book Review* or the *Times* daily edition, we would have spent the entire budget on two ads. Instead, we proposed spending all of the money on targeted talk-radio programs that dealt with quirky subjects.

Through negotiation, we reserved a reasonable number of spots over a one-week period. The creative helped, too, by using voices of children recounting experiences detailed in the book. The results were staggering. The spots reached precisely the audience we sought and the phones began to ring at the radio stations. Suddenly, people wanted to know all about this topic. One station even did a special on children's near-death experiences because of the large response to the radio spots. *Closer to the Light* had a first printing of only 6,000 copies. After the ad campaign, more than 100,000 books were printed.

That's an example of not going the traditional route when choosing the media mix. There's a vast range of possibilities. As in all parts of the marketing plan, proper selection of media requires setting a goal and then finding the best way to achieve it. This chapter tells you how to do just that.

THE MEDIA MIX: FINDING THE RIGHT RECIPE

The first question to ask after the creative idea is formulated is what media can best convey your message. A great variety of media are used for advertising, ranging from television, radio, newspapers, and magazines to billboards, signs, flyers, pamphlets, direct mailings, and transit advertising—including buses, subways, trains, and taxis—to novelties such as skywriting, lighted zipper signs on airplanes and buildings, blimps, sky banners hanging from planes, and ads on shopping carts. The media are as diverse as the settings for capturing the eyes or ears of the target markets.

NEWSPAPERS

This medium moves fast to hit the public and is inexpensive. It's no mystery that newspapers remain first priority in an advertising budget. In addition, different newspapers have different reputations. Some are conservative, serious, and respectable. Others are gossipy and sensationalistic. It's important to be selective about which papers to advertise in and to bear in mind whether its image suits the personality of your product.

Quick, Easy, and Cost-Efficient

Cost-efficiency is a major advantage of newspaper advertising. Advertising in newspapers is relatively inexpensive, running from less than $100 per column inch in a local weekly newspaper to more than several thousand dollars for multiple inches in a major metropolitan daily.

The response to newspaper advertising can be amazingly quick. You can judge whether an advertisement is effective by analyzing the sales figures by 1:00 P.M. the day the ad runs. Newspapers are an active medium: People want to absorb the information in the paper. They're habit-forming. People take them along to read on the train or bus on their way to work or in the diner as they sip coffee. Some feel naked without them and simply can't start the day without one. It's still a better read than the daily flash in the buyer's office. It is estimated that readers see at least 85 percent of the material in a newspaper, so ads have an excellent chance of getting noticed.

The lead time, or the time needed for the newspaper to have the ad in hand before it is printed, is quite short. It can be less than 24 hours. That's good to know in emergency situations, such as when a company goes bankrupt but must inform the public that its stores are still open for business. Sometimes bankruptcies imply store closings, but not always.

The Run for the Best-Seller List

An example of using the immediacy and short lead time of newspapers effectively can be seen in the newspaper campaign Ziccardi & Partners did for Colin Powell's book. Opinion polls were ranking Colin Powell, former Chairman of the Joint Chiefs of Staff, as a leading contender for the presidency, even though he hadn't thrown his hat into the ring. For months, he rode a wave of popularity that helped sell his autobiography, *My American Journey*. The book arrived in bookstores at a time when Powell seemed close to a decision on his candidacy. Everyone—including his publisher—was waiting for him to decide.

After launching the initial campaign for the book, Ziccardi & Partners prepared additional advertising; Powell's decision about whether to run would determine the direction of these follow-up ads. Because the advertising had to instantly reflect Powell's announcement, the immediacy and impact of full-page newspaper ads, capturing the moment of decision, was the only way to go. Ziccardi & Partners had an ad at the *New York Times* fewer than 24 hours after Powell's announcement.

Exhibit 7–1, Colin Powell's original *New York Times* ad, ran in September of 1995, and focused on the man who could be president. Exhibit 7–2, Colin Powell's *New York Times* ad that ran after he declared he was not a presidential candidate, focused on the man, his roots, his family, and his life.

In this electronic era, newspapers are still ubiquitous, though readership and revenues are declining as more people watch TV and log onto the Internet. The vast majority of the population reads a newspaper every day or several days of the week, even though the papers remain cumbersome, difficult to fold, and divided up into sections. The plus side for advertisers is that in each section, there is editorial material appealing to different audiences. This format allows you to advertise in the section that your customers read.

Exhibit 7-1
COLIN POWELL: *MY AMERICAN JOURNEY/*
FIRST *NEW YORK TIMES* AD

You'VE READ THE HEADLINES —
Now READ THE BOOK!

" [Political] matters account for about 10 of the 643 pages of
My American Journey. The politically obsessed are likely to skim
through the rest. That is a shame because the whole book is must
reading for anyone who wants to reaffirm his faith in the promise
of America.... A profound and moving story of immigrant
achievement.... A particularly interesting life in our times. "
— *The Wall Street Journal*

"Fascinating."
— *The Washington Post Book World*

"Compelling."
— *USA Today*

"Endearing and well-written."
— *The New York Times Book Review*

A Main Selection of the Book-of-the-Month Club
Also available as a Random House AudioBook and in a Random House Large Print Edition
Preview *My American Journey* on-line at http://www.randomhouse.com

RANDOM HOUSE

142

International Bestseller — Over 1.6 Million Copies in Print

A GREAT
SUCCESS STORY
OF OUR TIME.

"I have had a great life, and this is the story so far. It is a story that could only have happened in America."
— FROM THE PREFACE

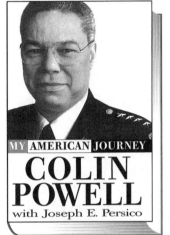

He was born to a working-class immigrant family in the Bronx. He became the national hero America wanted to draft into the presidency. Colin Powell's journey is the embodiment of the American dream. And his story is inspiration for us all. It is the story of a boy who found his calling in the Army. Of a husband involved in a 33-year love affair with his wife. Of a father deeply devoted to his family. And of a leader who rose to the challenge of his times. Here is a stirring account of a life richly lived, a brilliant portrait of determination, faith, and achievement.

MY AMERICAN JOURNEY
COLIN POWELL
with Joseph E. Persico

The Wall Street Journal
"A PROFOUND
AND MOVING STORY."

The New York Times Book Review
"ENDEARING
AND WELL-
WRITTEN....
Mr. Powell truly has, as he says of himself, 'lived the American dream.'"

The Washington Post Book World
"FASCINATING.... The stirring, only-in-America story of one determined man's journey from the South Bronx to directing the mightiest of military forces."

A Main Selection of the Book-of-the-Month Club

Also available as a Random House AudioBook and in a Random House Large Print Edition

RANDOM HOUSE

Preview *My American Journey* on-line at http://www.randomhouse.com

Aging, Ink Spots, and Repro Quality

The poor reproduction quality of newspapers is their distinct disadvantage. The fine stitching or detailing of fashion products could get lost in a reproduction that's overly dark.

Newspapers age quickly and turn old in a day. They get discarded sooner than magazines. Therefore, it may be a good idea to repeat a successful newspaper ad for several days to maximize exposure and optimize sales. It may seem minor that the ink rubs off on your hands, but it's irritating and another reason for throwing out a newspaper quickly.

MAGAZINES

The magazines one reads reflect an individual's interests and lifestyle and the image he or she wants to project. For advertisers, magazines can be useful for upgrading image, if the magazine is chosen with an eye to the market's perception of the magazine. While some gossip magazines would detract from a company's reputation, many magazines such as *Town and Country* or *Departures* can support a luxury image. Magazines range from general-interest formats covering the globe, such as *Time,* to specialty-interest magazines, such as *Gourmet* and *GQ*. Specialty magazines provide the format for more detailed, informative advertising on products geared to the groups that read each magazine. Magazines also offer excellent color reproduction quality.

Longer Shelf Life and Higher Quality

Magazines have a longer life span than newspapers, up to two months or more. Thus ads remain in the hands of the readers longer and are likely to be noticed more than once. For example, *National Geographic, Architectural Digest, Reader's Digest,* and *Martha Stewart Living* are all known to linger in living rooms for months at a stretch.

More so than newspapers, magazines have a pass-along readership. They are borrowed and saved in barbershops, the waiting rooms of doctors' and dentists' offices, and on airplanes. That means there's always a larger audience than the paid circulation.

Greater Expense and Effort for the Reader

Magazine ads can be expensive, running from less than a thousand dollars to more than a hundred thousand dollars for a one-page, one-time insertion. (One page in *Parade* costs $647,000.) Weigh carefully how many of the readers fit your target market and how many readers are not in your target market. You pay for both!

Magazines also have a longer production lead time than newspapers, some as long as three months. Additionally, both newspapers and magazines are nonpassive media. In other words, they must be read and absorbed by the reader. There's some effort involved. Television and radio require less concentration. Do you have a lazy audience, one that rarely reads, or an audience that devours printed material? The effort and concentration required can be both an advantage and a disadvantage, depending on your audience.

There are research companies, such as Starch (914-698-0800) and Nielsen (212-708-7580), that can help determine what newspapers and magazines an audience is predisposed to or whether they are totally glued to the TV set. This will help you modify various aspects of the ad and choose the best combination of print media for the advertising strategy.

Overcoming Magazines' Constraints

Be imaginative in the creative. Finding creative solutions to work within the limitations of a specific medium can often generate positive results. Our agency created a new logo for Company by Ellen Tracy as part of a reimaging strategy for this client in 1995. Our challenge was to get the most brand recognition and impact with this new logo—and to do it cost-effectively. The solution came with some creative media thinking.

Our allocation for the March and April 1996 issues of *Elle* magazine was for four pages total. Originally we thought our best option was to do a two-page spread in the March issue and a single page in the April issue. However, the most important part of the advertising strategy was logo registration, and with a little creative thinking we came up with an even better solution. For the March issue, we elected to run a two-page spread and three one-third vertical pages, strategically placed in other parts of the book. In the April issue, we concentrated again on registering the Company logo by simply repeating three one-third verticals to reinforce the image. As shown in Exhibit 7–3 (a, b, c), Company verticals in *Elle,* these one-third page positions were negotiated to run against editorial (one even ran on the masthead page) and focused primarily on the logo. It gave Company by Ellen Tracy a total of five registrations in the March issue and three registrations in the April issue, giving the impression that the Company logo owned the book, while stretching the effectiveness of the available media dollars. The main focus of the campaign, the two-page spread, can be seen in Exhibit 7–4.

Another opportunity to stretch the value of a magazine plan is to take advantage of the various merchandise programs, or value add-ons, that magazines offer, either as a regular promotional enhancement or that can be negotiated on a customized basis, as an element of a schedule. A range of merchandising programs may be available that can be directed toward specific marketing goals or audience segments. These programs, at their best, provide the advertiser with another way to promote its product—at no extra cost—and associate it with a publication that is highly regarded. The hope is that some of the magazine's prestige will rub off on the advertiser's product.

Vogue magazine provided a significant value-added program when it offered advertisers the opportunity to use *Vogue's* self-promotional outdoor advertising campaign, tying in advertisers' names with the tag line "See You in September Vogue." Both the magazine and the advertisers used their name equity to promote themselves and each other. Some of the more well-known advertisers who came on board for this promotion were Gucci, Giorgio Armani, Gianni Versace, Richard Tyler, and Ellen Tracy.

Build relationships with key players. Frequent contact with magazine sales staff and senior management has proven crucial as a source of insight into a magazine's upcoming promotional plans and directions. Another source is the magazine's own advertising, which often publicizes new and innovative programs.

In 1992, *Harper's Bazaar* realized a transformation in the hands of its new editor, Liz Tilberis. To bring her vision to reality, Tilberis brought in some of the best talent in fashion journalism, including creative director Fabien Baron, photographers Patrick Demarchelier and Peter Lindbergh, fashion director Tonne Goodman, and beauty and fashion news director Annemarie Iverson, each of whom were playing an important role at the "world's most beautiful fashion magazine." A major media campaign was

Exhibit 7–3a
COMPANY BY ELLEN TRACY/*ELLE* MAGAZINE VERTICALS

BE GOOD

COMPANY

ELLEN TRACY

ELLE

Régis Pagniez
PUBLICATION DIRECTOR

Amy Gross	Gilles Bensimon
EDITORIAL DIRECTOR	CREATIVE DIRECTOR
Elaina Richardson	Marin Hopper
DEPUTY EDITOR	STYLE DIRECTOR
Adam Smith	Nicole Crassat
ART DIRECTOR	EUROPEAN FASHION DIRECTOR

FASHION

SENIOR FASHION EDITOR	Marybeth Schmitt
SENIOR STYLIST	Fanny Pagniez
STYLISTS	Isabel Dupré, Natalia Cañellas
SENIOR MARKET EDITOR	Michelle R. Morgan
SENIOR ACCESSORIES EDITOR	Ellyn Chestnut
MARKET EDITORS	Lisa Fernandez, Ashley Kennedy (Accessories)
BOOKINGS/PRODUCTION DIRECTOR	Cynthia Weinstein; Hillary Boylan (Associate); Selene Milano (Assistant)
ASSOCIATE	Gina Kelly (Fashion)
ASSISTANTS	Ninotchka Garcia (Fashion), Samantha Jones (Fashion),
	Jon Moore (Fashion), Marie Paillard (Accessories),
	Lora Phillips (Fashion), Paula del Rio (Stylist)
FASHION CREDIT COORDINATOR	Tricia Schreiber
CONSULTING FASHION NEWS DIRECTOR	Ruth La Ferla

FEATURES

SENIOR FEATURES EDITOR	Patricia Towers
SENIOR ARTICLES EDITOR	Roberta Anne Myers
WRITERS AT LARGE	Lisa Kogan, Vanessa V. Friedman
RESEARCH EDITOR	Brantley Bardin
ARTICLES EDITOR, COPY	Marisa Cohen
ARTICLES EDITOR	Jennifer Pierce Barr
WEST COAST REPORTER	Jennifer Scruby
ASSOCIATE ARTICLES EDITOR, COPY	Diane Stegmann
ASSOCIATE FEATURES EDITOR	Jennifer Weisel
ASSOCIATE EDITOR	James Patrick Herman (Research)
ASSISTANT EDITOR	Kathryn Pottinger (Fashion News)
ASSISTANT TO THE EDITORIAL DIRECTOR	Nell Casey
EDITORIAL ASSISTANTS	Alanna Fincke, Janice Lee, Katherine Rosman

BEAUTY AND HEALTH

BEAUTY/FITNESS DIRECTOR	Jean Godfrey-June
ASSOCIATE EDITOR	Sara Atkinson
EDITORIAL ASSISTANT	Rachael Combe

ART AND DESIGN

SENIOR ASSOCIATE ART DIRECTOR	James Stoffel
ASSOCIATE ART DIRECTOR	Anna Starr
ART PRODUCTION EDITOR	Andrea Legge
ASSISTANT TO THE PUBLICATION DIRECTOR	Alison Pryor
ASSISTANT TO THE CREATIVE DIRECTOR	Darlene Gillard-Jones

PHOTOGRAPHY

PHOTOGRAPHY DIRECTOR	Alison Morley
ASSOCIATE PHOTO EDITOR	Quintana Roo Dunne
ASSISTANT PHOTO EDITOR	Gena Merberg

PRODUCTION

PRODUCTION DIRECTOR	Lisa Loverro
PRODUCTION MANAGER	Mary Brecka
EDITORIAL SYSTEMS DIRECTOR	H. Scott Jolley
PRODUCTION ASSISTANTS	Heather Karp, Linda Fernbacher
CONTRIBUTING WRITERS	Eric Alterman, Marion Asnes, E. Jean Carroll,
	Polly Frost, Meryl Gordon, Jesse Green, Pam Houston,
	Elizabeth Kaye, Oni Faida Lampley, Rosemary Mahoney, Susan Morgan,
	Coco Myers (Style), Judith Newman, Amy Pagnozzi, Richard Panek,
	Degen Pener, B. Ruby Rich, Paul Schneider, Michelle Stacey,
	Elizabeth Stone, Cheryl Lee Terry, Meg Wolitzer
CONSULTING EDITORS	Peggy Cooper Cafritz, Joni Evans, Lise Friedman, Deborah Hughes,
	Vincent Longo (Beauty), Gabrielle Reece (Fitness), Tabitha Soren
BUDGET DIRECTOR	Anita Young
NEW MEDIA EDITOR	Tess Ghilaga
ASSISTANT TO THE MANAGING DIRECTOR	Rebecca Governale
EDITORIAL BUSINESS MANAGER	Lorraine Pharaoh-Brandon
INTERNATIONAL BUREAU CHIEF	Kristen Ingersoll
OFFICE MANAGER	Darrell Thorpe

Jean L. Fomasieri
VICE PRESIDENT/MANAGING DIRECTOR

HACHETTE FILIPACCHI MAGAZINES, INC.	Chairman, Daniel Filipacchi
	President, CEO and Chief Operating Officer, David J. Pecker
	Executive Vice President and Editorial Director, Jean-Louis Ginibre
	President, Hachette Filipacchi New Media, Paul De Benedictis
	Senior Vice President, Global Advertising, Paul DuCharme
	Senior Vice President, Director of Corporate Sales, Nicholas Matarazzo
	Senior Vice President, CFO & Treasurer, John T. O'Connor
	Vice President, General Counsel, Catherine Flickinger
	Vice President, Manufacturing & Distribution, Anthony Romano
	Vice President, Circulation, David W. Leckey
	Vice President, Research & Marketing Services, Susan Smollens
	Vice President, Communications and Special Projects, Keith Estabrook
	Vice President, Magazine Development, Marcia Sachar
	Vice President, Director of Creative Services, Corporate Sales, Lynn Chaiken
	Creative Production Director/Global Mktg., Jean-Pierre Labelut
	Senior Vice President, Corporate Sales, Detroit, H.E. (Bud) Allen
	VP, Advertising Director Global/Corporate Beauty & Fashion, Tracee Kiner
	Manager, Global/Corporate Beauty & Fashion, Timothy R. O'Connor

HFM
Hachette
Filipacchi
Magazines

34 ELLE / MARCH 1996

Exhibit 7–3b
COMPANY BY ELLEN TRACY/*ELLE* MAGAZINE VERTICALS

shopping guide

Q2 Cable television's resource for the latest news in style, home, health, beauty, travel, and family. Catch us live, five days per week. Check your local cable guide for listing.

COVER
Silk **shirt**, $595, and cotton **pants**, $525, by *Gucci*, available at Gucci (NYC, Beverly Hills).

CAMERON DIAZ
Page 77: **Dress** and belly **chain** by *MAG*.

TIMOTHY HUTTON
Pages 94: **Shirt** by *Agnès B.*, **T-shirt** by *Calvin Klein Underwear*, **Jeans** by *Paul Smith*. Page 95: **Ensemble** by *Prada*. **T-shirt** by *Levi Strauss*.

FASHION NOTEBOOK
Page 184: All clothing by *Romeo Gigli Jeans*, available at Ron Ross (Studio City, CA), Ruth Shaw (Baltimore), Untitled (NYC). (At left) Dark denim **jeans**, $120. Denim **jacket**, $198. (At center) Silk **vest**, $92. **Skirt**, $140. (At right) Gold **jacket**, $290. Striped **top**, $55. Stonewashed **jeans**, $120. Page 194: (1) **Earrings** at Fred Leighton & Seaman at Bergdorf Goodman; (3) **Bracelet** at Seaman Schepps (NYC); (4) **Ring** at David Webb (NYC, Houston, Beverly Hills); (5) **Earrings** at select Saks Fifth Avenue; (6) **Earrings** at Bergdorf Goodman; (7) **Necklace** at Neiman Marcus, Stanley Korshak, to order at Bergdorf Goodman; (8) **Ring** at Camilla Dietz Bergeron, Ltd.; for information, call (212) 794-9100.

GREAT STYLE
Page 202: **Bag** by *Bruno Magli*, $400, at Bruno Magli stores nationwide in May. **Shoe** by *Patrick Cox*, $290, at Patrick Cox (NYC). **Belt** by *Liz Claiborne Accessories*, $22, at Lord & Taylor, Dayton's, Hudson's, Marshall Field's. **Bag** by *Calvin Klein*, $950, at Calvin Klein (NYC). **Shoe** by *Gucci*, $490, at Gucci (NYC, Beverly Hills). **Bag** by *Judith Leiber*, $1,055, at select Saks Fifth Avenue, Neiman Marcus, Bergdorf Goodman. Page 206: **Bag** by *Lulu Guinness*, $345, at Bergdorf Goodman. **Bag** by *Gucci*, $770, at Gucci (NYC, Beverly Hills). **Bag** by *A Line Anne Klein*, $55, at Anne Klein Boutique (Manhasset, NY), The Pocketbook Man (Honolulu). **Bag** by *Serpui Marie at Aprapo* at Barneys New York. **Bag** by *Dolce & Gabbana* at Bergdorf Goodman, select Saks Fifth Avenue.

GUCCI'S NEW SENSUALITY
Pages 263–267: All **clothing** and **shoes** by *Gucci* at Gucci (NYC, Beverly Hills).

THE CHARM OF PRADA
Pages 269–273: All **clothing** by *Prada* at Prada (NYC, Beverly Hills), Neiman Marcus. All **shoes** and **sandals** by *Prada* at Prada (NYC, Beverly Hills). Page 271: **Sunglasses** by *Christian Roth for Optical Affairs*. Page 272: **Glasses** by *Paul Smith*. Page 273: **Watch** by *Oris*.

DONNA KARAN PARES DOWN
Sunglasses by *Christian Roth for Optical Affairs*; *Alain Mikli*. Page 275: (At left) **Dress coat** at Sarah's (Pensacola, FL). **Skirt** at Bergdorf Goodman. Gabby (Great Neck, NY), Macy's West/Bullock's, Nordstrom. **Sandals** at Saks Fifth Avenue, Neiman Marcus. (At center) **Halter** and **skirt** by *Donna Karan*. **Sandals** at Bloomingdale's. (At right) **Jacket** by *Donna Karan*. **Pants** at Saks Fifth Avenue, select Nordstrom. **Shoes** by *Donna Karan*. Page 276: (At left) **Jacket** at Nordstrom (San Diego, Costa Mesa, L.A.). **Pants** at select Saks Fifth Avenue, select Nordstrom, Dayton's, Hudson's, Marshall Field's. **Sandals** at Bloomingdale's. (At center) **Jacket** at Gabby (Great Neck, NY), Charles Sumner (Boston, Chestnut Hill, MA), select Nordstrom. **Skirt** at Gabby (Great Neck, NY), Nordstrom. **Sandals** at select Saks Fifth Avenue, Neiman Marcus. (At right) **Shell**, **skirt**, **shoes** by *Donna Karan*. Page 277: (At left) **Dress** by *Donna Karan*. **Sandals** at select Saks Fifth Avenue, Neiman Marcus. (At center) **Top** at Gabby (Great Neck, NY), Barbara Jean, Ltd. (Little Rock, AR), Gazebo (Dallas). **Pants** at Gabby (Great Neck), select Nordstrom. **Shoes** by *Donna Karan*. (At right) Tank **top** at Bergdorf Goodman, Gazebo (Dallas), select Nordstrom. **Skirt** at Bergdorf Goodman, Gazebo (Dallas), Macy's West/Bullock's, Bloomingdale's. Page 278: (At left) **Dress** at Neiman Marcus. **Sandals** by *Donna Karan*. (At center) **Shirt** at select Saks Fifth Avenue, Bloomingdale's, Barbara Jean, Ltd. (Little Rock, AR). **Skirt** at Neiman Marcus, select Saks Fifth Avenue, Barbara Jean, Ltd. (Little Rock, AR). **Shoes** by *Donna Karan*. (At right) **Jacket** at Bergdorf Goodman, Saks Fifth Avenue, select Nordstrom. **Skirt** at Bergdorf Goodman, Saks Fifth Avenue, Macy's West/Bullock's. **Sandals** at select Saks Fifth Avenue. Page 279: (At left) **Top** at Barneys New York, Nordstrom (Salt Lake City, UT). **Skirt** at Barneys New York, Bloomingdale's, Neiman Marcus, Nordstrom. (At center) **Dress coat** by Donna Karan. (At right) **Vest** at Barneys New York, Bloomingdale's, select Nordstrom.

CALVIN KLEIN'S NEW BODY IMAGE
Pages 281–285: All **clothing** and **shoes** by *Calvin Klein*. Page 281: **Top** at select Calvin Klein stores, Bergdorf Goodman, Adele Kauff (Great Neck, NY). Page 282: **Dress** at select Calvin Klein stores, Mario's (Seattle, Portland, OR), Ron Ross (Studio City, CA). Page 283: **Coat** at Saks Fifth Avenue, Calvin Klein (NYC, Dallas). **Shirt** at Calvin Klein stores, Neiman Marcus, Mel & Me (Cranston, RI). **Pants** at select Calvin Klein stores, Barneys New York, Mario's (Seattle, Portland, OR). **Pumps** at Calvin Klein (NYC), Bergdorf Goodman (after April 1), Neiman Marcus. Page 284: **Sweater** at Calvin Klein (NYC, Palm Beach), select Nordstrom, B. Barnett (Little Rock, AR). Page 285: **Top** and **pants** at Calvin Klein (NYC).

SAFARI IN THE URBAN JUNGLE
Page 287: **Shirt**, $42, at Banana Republic. **Skirt**, $207, at Anastasia (Newport Beach, CA), >

ELLEN TRACY

COMPANY

BE GOOD

Exhibit 7–3c
COMPANY BY ELLEN TRACY/*ELLE* MAGAZINE VERTICALS

health

examine hundreds of patients before you can see a pattern that defines their problems as a real disease and not just a series of random complaints. Researchers at CDC and NIH didn't do this, yet they were charged with making some incredibly important decisions about how CFS should be pursued. They didn't think CFS was an important disease, and they decided not to waste much time or money on it.

Today, independent scientists have identified clinical markers for CFS, but the government agencies won't recognize their work. For instance, the disease can show up in simple blood tests like the form of extremely low blood-sedimentation rates, yet most doctors aren't even aware of this. If the government says CFS isn't a real illness, then that's what physicians in the field say too.

NK: What is the significance of the title *Osler's Web?*
HJ: Sir William Osler was an eminent clinician who taught medicine at Cambridge in the first part of the century. He extolled the virtues of listening to the patient, of being sensitive to what the ill person was saying. CFS was dismissed by people at the federal health agencies who thought all these crazy women who say they have a problem would get over it and the disease would just go away. But it's *not* going away.
NK: How do the politics of CFS compare with those of AIDS?
HJ: In 1982, before HIV was discovered, *The Journal of the American Medical Association* published an article saying it was unlikely that AIDS was caused by a virus alone. Back then, investigators emphasized the personalities of AIDS >

how casual is casual transmission?

The stockpile of evidence Hillary Johnson has amassed about CFS makes one alarming conclusion seem inescapable: The disease may be contagious—and worse, it could be casually transmitted. In *Osler's Web*, Johnson tracks cluster outbreaks around the country and meticulously reports ten years of scientific evidence garnered by independent clinicians and researchers, the culmination of which suggests that you can catch CFS. The problem is, without government grants to turn the most substantial medical hunches into hard proof, no one knows for sure exactly what causes CFS or how it's passed. According to Johnson, CFS researchers suspect it's triggered by an infectious viral agent. Unlike HIV, which is so fragile it can't survive outside the body, this predator seems to require a lot less than sexual contact to infect. Johnson details a preliminary study of a traveling orchestra plagued by CFS that showed the closer the physical contact—from sharing an eating utensil to sharing a bed—between a person with the disease and a person without it, the more likely it was to be transmitted. On occasion, the families, co-workers, or schoolmates of a CFS sufferer fall ill after being exposed. More than half of the patients in a 1992 Harvard study reported that someone close to them, either at home or at work, also had the disease. But experts can only speculate whether it's passed through the air like tuberculosis, through saliva like mononucleosis, or by physical contact—say, shaking hands—like a cold. Some doctors have reported patients who came down with CFS after a blood transfusion; a nurse in a CFS-dedicated clinic contracted the disease when she accidentally stuck herself with the needle she'd used to draw blood from an infected person.

The good news: As mysterious as it is, CFS seems to follow the protocol of many known infectious diseases. Only a small percentage of those exposed contract it. And it's highly unlikely that people who have it are infectious all the time. That many people live with CFS and no one around them ever becomes ill is a hopeful indicator that the window of infectiousness is quite small. —JENNIFER WEISEL

149

Exhibit 7–4
COMPANY BY ELLEN TRACY/*ELLE* MAGAZINE SPREAD

launched to announce the "new" *Harper's,* and advertisers who were in the premier issue enjoyed greater visibility through significantly increased circulation.

Explore the merchandising offerings regularly provided by a magazine before attempting to develop a custom program. The magazine's own programs are usually based on features, benefits, or values intrinsic to the magazine, that is, the things it does best, and therefore offers advertisers a persuasive platform for their communications.

TELEVISION

In large, worldwide advertising agencies, television is the name of the game. It's where the big bucks are placed and where the recognition factor is the highest. Combining the sound and immediacy of radio with the color of magazines and the excitement of motion, television advertising can effectively capture the attention of the target market, provided the viewing habits of the desired audience are understood—a matter of determining how much and exactly what television shows your market watches. Television can demonstrate how to use a product and, when done well, is best for branding or rebranding a product or image. For example, in the mid-1990s Wonder Bread began replaying part of its memorable "Helps build strong bodies 12 ways" slogan on TV. Television makes national and regional advertising more feasible. There can be a single, unifying countrywide campaign supported by a more flexible campaign that varies from region to region.

Pros and Cons in a Nutshell

The broad audience coverage of television can be an advantage or a disadvantage. Television has a low cost for the number of people who see the ad, but not everybody who views the ad is a potential customer. From that perspective, television is expensive. For the 1996 Super Bowl, advertising time ran at a minimum cost of $1 million for 30 seconds, depending on how early in the game the advertisement ran. The earlier, the more desirable—and more expensive—since there's a good chance the TV audience will be larger at the outset of the game. A contest that's a blowout by halftime spells defeat for second-half advertisers because many people will switch channels after figuring the outcome has already been decided.

However, the number of households that watch at least part of the game is enormous. It's been estimated that more than half of the television sets in America tune into the Super Bowl. The question becomes who watches what commercials and who splits for the kitchen to grab a beer when the commercial starts. Even the most serious couch potatoes don't necessarily sit passively fixated on the TV screen during the commercials.

Moreover, modern technology has enabled viewers to ignore commercials by cutting off the sound or channel surfing. Videotaping is an advertiser's nightmare. Consumers can fast-forward something that's prerecorded, bypassing commercials entirely. In addition, RCA manufactures two types of VCRs that automatically pause during commercials.

Even with the high costs and risks, because of its potential to reach a vast, global audience, television advertising remains highly prestigious and perhaps the best venue for strengthening brand awareness or introducing new products or marketing campaigns.

Use TV to Your Advantage

The solution is to make commercials more compelling, more involving, more intrusive, and more entertaining. Relying less on laboratory research and more on capturing the viewer's interest is the goal. Of course, if your commercial runs after a poor commercial by another advertiser, it probably won't matter how good it is. The audience will have already zapped it. You should concentrate on negotiating for the first position in a commercial break—referred to as the A pod position—as a way of ensuring that your commercials are at least masters of their own fate.

Stretch your production dollars. When you are given limited budgets to advertise on television, there is always a conflict in having enough money for the production without compromising the reach and frequency of the media buy. Here, again, resourcefulness in the creative approach is imperative.

Such was the case when Ziccardi & Partners was given the assignment of advertising Stephen King's book *Insomnia*. The production budget would not allow for shooting live action without cutting heavily into the media buy. Animation was a consideration, but not from a high-priced animation house.

The answer to this assignment was found in our agency's in-house computer graphics department. We created a concept that we were able to design on our own computer system, thereby limiting the amount of money spent on animation. We then took it out of house, using CGI animation

Exhibit 7–5
STEPHEN KING: *INSOMNIA*/TV STORYBOARD

PRODUCT: *INSOMNIA*
TITLE: *INSOMNIA*-WALKING MAN
PROGRAM: :15
STATION:

[1] New from Stephen King...

[2] Derry, Maine is a quiet little town. Until some unexpected guests arrive...

[3] First they haunt people's dreams...

[4] Then they steal their sleep.

[5] Now, Derry is caught in a waking nightmare...and only one man has the power to end it—if he sees the light.

[6] *Insomnia*. The number one national bestseller—now in paperback. *Insomnia* by Stephen King. He will scare you sleepless.

153

technology compatible with our own designs to make the spot come to life. Once a dramatic soundtrack was added, the result was a powerful spot that left us with enough money to make an influential media buy, helping take *Insomnia* to the top of the best-seller list. Exhibit 7–5 is an illustration of the *Insomnia* concept storyboard that was first presented to the client.

Remember, a poor television commercial can do more than cause your audience to simply tune out; it can distort the message and tarnish the corporate image. It is vital to choose the proper execution for your message and the right media for the target market.

The Influence of Cable

In television, with more than 62 percent penetration of all U.S. homes, cable has become the predominant means of video reception in the United States. This means not only that viewers now have a vastly larger number of choices in viewing but, more importantly, the long-held distinction between cable and broadcast programs has disappeared. In addition, where once there were only three television networks that, in combination, commanded more than 80 percent of all television viewing, there are now at least six entities that claim to offer some form of network, and these six combined comprise less than 60 percent of all viewing.

TV audiences are fragmented because of the myriad choices available. While television remains a mass medium, it takes a lot more announcements on a far larger number of programs to reach the same number of viewers as in the past. Recent developments such as the commercial availability of direct transmission satellite signals and the proliferation of pay-per-view shows have further complicated the television marketplace while increasing audience fragmentation. For the marketer, this poses new challenges. It means choices have to be made more carefully considering the different networks and on-line services.

RADIO

While radio cannot offer an advertiser graphic representation like television or magazines, it often makes up for this limitation. Frequency, immediacy, and the loyalty of an audience to a radio station or announcer all add to the power of radio advertising.

Factor into the equation the power of bluntness and the mass appeal of crudity. Witness the popularity of shock jocks such as Howard Stern, who takes on anything and anybody, using off-color language and covering topics such as sex, himself, and his wife. His show invites audience participation and arouses emotions; someone listening is likely to stick with it through the commercials and remember the spots as well.

The Benefits of Radio

There are considerable benefits to using radio. Radio is less expensive than television. Easily targeted to local and regional listening audiences, it is a natural for department stores, car dealerships, hotels, theaters, restaurants, and any other company that does business locally. Radio is also effective in reinforcing messages that are in newspapers, magazines, and TV.

Many radio talk-show hosts—Don Imus and Rush Limbaugh, for example—command loyal audiences who listen regularly to their programs, which is a major advantage to advertisers. Radio also provides marketers with opportunities for hybrid ad strategies. Since some radio shows are broadcast nationally, advertisers can get national coverage while focusing their efforts and expenditures on key markets promising above-average sales potential. This hybrid approach is often used by publishers who have a need to ensure some level of national exposure but must also concentrate on markets that account for the majority of book sales in this country.

At Ziccardi & Partners, we have found that the key book markets are generally New York, Los Angeles, San Francisco, Washington, D.C., and Chicago. By developing media plans that use network radio to provide national coverage to create a certain level of support everywhere the book is sold, we can then use local schedules in key markets to greatly increase interest in the book. This strategy has proven highly effective for book advertisers because a key component of successfully marketing a book is word-of-mouth support. These markets, in addition to being the strongest in book sales, also comprise the thought leadership in this country. They are the centers of broadcasting, government, fashion, publishing, and entertainment. They are the markets that set the trends for the entire country; if a book can be successful in these markets, it is almost assured of becoming a national best-seller.

Listen to the Flip Side

Radio messages are fleeting. An ad runs for 30 to 60 seconds and then—as with TV—it's gone. It's easy to miss. And you don't get a second chance to hear it right away. The audience needs to listen carefully to catch all of the details of the message. In addition, programs like "War of the Worlds" are rare, and rarely does one listen to radio with undivided attention. We tune in but don't completely tune out the rest of the world. The radio is a companion when we're raking the leaves or driving the car, but we still focus on the task at hand or the traffic ahead.

Frequency is key to radio. The activities we engage in as we listen to radio interfere with how well we absorb information from the radio. Therefore, radio messages must be repeated with some frequency. Exactly how many times the message must be repeated for it to sink in depends on a multitude of qualitative and quantitative variables. Many studies suggest that at least three exposures are necessary before there is any significant level of persuasion. Whatever the frequency of repetition considered sufficient, the goal of any radio effort should be to maximize the number of people effectively exposed.

OUTDOOR

Transit

In metropolitan areas, transit advertising is used to convey information on topics ranging from food to fashion to health issues to Broadway shows. It is inside the subways, atop taxi cabs, stretched along the sides of buses, and on bus shelters. Subways, trains, and taxis have advertising cards. Airlines typically have advertising in the airport, and some airlines are even experimenting with advertising on the sides of their planes.

In Your Face and above Your Head

The major benefit of transit advertising is that there's a captive audience. The ads can't be avoided, unless you shut your eyes. Consider the type of transit and how well it supports the message and image of the product or store. Some forms of transit advertising, such as those found in airports and commuter train stations, are perceived as more upscale than others, such as those found in subways and taxis. But outdoor signs can be used for middle- to upper-class products and stores, while cards advertising services, trade schools, or courses in bartending or cosmetology generally target the lower and middle classes. You may do well to advertise in airports and not in subways or taxis, depending on the perceptions of your target market.

Billboards

Billboards seem to be getting bigger and more ubiquitous. They're all over highways, atop skyscrapers, and on construction sites promoting upcoming stores. Calvin Klein and Nike, with its giant swoosh logo that it hoists above its NikeTown stores, believe in oversized messages. Such a giant stamp can create excitement and suspense about what is coming. Even for companies with small followings, billboards provide an opportunity to play it up big—sometimes bigger than a company's reputation.

Kenar, a clothing manufacturer, has been a survivor on Seventh Avenue but hardly a household name in fashion. The company once decided it wanted to change all that by putting up a huge billboard—featuring supermodel Claudia Schiffer—in the heart of Times Square. Kenar still isn't a household name, but the company has been slowly gaining recognition. Many retailers and competitors are starting to take the brand more seriously, as it continues to step up its advertising with full-page ads in the *New York Times,* other forms of outdoor advertising, and PR efforts tying into charities.

Disadvantages of Billboards

The message of a billboard is generally limited to a few words, a single concept, a very simple message, since the audience is usually in motion—either walking, driving, or riding in a bus. Because a billboard may be viewed by the same person several times a day, depending on his or her movements, the sign can become boring and lose its impact.

Flyers

Have you ever seen an intriguing flyer? Or been handed one and said to yourself, "Hey, this is great"? It's rare. Among the most obnoxious are those that resemble dollar bills but are actually plugs for 900-number phone services. In major urban areas, where the pedestrian traffic is enormous, such as midtown Manhattan and 34th Street, flyers are impossible to avoid. Leafletters are aggressive. They served subpoenas in past careers. Everything from Chinese takeout to topless clubs to men's suits on sale is advertised on flyers. If you don't get it slapped in your hand, it's probably on your windshield. Call it leaflittering.

Point-of-Purchase Materials

Store signs are one of the oldest forms of advertising. Signs indicating the locations of guild craftsmen have been found in ancient Roman ruins, such as Pompeii, as well as in Greek ruins. Signage is very important in your campaign to capture attention and entice consumers at the point of purchase. In large stores, it's particularly important to have clear, easy-to-read signs that designate different merchandise departments and service sections. Target is considered to have the best signage in the discount industry. Discount and department stores are difficult enough to shop. Don't make it harder.

Properly designed, signs enhance the exterior of a store or showroom and its overall image. If a sign has too much information, it can be confusing. In other cases, there are just too many signs. Some of the nation's older highways, such as Route 1, are so visually cluttered that many drivers avoid them.

Novelty

Advertising venues such as skywriting, banners trailing behind planes, zipper signs on buildings, and blimps are considered novelty media and are suitable for certain seasons and products. Banners trailing planes are great for consumer ads for restaurants and bars near the beaches but may not be appropriate for an upscale establishment. Skywriting can only be used when your target market will be out of doors and the wind is low. Lighted zipper signs on airplanes and buildings can garner a great deal of attention. Zipper signs (made up of a series of lights that digitally spell out a message) have been used on buildings for decades, as evidenced by the ads in Times Square in New York City.

Blimps can be seen from several miles and certainly get noticed. When flown above the target audience, blimps can be an effective adjunct to an advertising campaign—particularly during special events such as the U.S. Tennis Open and the Super Bowl, which are viewed by both local audiences and a national television audience.

Other forms of novelty advertising are cards on supermarket carts and stall cards. Supermarkets have started advertising special products on the outside and inside of shopping carts. Shoppers can see the ads and are reminded of products that they may need. This is a practice that sparks impulse purchases. One advertising agency has begun to buy advertising space in toilet cubicles in rest rooms. The idea is that this is a place where people spend time and may want something to read. New novelty paid advertising can be useful as an attention-getting device but cannot be used on an exclusive basis. Again, the proper match between target market and media placement is important.

The New Media

In the 1990s, the term *new media* entered the lexicon of marketing. It has come to represent an individualized specialty within the world of marketing. Advertising agencies large and small, as well as many marketers, have devoted significant resources to the amorphous new media and many even have departments for, or at least a director of, new media.

It should be recognized that the term reflects, for the most part, new *electronic* media. More specifically, many times the term refers to *interactive* media. The buzzwords are often associated with the new media environment—for example, cyberspace, the information superhighway, the Internet, the electronic community, or virtual reality. These all encompass elements of electronic technology and varying degrees of interactive participation.

Levi's, arguably *the* denizen of American pop culture, has established a World Wide Web site on the Internet with the help of the advertising agency Foote, Cone & Belding. The company is unifying all of its brands in one global campaign on the Web. The site seeks to be informative, entertaining, and interactive, with a much broader focus than the company's individual TV spots, print ads, or outdoor billboards.

Home computers, which in 1995 were in one out of every three households in America, represent the new frontier in marketing communications. Through such on-line services as CompuServe, Prodigy, and America Online, millions of computer users, both at home and on the job, have access to the Internet. Between browsing, chatting, using CD-ROMs, and e-mailing, many people, particularly teenagers and those under 40, spend more time with their computers than any other electronic or print media.

The Coors Brewing Company is seizing the opportunity in the young-adult market with electronic media. Its clear malt beverage, Zima, occupies a premier spot on the Web. In one of the first attempts by a packaged goods company to have a presence on the Web, Zima and the site's creator, Modem Media, have used the Web for both consumer research and audience entertainment. By having surfers sign up for Tribe Z (so users can access certain areas of its vast Web site and get weekly updates), it is tapping into a whole new opportunity for consumer research.

In many cases, computers have supplanted TV and books as forms of recreation and learning tools. Saturn, a division of General Motors, uses its Web site to allow current and potential customers to get information about Saturn models and chat with Saturn owners. Saturn has designed the site with simple graphics to coincide with the nature of the Saturn buyer. Since Saturn buyers don't go for expensive, frilly options, the approach to the Web site is functional, with a focus on providing information.

The real potential behind the new electronic media lies in its capacity for interactive communications—consumers can respond directly to a message, ask questions, engage in a dialogue, and order a product on demand. This interactivity has become the mantra of new media zealots.

Although most of the focus on interactive communications is tied in with the ongoing development of personal computing, there have been many interactive innovations in other areas as well. From magazine ads that play a tune to supermarket kiosks that plan a menu based on an individual's dietary and taste preferences to the mass-market, middle-American appeal of home-shopping programs, interactivity is busting out all over.

Of course, the phenomenon is still too new to assess its merits and gauge its success. In addition, most efforts in the new media and interactivity are spent figuring out just what's available and how to buy and use it. Because it is so new and unfamiliar, the real cornerstone of advertising and competitive marketing, message creativity, is still sorely lacking. There remains a stunning simplicity and sameness to the thousands of ads on Prodigy or the Web sites that have been established on the Internet. Only when the technology is fully grasped and the audience delivery potential understood and mastered will significant dollars be funneled into interactive communications and away from current mainstream media.

MEDIA: HOW TO MAXIMIZE THE BUCKS

It is not just a matter of choosing a certain media mode and a vehicle within that mode. It is critical to know the best combination of media choices based on the advertising budget. You want to maximize the size of the target market exposed to the advertising message, known as maximizing the *reach*. Also, maximize the number of times that the customer audience receives the message, which is known as maximizing the *frequency*. Often, due to the constraints of operating within a budget, there's a trade-off between reach and frequency.

Research the demographics and psychographics of the readership, viewership, and listenership of the media using the services of media research specialists or buy computer programs that will have you key in the page rates and the readership information for each of the media being considered. This computer software is invaluable in helping uncover the most economical use of ad dollars, though, ultimately, it's your decision on how to allocate the budget to meet the advertising goals. Machines and research go only so far. At some point, leap into the advertising game and see whether the market behaves as the research predicts or if the consumers react in a contrary fashion. Use your intuition—it's a valuable tool whose benefits are not often addressed in grad school!

THE MEDIA PLAN: HIGH-PROFILE OR LOW-KEY?

The Written Plan

The written plan is a statement of the types of media that will be used to carry the advertising message to the target market. It should include a description of the format of the ads and the type of media to be used for each advertisement. Your analysis of the media and the reading, viewing, listening, and commuting habits of the targeted audience should be thoroughly spelled out.

Do Research

Media research involves an examination of the various media vehicles; the advantages, disadvantages, demographics, and psychographics of each of the audiences; and the costs of each. Sources of this information include the media, Simmons Market Research Bureau, MediaMark Research, the Purchase Influence Study, VALS2 (a qualitative analysis of psychographics by SRI International), and PRIZM, a geodemographic analysis by Claritas Corporation of lifestyles within zip-code clusters. Media research companies and the media departments of companies are also responsible for keeping media planners current on emerging or submerging trends, technologies, and customer demands.

Return to the Marketing Plan

For an initial direction in what, when, where, and how much media to run, return to the marketing plan. Review the products and services, target market definition, competition, and objectives. For each target market, determine the seasonality, geography, and communications strategy—the reach and frequency—of the advertising campaign.

Geography

The target market dictates where you choose to place ads. Advertise not only in areas where you know sales are good, but also where the target market is situated. To strengthen market share where sales are already strong, advertise products to remind customers to buy them. To increase market share where sales are weak, persuade your competitor's customers of the advantages of your products, but make sure that you have good distribution support. When the advertising works, a demand for the product is created.

Reach and Frequency

The next step is to determine how much advertising to run and how often. The reach of an ad is defined as the percentage of the target audience exposed to it at least once during a four-week period. The frequency is the average number of times those people are reached in that time span.

Other key terms are rating points and gross rating points. Each rating point represents 1 percent of the market. Gross rating points are a summation of what percentage of the target market watched or listened to a program. Gross rating points (GRPs) can be calculated by multiplying reach by frequency. In general, to increase frequency, decrease reach in a target market, unless it's possible to increase the total advertising budget.

Having calculated the GRPs for your ad, the geography, and the seasonality, now choose the program time that matches the desired GRPs. Nielsen ratings indicate how much of the total population watches which shows. Then it is up to you to determine how much of your target market is within that audience to know whether that program is a good media buy.

MEDIA PLANNING IS A LITTLE LIKE JOURNALISM

Are you approaching a comprehensive media plan? Think of how you would start a newspaper story—using the five Ws of journalism: who, what, when, where, and why. The *who* relates to the target audience. Make sure you have a firm grasp on who you are directing your message to. Once you have a clear understanding of the target market and how it spends its time, you'll be in a much better position to evaluate the type of media noise that it sees or listens to most frequently.

What refers to the creative message. If it's a big idea whose message relies on visual communications, obviously the choice of medium is not going to be radio. *When* is also an important question. If your product is such that the message needs to be told at a specific period or time of the year, certain media may need to be excluded. If Solarcaine, the sun product, broke its summer campaign on television, that would be akin to media suicide. Who's watching TV when everyone's at the beach? It would be better to put the message on aerial banners and radio.

Where is answered with the right media selections. Do you choose TV or radio; outdoor or indoor; *Vogue* or *Harper's;* PBS or NBC? Select the media wisely. Finally, ask *why*. This is, in effect, the media rationale. For example, if your only recommendations are magazines, maybe it's because your target market has an affinity for upscale editorial. Maybe your limited budget can buy high levels of media noise if you limit your commitments to one medium. In that case, select only the best one under the circumstances.

Taking the journalistic approach to media planning is a simple, straightforward way to ensure an efficient plan.

8 | Creative Adaptation for the Media

"It's OK for *Vogue*, DZ,
now what do we do for *Bowling Today?*"

SAY YOUR CAMPAIGN WILL HIT *VOGUE,* the *New York Times,* and the *Village Voice.* Ads that are appropriate for one magazine or newspaper may not be right for another. Just as you always bear in mind who your customers are and what they want, you must consider who is buying the *Times* or the *Daily News.* Obviously, it's not the same customer. You have to choose the right venue.

For example, Peter Benchley's book, *Beast,* was his long-awaited follow-up to *Jaws.* The release was scheduled right before summer and the timing had a strong impact on the media chosen. While Ziccardi & Partners did create newspaper ads and radio spots for the campaign, the most effective medium we used was aerial beach banners. Outdoor advertising was perfect for the time of year, and the aerial banners were ideal for a Benchley book. Once we had chosen the medium, we had to tailor the creative to it. The message, accompanied by a huge shot of the book jacket, was simple yet effective and quite ominous in tone: "There's something in the water . . ." The book catapulted on the *New York Times* best-seller list. Certainly, the advertising helped to hype sales because it was shaped by the medium in which it ran. That, too, is part of the creative process. Ads must always complement their media. This chapter offers the nuts and bolts on adapting the creative to the right media.

THE MEDIA AFFECTS THE CREATIVE

Like chess, in which every game poses a new challenge, each advertising situation requires a different strategy and set of moves. The pieces in the creative game of advertising include the headline, photography, illustration, logo, copy, white space, and floor line. In an ad, as in a game of chess, you don't necessarily use all of the pieces at your disposal. You manipulate them differently to suit the situation.

An ad placed in the *New York Times* should have a completely different attitude and look than one placed in *Vogue*. Its character and personality should also be distinct from an ad placed in the *Village Voice*. Similarly, an ad in *Vogue* should be different from one in *Wired,* and a radio spot for a top-40 rock station is produced differently than one for a classical music or easy listening station.

There is no such thing as "just a magazine ad." Magazine advertising is not as simple as saying, "Let's put together an ad to run in a dozen different magazines." Consider the magazine or magazines the ad will appear in, and determine whether the ad presentation is compatible with the image of the magazine and is targeted to its readership. It is also important to ask when the ad will run and if there is a special issue dedicated to a particular theme. If there is, find out whether there are any special promotional tie-ins to participate in, giving the client added value.

Production idiosyncrasies must be considered as well. A newspaper ad does not generally reproduce with the quality of a magazine ad. Color in newspapers may not appear as vivid. The detailing on sweaters and dresses may be hard to make out, and textures may get washed away in a sea of black ink. Speedo activewear ads, for example, look fine in newspapers because the ads show functionality, high performance, and modern styling, rather than texture, fashion, and detailing—the kind of elements that are tough to bring out in newspapers.

An ad in one magazine may reproduce differently in another, and sometimes all the work and creativity gets stifled by a shoddy production process. For maximum impact, get familiar with the quality of the publications in which you are placing the ad and create the ad bearing in mind where it will run.

NEWSPAPERS

The newspaper reigns as the advertising medium that accounts for the single largest volume of advertising dollars. Its popularity results in unique challenges: Because the limited space is crowded with competitors' and noncompetitors' ads, attracting and holding the consumer's attention becomes more difficult. It's important to outshine the competition through ads that are distinctive, original, riveting, and memorable.

At Zicccardi & Partners, we use the following guidelines in creating newspaper ads.

Newspaper Creative Guidelines

Find a Unique Format

Make your ad instantly recognizable by developing a format. Be consistent in format, yet fresh and imaginative with every new ad. For Random House's Modern Library, as shown in the sample in Exhibit 8–1a, we use the same format with every ad, varying only the graphic elements within. The ads automatically stand out against their competition. The format for Signet Paperbacks is accomplished by using a movie ad approach—large graphic elements with big author name and title, as you can see in Exhibit 8–1b.

Keep It Organized

Use an organized layout that guides the reader's eye through the ad easily and in proper sequential order, that is, from headline, to illustration, to copy, to price, to store name or product logo. It doesn't have to be a magnificently beautiful ad to accomplish this goal. In its Valentine's Day ads in 1996, The Wiz used a simple yet symmetrical format, with a curved headline reading "This is Valentine's Day," followed by the line "Say It With Music." The curved headline helped frame the ad around a vintage Hollywood photo of a man—possibly Rudolph Valentino—planting a kiss on a woman. At either side of the photo are the covers of CDs from different recording stars—suggested selections for Valentine's gifts. Lower in the ad is a plug for a contest (no purchase required, with a Club Med trip as the prize) sponsored by The Wiz. Even further down, discreetly listed, are the prices, the Wiz logo, and its 800 number. The ad is hardly gorgeous, but its effective arrangement of several necessary elements helped communicate the message and guide the reader's eye smoothly through it.

Exhibit 8–1a
RANDOM HOUSE
MODERN LIBRARY/
UNIQUE FORMATS

NEW FROM
MODERN LIBRARY

**THE COLLECTED ESSAYS
OF RALPH ELLISON**
Edited by John F. Callahan
Preface by Saul Bellow

"The collection celebrates Ellison's
great talent...and, most important,
his depth of insight into the American
dilemmas of race and culture."
—*The Boston Globe*

"Elegantly written, beautifully
composed, and intellectually
sophisticated."
—*Los Angeles Times*

A RAISIN IN THE SUN
Lorraine Hansberry

"Will remain an inspiration
to generations yet unborn."
—Dr. Martin Luther King, Jr.

"It is as if history is conspiring
to make the play a classic."
—*The New York Times*

**SOUTH TO A VERY
OLD PLACE**
Albert Murray

"Incredibly inventive...Nobody,
but nobody, has ever captured
Southern black speech, in all its
deep humanity and signifying
boastfulness, like Albert Murray."
—Charles Monaghan

"A highly syncopated memoir
of youth and a celebration of
U.S. Negro culture."
—*Time*

THE FIRE NEXT TIME
James Baldwin

"Sermon, ultimatum, confession,
deposition, testament, and
chronicle...all presented in
searing, brilliant prose."
—*The New York Times Book Review*

"Baldwin uses words as the sea
uses waves, to flow and beat,
advance and retreat, rise and
take a bow in disappearing."
—Langston Hughes

Also available from The Modern Library

GO TELL IT ON THE MOUNTAIN
James Baldwin

INVISIBLE MAN
Ralph Ellison

CANE
Jean Toomer

MODERN LIBRARY

Exhibit 8–1b
TOO DAMN RICH/VARYING GRAPHIC ELEMENTS

Many ad designers make the mistake of thinking that different typefaces, borders, and reverses add to the interest of the ad. On the contrary, these devices are distracting and can render an ad difficult to read. Such was the case with newspaper ads in 1996 for UNITE, a new union formed through the merger of the ILGWU and ACTWU. In one ad, six different typefaces were used, a seemingly arbitrary box was placed around the word *changes,* and a few paragraphs seemed randomly placed on the page. The ad was tough to read, and its important message—that 300,000 garment and office workers had united to fight for better working conditions and wages— could have been delivered with greater clarity.

Exhibits 8–1c and 8–1d are two examples of how a type-intensive ad can still be well organized. While there are many elements on the page, the eye reads easily from top to bottom, absorbing the important selling points in order of priority.

Place One Element Prominently

Pick one element and make it dominant. The art or headline is usually the most prominent element in the ad. These are the two components that attract attention first and ensure notice. One year Ford used a big, booming headline, "We Buried 'Em At The Beach," to underscore its victory at the Daytona 500. The ad tied the winning performance to Ford-developed safety features, and the headline telegraphed that with impact.

In the ads shown in Exhibits 8–1e and 8–1f, there is one element that dominates the ad and is sufficient to sell the book. In the first, the title is all you need. In the second, the author's name sells the book better than anything else.

Use Benefits in Headlines

It's smart advertising to mention in the headline a benefit beyond the obvious. Don't say: "Loehmann's. Designer dresses regularly $999—on sale $499." Say, "When you pay $499 for a $999 designer dress, that's $500 more you can spend tuning up the Rolls." Headlines for Chase Manhattan, for example, say "Me and my peace of mind." That's the real benefit, besides the obvious one—that you can use the Chase Better Banking Card to access any of the 150,000 Chase ATMs around the world.

Use White Space Effectively

White space can focus attention on the words or illustrations that count. In one Bloomingdale's coat-sale ad, about a quarter of the space was

171

Exhibit 8–1d
NEANDERTHAL/WELL-ORGANIZED TYPE-INTENSIVE AD

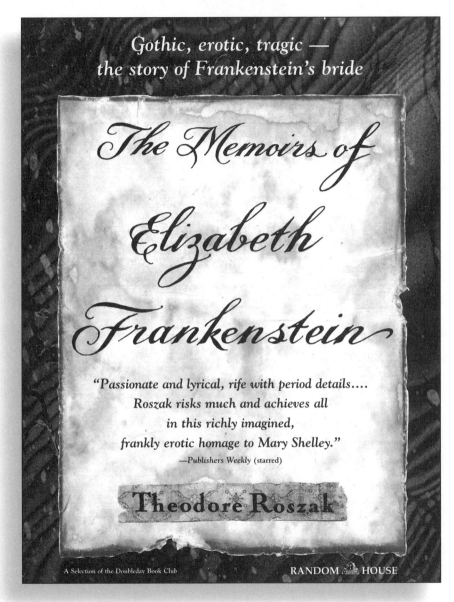

Gothic, erotic, tragic —
the story of Frankenstein's bride

The Memoirs of

Elizabeth

Frankenstein

"Passionate and lyrical, rife with period details....
Roszak risks much and achieves all
in this richly imagined,
frankly erotic homage to Mary Shelley."
—Publishers Weekly (starred)

Theodore Roszak

A Selection of the Doubleday Book Club   RANDOM HOUSE

Exhibit 8–1f
RECESSIONAL/ONE DOMINANT ELEMENT

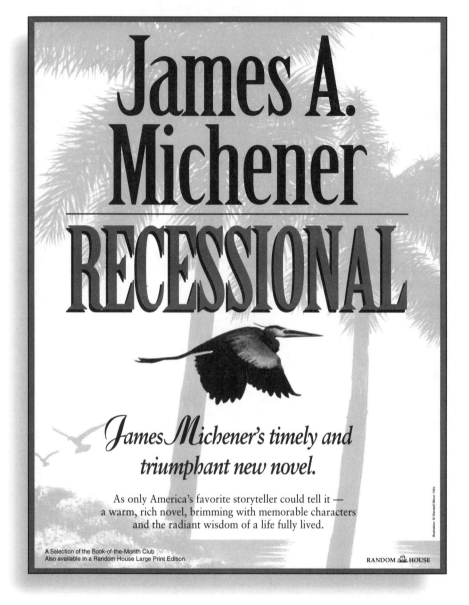

174

white space, which drew your eyes to the big "30% to 60% off." White space can also be used as an artistic design element. A large *New York Times* house ad, with few words and much white space, had a photograph of the earth taken from high in space. The circumference was muted for an atmospheric, almost celestial effect. The headline was big and simple—"Some Promise You The World. We Deliver"—and created a play on the advertising message for a special home-delivery rate. This was also a good example of an ad that's not overcrowded with information.

When a lot of information is required (perhaps for a one-day sale that lists a multitude of marked-down brands and items), be sure to use a well-organized grid format. Department stores and other promotional specialty stores typically pack plenty of information into their ads, illustrating good prices on a wide array of products. One Gristede's/Sloan's ad listed 40 items, including coupons, in an organized way—in four columns and categorized by food classification, such as produce, deli, or dairy. Coupons was a separate category. The Food Emporium also crams plenty of item information into its ads, but flags the most special offers for club members with checkerboard designs above the items.

The ads used in Exhibits 8–1g and 8–1h are good illustrations of how the use of white space draws your eye to the most important elements. In *Enigma,* your eye immediately goes to the words on the page because of the way they are spaced. In *Brando,* the photo grabs your attention.

Write Crisp Copy

Make the copy interesting and readable. Don't be too clever. Don't get cute, and avoid unusual or difficult words. Reinforce brand names: They're powerful, and a brand name that's well positioned represents quality to the customer. Including brand names also opens the door for a store to take advantage of co-op allowances from manufacturers.

The headlines in the ads shown in Exhibits 8–1i and 8–1j tell the story with a minimum of words. The copy gets right to the point and leaves more space in the ad to accommodate graphic elements.

Include the Details

Don't forget details. In fact, you can use them to your advantage in trying to tell the creative story. Don't throw in the kitchen sink, but give the relevant facts that will let the customer know the where, when, what, and why of

Exhibit 8–1g
ENIGMA/EFFECTIVE USE OF WHITE SPACE

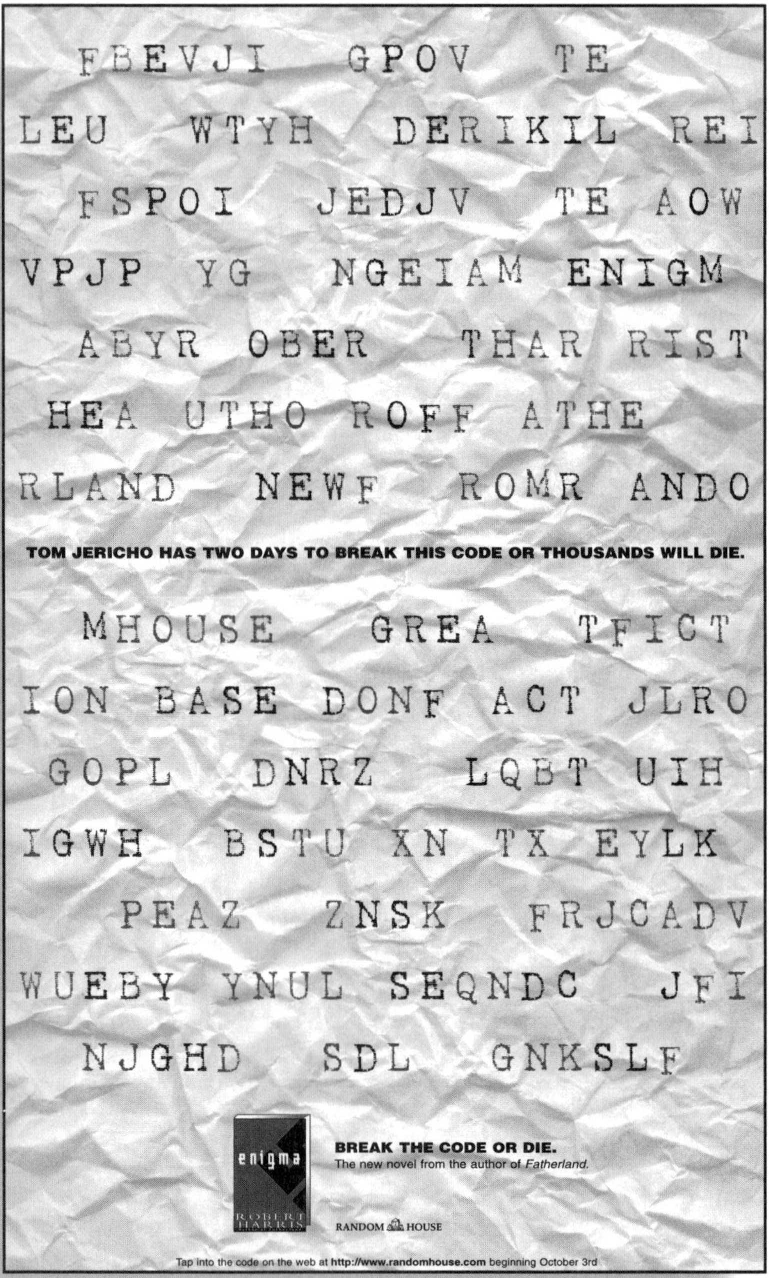

Exhibit 8–1h
BRANDO/EFFECTIVE USE OF WHITE SPACE

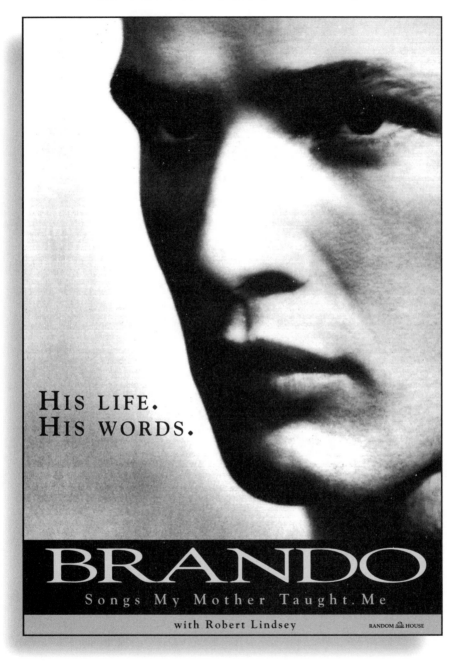

HIS LIFE.
HIS WORDS.

BRANDO
Songs My Mother Taught. Me
with Robert Lindsey   RANDOM HOUSE

Exhibit 8–1i
THE WORKS/CRISP COPY

JIM HENSON

THE WORKS

The Art, the Magic, the Imagination

A loving, joyful tribute, filled with nice people (Candice Bergen,
Harry Belafonte, Frank Oz), fantastic color illustrations (the definitive
portrait of Cookie Monster), secrets (how Miss Piggy did the
water ballet) and the quintessential Jim Henson: a man who
created a universe and changed our world.

RANDOM HOUSE

Exhibit 8–1j
BAD AS I WANNA BE/CRISP COPY

shopping at your store. The floor line at the bottom of the ad is the appropriate place for this information. The majority of newspaper and magazine ads include floor lines. Nordstrom, for example, runs in minuscule print at the bottom of an ad the relevant phone numbers and locations and a note about shipping charges on mail and phone orders. It's small enough not to detract from the main message that Nordstrom carries a full range of products.

The ad for the runaway best-seller, *Primary Colors,* shown in Exhibit 8–1k, has a big story to tell. Many copies have sold, and the critical reviews have been wonderful. The details are laid out in a way that is reader-friendly and used to advantage in telling the creative story. At Ziccardi & Partners, we now also include that all-important Internet address in many of our publishing ads.

Incite Action

Trigger immediate action by using such catch phrases as "limited supply," "act now," "this week only," and "one day only." Princeton Ski Shops went all out with full-size ads during the winter of 1996, promoting a huge clearance sale held at Giants Stadium in the New Jersey Meadowlands. It had a headline, "Now is the time to buy," and the message, "The largest ski, snowboard and winterwear blowout in history! Save 80% off everything in stock on sale." The word *blowout* was repeated three times in the ad. Andriana Furs ran an ad plugging its "Dream Sale" for "4 Days Only!" while Macy's frequently advertises "Take another 30 to 50 percent off" on certain fashion items for a "one day only" sale. "Super Saturday" is another catchphrase used in retail ads. Such hyperbole can work if it's not overused. Otherwise, it pushes credulity, and customers sense the ads are disingenuous. Exhibit 8–1l, the ad for *Tap, Tap,* a book by David Martin, is an example of an ad that is a call to action in a slightly different way.

MAGAZINES

Magazines have some very special features. They are printed on quality paper that provides excellent reproduction and have a longer shelf life than most other print media. In addition, special-interest publications, such as *Golf & Tennis, Elle, Architectural Digest, Gourmet,* the *Utne Reader,* and *Romantic Times,* provide opportunities for segmented marketing.

Exhibit 8–1k
PRIMARY COLORS/INCLUDE THE DETAILS

In case you're keeping score, here's who's winning the primary wars:

0 — Robert Dornan
0 — Richard Lugar
4 — Alan Keyes
12 — Lamar Alexander
71 — Pat Buchanan
76 — Steve Forbes
742 — Bob Dole
1,167,000* — ANONYMOUS

(Delegates committed through 3/13/96)

#1 NATIONAL BESTSELLER

AMERICA HAS VOTED, AND THE WINNER IS

PRIMARY COLORS!

*Over one million copies in print

"Congratulations, Anonymous, whoever you are."
— Christopher Buckley, *The New Yorker*

"The author knows politics...and writes like a dream."
— *The Boston Globe*

"*Primary Colors* is a scream....It is written perfectly."
— Mary McGrory, *The Washington Post*

"*Primary Colors* is the best book I never wrote."
— Mark Miller, *Newsweek*

Also available as a Random House AudioBook   A Selection of the Book-of-the-Month Club   http://www.randomhouse.com/site/election96/

RANDOM HOUSE

Exhibit 8–1I
TAP, TAP/A CALL TO ACTION

David Martin is "compelling and terrifying.*" If you don't agree, you get your money back.**

From the bestselling author of *Lie To Me* — a dark, thrilling novel of good, evil, and the ultimate revenge.

"David Martin is a heartbreakingly deft chronicler of human passion."
— James Ellroy

What if your best friend started killing your worst enemies?

RANDOM 🏠 HOUSE

TAP, TAP
DAVID MARTIN
AUTHOR OF *LIE TO ME*

**If after reading *Tap, Tap*, you feel it's not worth the purchase price, return the book and your cash register receipt within fourteen days of purchase and we'll send you a check for the price you paid. Offer expires March 31, 1995. Return to: *Tap, Tap* Rebate Offer c/o Random House, Inc., P.O. Box 709, Westminister, MD 21158-0709

* *The Washington Post*

182

Magazine ads should be designed to fit the tone of the magazine. Audiences vary from one magazine to another; the creative approaches, including copy, should be tailored to each magazine.

Magazine Creative Guidelines

Design and Write to the Demographics and Psychographics of the Audience

Johnny Walker Black Label Scotch has a reputation as a quality, stylish, old-line brand tied to tradition and bearing a masculine image. However, the company has sought to appeal to new audiences by reshaping its image so it's less tied to tradition and typical masculine imagery. For example, a Johnny Walker ad in *New York* magazine had the headline "Dare To Discover the Possibilities of a New Perspective" set above a picture of a young painter at his easel on a beach drenched in a shimmering sunset's gold and orange hues, evoking the warm color of whiskey. The ad's look and message, which offered a new perspective on an established product, was designed to appeal to *New York*'s young, ambitious, trendsetting readership.

Tap into the Audience's Needs

Appeal to the specific needs, wants, and desires of the magazine audience. ABR advertises its benefits administration services in *Forbes,* targeting businesspeople and Wall Street. It knows many businesses are struggling and downsizing and may want to hire outside help to manage certain internal operations so they can focus on their core business objectives and plan ways to "steal" customers. Corporate jet companies and makers of expensive automobiles such as Lexus also advertise in *Forbes* or *Fortune* magazine to appeal to corporate executives who control national and international businesses and command six- or seven-figure salaries.

Develop a Strong Positioning Line

Develop a strong positioning line that reinforces the attitude of the photography and vice versa. Diet Coke ads do a good job of that. One ad showed a close-up of a punk, streetwise couple with an in-your-face attitude, which fits with the positioning line, "Just For The Taste Of It." They're independent-minded, and the point is made that you don't have to be overweight to drink diet Coke.

Skip the Clichés

There's nothing worse than corny or clichéd copy in an ad, especially when it's used in ads for upscale products. It can be used, though, if there's a clever angle or spin. Godiva, for example, has an ad for ground coffee that reads, "Escape The Daily Grind," and one for chocolate that reads, "Not Only Absence Makes the Heart Grow Fonder." Baker Furniture ran an ad with a small headline reading, "It hasn't been business as usual for a long time." A smiling career woman is depicted working on a laptop placed on an elegant wood table's surface, next to a bowl of fruit and a coffee cup. The message sent is one of comfort and elegance and a better way of doing things.

Rely on Strong Visuals

Use a great headline or an arresting photograph to catch the reader's eye. Ralph Lauren's magazine ads launching a line of body treatments show a perfectly built, blond, Nordic-looking woman with a pout and a tank top that amplifies her assets, and bear the headline, "The Architecture of a Beautiful Body." On a separate page, oversized photos of bottles of body oil and body spray reinforce the bold, architectural theme and suggest a sense of power behind the product.

Absolut, the Swedish vodka brand, has also used a strong visual concept, but in an offbeat way. It has transformed a bottle into a celebrity. Since the mid-1980s, Absolut ads have been dominated by a giant photo of the brand's distinctively shaped bottle with the word *Absolut* and a short qualifying word such as *perfection* or *clarity* placed next to it. The original ad with the "Absolut Perfection" tag line had a halo above the bottle. More recently, there have been quirkier variations on the theme such as "Absolut Centerfold," with a picture of the bottle stripped of its label, and "Absolut Houdini," with the bottle missing from the picture and only a ring of moisture left on the table. This simple yet unusual campaign is marked by a strong visual element and shows a staying power that has helped catapult Absolut's market share.

A Designer's Visual Approach

The designer Ellen Tracy also has a very visual but understated and elegant approach. Ellen Tracy had always done beautiful ads, but it challenged our agency to take its advertising to the next level—to make it more unusual, to make it stand out in the clutter of other fashion advertising, and to appeal to its customer on a more emotional level.

We set out to develop a new, unique look to its advertising, along with a platform line that would evoke an emotional response. The line we came up with was a simple one: "What should I wear?" It's a phrase that was, is, and always will be the question that many women ask themselves every day. But as we later found in consumer focus groups, this line opened the door to deeper emotional issues for woman. It did not just address the issue of dressing for the day's or evening's activities. It was a question that cut right to the core of a woman's identity: Who am I? As a person at home, in business, with my friends, colleagues, and children? It was a strong personal-identity question that opened the door to many of these emotional issues.

We were on the right track, but the visuals would hold the key to a successful fashion campaign. Since the question was emotional, the visuals had to convey the same feeling as the copy. The advertising story was all about the different roles and parts of a woman's life. We had to bring the copy and graphics together in a way that would still give us the ability to show the clothing itself.

We developed a campaign of emotional imagery (which you can refer to in Exhibits 8–2a and 8–2b) using moody, environmental black-and-white photos on one page, faced on the opposite page by studio shots of the clothing. The insert told a story—of a woman's day from morning to night and how her Ellen Tracy wardrobe allowed her to accommodate all of the day's activities. The response to the campaign by the trade and consumers was immediate and enthusiastic.

The following season, the campaign evolved naturally. Keeping the "What should I wear?" positioning line, we changed the attitude of the environmental photography. We chose unexpected locations that included a pristine lake, a garden, the shingled roof of a country inn. But the key to developing the campaign came with the decision to bring the product into the environmental setting, as you see in Exhibit 8–2c. The contrast between the rural settings and the elegantly dressed Ellen Tracy models drew attention to the product in a very fresh way and won us the prestigious Photo District News Gold Award for best photography in all advertising categories.

Recently, Ellen Tracy's advertising has moved toward using an eight-page foldout in the major magazines to add multiple dimension to the

186

Exhibit 8–2c
ELLEN TRACY COLLECTION/PHOTO DISTRICT NEWS GOLD AWARD

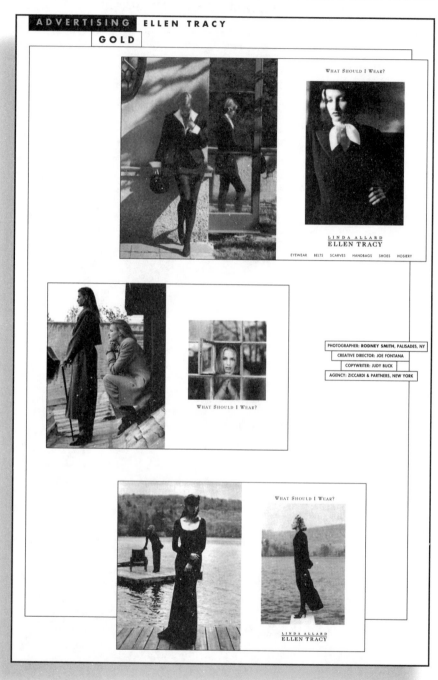

campaign. The emphasis in this part of the evolution was more strongly on the clothes, photographing them in simple settings. The positioning line is well-known by now, but to take it a step further and complement the graphic evolution, the eight-page story began with "What should I wear?" and paid off with "You know the answer." Exhibit 8–2 (d, e, f, g) depicts several pages from the insert.

Ellen Tracy's formidable design director, Linda Allard, says of the campaign, "The visual elements in our magazine advertising continue to be strong, dominant, and effective. The campaign simultaneously shows the clothes and builds imagery. 'What should I wear?' is a positioning line that has given Ellen Tracy strong brand identity. We continue to use it and keep it fresh by reflecting changes in the fashion marketplace."

DIRECT MAIL

Don't Confuse It with Direct Response

Many people still have not figured out the fundamental difference between direct mail and direct response, although there is a very distinct one. In our business we sometimes use the terms interchangeably, and that creates confusion. Very simply, here are the differences.

Direct mail uses the mail. It's a medium in itself, just like magazines or TV. It uses the mail to deliver an advertiser's message. Direct response is not a medium, but it uses many media, including newspapers, magazines, broadcast, and direct mail. Direct response uses one or more types of these media for the purpose of getting a response directly from the reader, viewer, or listener.

Segmented Marketing Raises the Importance of Direct Mail

The main advantage of direct mail is that it is the most segmented medium currently available. Segmenting breaks customers into groups according to common demographic, product usage, and purchasing characteristics. This breakdown allows for the analysis of which customer group is most likely to respond to a particular advertising or promotional offer. Each offer is then marketed only to those customers who will most probably respond. It is the most expensive medium per 1,000 reach.

189

Exhibit 8–2d
ELLEN TRACY COLLECTION/MAGAZINE INSERT

What should I wear?

Exhibit 8–2e
ELLEN TRACY COLLECTION/MAGAZINE INSERT *(CONTINUED)*

Exhibit 8–2f
ELLEN TRACY COLLECTION/MAGAZINE INSERT *(CONTINUED)*

You know the answer.

Exhibit 8–2g
ELLEN TRACY COLLECTION/MAGAZINE INSERT *(CONTINUED)*

L I N D A A L L A R D
ELLEN TRACY

With segmented marketing so popular today, and the development of highly sophisticated ways to manipulate and define consumer data banks, direct mail has become increasingly important to the advertising mix.

Direct mail has been a very successful medium for Ellen Tracy, working in conjunction with retailers such as Saks Fifth Avenue, Bloomingdale's, Marshall Fields, and Dayton Hudson. We've been able to target the Ellen Tracy customer using sophisticated computer lists, working in conjunction with the major retailers. Exhibit 8–3 is a piece we've done in conjunction with Saks Fifth Avenue.

Direct-Mail Creative Guidelines

Define your reason. This is elementary but sometimes so obvious it's overlooked. What is your objective? Is it to get more sales, build an image, attain more profitable sales, or whet the prospect's appetite?

Offer added value to increase projected responses. It could be a gift-with-purchase, a purchase-with-purchase (the cosmetic industry does this best), or any other incentive that makes the offer more opportunistic for the consumer. Try to include a guarantee and make it easy for the consumer to respond. Provide an 800 number.

Testing the Mail

Direct mail is a medium for testing, even more so than other media formats. Before making a major capital commitment and rolling out a large mailing, test the mailing lists on a sampling to observe the probability of responses relative to demographics, psychographics, and the merchandise or product.

Effective Uses of Direct Mail

The JA (Jewelers of America) International Jewelry Show

In direct mail, a targeted creative approach is extremely important. It must contain a headline that will grab attention and immediately telegraph the message. If that is accomplished, the reader is likely to get into the nuts-and-bolts details of the piece.

An example of this was in our agency's creative approach to the direct-mail pieces for the JA International Jewelry Show. The JA trade show is held at the Jacob Javits Convention Center in New York in

Exhibit 8–3
ELLEN TRACY COLLECTION/SAKS FIFTH AVENUE
DIRECT-MAIL PIECE

SAKS FIFTH AVENUE

Full-dress salute.

To Martha Graham, in bare feet and

flowing faille. To Audrey Hepburn, in

charcoal cashmere. To Jessye Norman

in gunmetal taffeta. To Sophia Loren in

black cut velvet. To Cat Woman,

Spider Woman and Wonder Woman.

To women.

ELLEN TRACY

February and July. Traditionally, the JA mailing pieces concentrated on merchandise and the enormous size of the show. But in 1994, for the first time in its history, the show faced serious competition from a new trade show in Las Vegas. There were plenty of reasons why the Vegas show would be more appealing than the New York show: Las Vegas is a great place to go to escape winter, to gamble, to see shows, and to play in the sun. The threat of losing exhibitors to Las Vegas was real. A new approach was necessary, one with a compelling look and that would provide surefire reasons why New York was the place to be.

First of all, we decided to take a more glamorous approach to the piece, presenting jewelry in a fashion context, which had never been done for the show. In Exhibit 8–4, we can immediately see the fashion impact and influence. Second, the headline spoke directly to New York's reputation as the center of the jewelry world: "Success is knowing where to show up."

Citibank Switzerland

Our direct-mail work for Citibank Switzerland is another example of how the right creative approach yields higher responses. Citibank Switzerland regularly solicits upscale individuals for large, long-term investment opportunities. But the creative approach to its direct-mail pieces did not address the lifestyle of its prospects. When the bank came to us for their Citiventure III brochure, we overhauled the look of the piece, showing illustrations of a sapling—seen in Exhibit 8–5—growing into a mighty oak tree with each turn of the page. It was accompanied by the headline, "Investing in tomorrow's growth." This approach gave a vibrant, more elegant look to an otherwise long and fact-filled piece.

Direct Mail Doesn't Have to Cost a Fortune

I held a dinner party last year during the week that Barbra Streisand performed her world tour concert in New York. I knew that several of the invited guests were die-hard Barbra fans, and in the spirit of good fun, I hired a Streisand look-alike, Susan Zimmerman, to perform at my apartment. Taken by her wit and charm, I invited her to stay for dinner. She mentioned that her bookings were not as brisk as she would have hoped and asked if I might have any promotional ideas to give her career a boost. She also mentioned, quite casually, that she had little money to spend. I couldn't resist helping this talented young woman.

Exhibit 8–4
JA JEWELRY SHOW/DIRECT-MAIL PIECE (FEBRUARY 1994)

197

Exhibit 8–5
CITIBANK SWITZERLAND/DIRECT-MAIL PIECE

Exhibit 8–6
SUSAN ZIMMERMAN/BUSINESS CARD

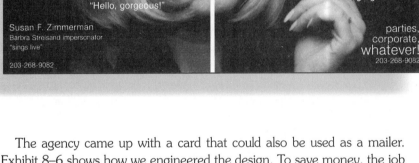

The agency came up with a card that could also be used as a mailer. Exhibit 8–6 shows how we engineered the design. To save money, the job was printed as one piece and then cut into four equal parts. Each part of the card was designed to be a stand-alone business card; the piece was also designed to be a four-part mailing to agents, hotels, and theaters. This low-budget program (it cost a mere $400) landed "Barbra" on two talk shows (*Rolanda* and *Maury Povich*), as well as a six-month tour of various cabaret theaters and clubs throughout the country. It worked like butta! Effective direct-mail ideas and executions do not have to cost a fortune.

OUTDOOR

No other advertising medium enables an advertiser to reach so many prospects as quickly, as often, and as cost-efficiently as outdoor advertising. Billboards, because of their size, can accommodate almost any kind of message. In a short time, billboards can deliver a large number of exposure opportunities. The size and placement of eye-catching outdoor signs offer an impact unmatched by any other medium, sending a larger-than-life message. Outdoor advertising, once considered a downscale medium, has emerged in the mid-1990s as one of the most effective media for upscale advertising, especially in the fashion arena. Again, the creative direction plays an important role in the impact of the outdoor advertising. It should, when possible, complement the billboard's location.

Driving the Message Home

For Izod's PGA line of shirts, we used a billboard extension to add to the creative impact. The billboard, illustrated in Exhibit 8–7, appeared on major highways leading into New York. The creative was a close-up shot of a golfer driving a ball off the tee. The flight of the ball was blurred, giving a sense that you're following its trajectory, which was extended beyond the billboard, creating the three-dimensional appearance of flying off the billboard and into the sky. A simple line of copy, "The Shirt for Sunday Drivers," appeared with the Izod logo. After the billboard went up, sales of the shirt in the New York market increased by more than 35 percent.

Beast Goes to the Beach

For Peter Benchley's book *Beast,* a long-awaited follow-up to *Jaws,* we took the outdoor campaign to selected beach locations, using aerial banners. The message, accompanied by a huge shot of the book jacket, was again simple but effective: "There's something in the water . . ." The book catapulted to No. 1 on the best-seller list.

Outdoor Creative Guidelines

Use Bold, Simple Visuals

The layout and the illustration need to be big, bold, and beautiful. The colors should be bright and the background simple and uncluttered. Take advantage of the space available in outdoor posters: Showing products larger than life is the way to add impact. Remember, you're trying to reach an audience that is generally in motion—people driving or walking by, not stopping for a cigarette break. Keep the visuals simple, with few elements and an uncluttered background.

Exhibit 8–7

IZOD: "THE SHIRT FOR SUNDAY DRIVERS"/BILLBOARD

Keep the Copy Clean

You're aiming for a moving target, so the message has to be understood in just a flash of the eye. The words should be short, and the type should be easy to read.

RADIO

Some people believe creating radio advertising is easy: Combine an announcer, a little music, and a few sound effects, and you're all set. It's a one-dimensional medium—sound only—what could be so difficult? But that's the very reason why writing *good* radio is so difficult. It's limited by virtue of not having a visual component to work with. However, in the hands of a skilled radio writer and producer, a radio ad represents a tremendous opportunity to paint emotional images more powerfully than in any other creative medium. In a radio campaign with the proper words and message, the listener is forced to create a mental picture.

Radio Creative Guidelines

Grab the Listener's Attention Immediately

Use an arresting, attention-getting device to draw in your listener from the outset. If you fail to do this, the rest of the spot may fall on deaf ears.

Repeat Key Points

You don't have the advantage of using titles on a screen or relying on someone to linger on a page. Repeat the product name and other relevant information so it sinks in. Many times, the end of the spot is the perfect place for another go-around with the most important fact. The last thing listeners hear is the one they will remember most.

Be Concise

No matter what creative approach you use, get right to the point and keep it simple. Brief sentences and short words are the ones that linger.

Focus on the Big Idea

Too many radio writers make the mistake of overwriting and trying to cram many thoughts into one spot. Determine the essential message and make it the focus. If your client has additional information to convey, consider writing it into a series of spots to run in rotation.

Talk to Your Audience

Know whom you are selling to. There is no broad definition of the radio consumer; the medium is very targeted. It is your responsibility to reach that audience with the right creative idea, written in the appropriate language.

Create the Big Finale

The ad should build to a climax. You run the risk of losing your listeners in the middle of the spot, especially if it's bogged down in details. Build to a big ending and leave them wanting more.

Promoting an Unknown Name through Radio

Once you've digested these guidelines, it's time to write and produce the spot. Consider the challenges and how to address them creatively. Some situations, such as advertising a new book on radio, are tough. When the author is famous, a good part of the advertising strategy is solved, since the author's name alone can be the strongest selling point for the book. But when the author is unknown, there's an immediate disadvantage, especially when the publisher expects it to be a breakout book for the author and wants big results. Time to panic? Don't. Consider taking a strong creative approach—one that will draw listeners in and pique their interest, even if they have never heard of the author.

Such was the case when we were given the advertising assignment for *Spandau Phoenix* by Greg Iles. It was the fact-meets-fiction story of Rudolf Hess and a secret he left behind in Spandau Prison. The client wanted the paperback version to have a strong mass-market appeal.

We took a nontraditional approach with the creative angle, beginning with the sound of footsteps on a concrete floor and a man talking in a thick Eastern European accent, as scripted in Exhibit 8–8. The opening line of his speech hides the fact that it is a book commercial and draws the listener in immediately: "I was there when it all happened. I was one of the last to see Rudolf Hess alive . . ."

Is it a news report? A promo for a TV miniseries or a news magazine show? When listeners are not sure, they continue to listen. And when they're drawn into the spot, they are yours when the time comes to give them the sell. Our radio campaign for *Spandau Phoenix* helped to make

Exhibit 8–8
SPANDAU PHOENIX/RADIO SCRIPT

Footsteps	**Client:** Penguin USA **Title:** *Spandau Phoenix* **Media:** Spot Radio **Length:** :60 **Version:** "Footsteps"

(Man's voice has Eastern European accent. Delivery is slow and deliberate)

SFX: *Man's footsteps on concrete floor — pacing.*

MAN: I WAS THERE WHEN IT ALL HAPPENED. I WAS ONE OF THE LAST TO SEE RUDOLF HESS ALIVE AT SPANDAU. HE HANGED HIMSELF IN HIS CELL, YOU KNOW — THE FAMOUS PRISONER NUMBER SEVEN.

THEY WERE ALL JUST WAITING FOR THE OLD MAN TO DIE. THEN THE BULLDOZERS CAME, AND SPANDAU PRISON WAS NO MORE.

MUSIC: *Enters with ominous, sustained tone — builds over remainder of spot.*

MAN: BUT THEN, THEY FOUND IT. A FEW SHEETS OF PAPER IN THE RUBBLE. *A DIARY.* I DON'T KNOW WHAT IT SAID, BUT *EVERYONE* WANTED IT. THE AMERICANS. THE GERMANS. THE ISRAELIS. THE RUSSIANS.

IT WAS AS IF HE ROSE FROM THE ASHES — LIKE THE PHOENIX. AND THE HORROR BEGAN AGAIN…

MUSIC: *Sting, then continues.*

ANNCR: *SPANDAU PHOENIX* BY GREG ILES. A LONG-BURIED NAZI SECRET ERUPTS INTO AN INTERNATIONAL NIGHTMARE AS FACT MEETS FICTION IN THIS ELECTRIFYING NOVEL.

SPANDAU PHOENIX. JOHN GRISHAM CALLS IT "A SCORCHING READ."

SPANDAU PHOENIX BY GREG ILES.

NOW A SIGNET PAPERBACK.

the book a success, catapulting it to the top of the *New York Times* best-seller list. Our agency won the International Broadcasting Award for best radio spot of 1994.

Getting Outrageous with Radio

Another example of creative problem solving on radio was for a special summer promotion that Penguin USA was running. The message was somewhat complicated: Buy paperback No. 1 (tell a little about the book) and paperback No. 2 (tell a little about that one, too) and you'll get paperback No. 3 (tell a little about that one, too!) for free. If we had approached this spot with straight sale copy, it would have gone over like a lead balloon.

Our answer came by using an out-there idea—some effective sound effects and creative casting, using the famous announcer Larry Kenny doing a very convincing and comical portrayal of a talking dog. Fade up beach sound effects. The dog complains that he's at the beach with his family but that no one is playing with him, as the script in Exhibit 8–9 reveals. Mom's too busy reading paperback No. 1, Dad has paperback No. 2, and Grandpa's ensconced in free paperback No. 3.

A Nostalgic, Emotional Approach

When we were asked to create a Special Olympics spot for Izod, the approach became more serious and inspirational, as can be seen in Exhibit 8–10. The objective was to communicate that the Izod shirt has been a great American tradition for three generations and can be compared to the great Olympic tradition:

> As a boy you wore Izod because your heroes did. As a man you wear it just because you know it's the best . . .

Using anthemlike Olympic music, we drove the point home at the end of the spot:

> . . . look for the crocodile and consider it a reminder—of a boy's dreams, a man's accomplishments, and how far you've come.

The tag line brought it all together:

> Izod. For the boys we were, the men we are.

Exhibit 8–9
RAGE OF INNOCENCE, FORBIDDEN ZONE/RADIO SCRIPT

██████████		
Talking Dog	**Client:**	Penguin USA: *Rage of Innocence /Forbidden Zone*
	Title:	"Talking Dog"
	Media:	Spot Radio
	Length:	:60

Dog (AVO) intersperses pants and woofs at will

SFX: *Beach sounds — surf, children playing, etc.*

DOG: BOY, THIS REALLY IS A DOG'S LIFE. WE'RE SUPPOSED TO BE ON VACATION, BUT I CAN'T GET ANYONE TO PLAY WITH ME.

I GO OVER TO MOM AND I BRING HER THE BALL, BUT SHE'S TOO BUSY READING THE WHITLEY STREEBER PAPERBACK, WHAT'S IT CALLED? OH YEAH (SARCASTI-CALLY), *THE FORBIDDEN ZONE.* OOH, SPOOKY, SPOOKY. I WANNA PLAY FETCH!

SO I GO TO DAD, I BRING HIM THE STICK, BUT HIS NOSE IS IN A BOOK TOO. "NOT NOW, BOY," HE SAYS. "DADDY'S READING *THE RAGE OF INNOCENCE* BY WILLIAM PEASE. MURDER. INTRIGUE. COURTROOM DRAMA. BE A GOOD BOY AND GO PLAY." GREAT. I'LL BE A GOOD BOY — JUST THROW THE STICK, OKAY?

SO I GO TO MY LAST HOPE, GRANDPA. HE *LOVES* ME. BUT NOT NOW. HE'S TOO BUSY READING THE FREE BOOK THAT MOM AND DAD GOT FOR BUYING BOTH *THE FORBIDDEN ZONE* AND *THE RAGE OF INNOCENCE.* THAT'S THE LAST TIME I'LL EAT HIS BRUSSELS SPOUTS. (GRRR)

ALRIGHT. SO LET'S REVIEW MY OPTIONS. MOM'S READING *THE FORBIDDEN ZONE* FROM ONYX BOOKS. DAD'S READING *THE RAGE OF INNOCENCE* FROM SIGNET. GRANDPA'S READING THE FREE PAPERBACK THEY GOT WITH THE SPECIAL OFFER. (SADLY) AND MY VACATION IS HISTORY.

JEEZ. MAYBE I'LL RUN AWAY. (PAUSE) MAYBE I'LL LEARN HOW TO READ!

Exhibit 8–10
LACOSTE/RADIO SCRIPT

The Olympic Tradition	**Client:** Lacoste **Title:** "The Olympic Tradition" **Media:** Spot Radio **Length:** :60

MUSIC: *Emotional, anthemlike*

AVO: THE OLYMPIC TRADITION.
TO A BOY, IT MEANS HEROES.

THE OLYMPIC TRADITION.
TO A MAN, IT MEANS BEING THE BEST. SETTING A
STANDARD OF EXCELLENCE THAT OTHERS ASPIRE TO.

LACOSTE WAS BORN IN THAT SAME GREAT TRADITION.
AND FOR THREE GENERATIONS, THE SHIRT WITH THE
CROCODILE ON IT HAS BEEN THE ONE THAT SET THE
STANDARD.

LACOSTE.
AS A BOY, YOU WEAR LACOSTE BECAUSE YOUR HEROES DO.
AND AS A MAN, YOU WEAR LACOSTE JUST BECAUSE YOU
KNOW IT'S THE BEST. A PART OF YOUR OWN TRADITION
OF EXCELLENCE.

LACOSTE.
LOOK FOR THE CROCODILE AND CONSIDER IT A
REMINDER OF A BOY'S DREAMS.
A MAN'S ACCOMPLISHMENTS.
AND HOW FAR YOU'VE COME.

SFX: *Applause builds, then fades*

AVO: LACOSTE. FOR THE BOYS WE WERE,
THE MEN WE ARE.
AVAILABLE AT THE MACY'S NEAREST YOU.

MUSIC: *Fades*

The approach was extraordinarily simple, but the inspiring words and use of the right announcer, John Henry Kurtz, made it very effective.

TELEVISION

The power of television advertising sets it apart from other media. There is no better way to reach such a mass audience at home and have it focus on your message. Because of this power and because television is regarded as an entertainment medium, ads must be both believable and entertaining: believable because your ability to persuade is paramount and entertaining because that's why people watch TV. But commercials are generally perceived as annoying interruptions to the enjoyment—like rough patches in an otherwise smooth ski run. We often feel that there are just too many commercials, particularly when engrossed in a good movie. They seem to come just at the crucial moment and spoil the flow.

TV Creative Guidelines

Whatever creative direction you decide to take, there are still guidelines to follow, similar to those in other forms of advertising.

Focus on the Strongest Selling Point, Open Strong, and Use the Right Technique

Using the creative strategy template in Exhibit 6–1 as a guide, distill the selling points down to the few strongest. Remember that, as in radio, if there are too many facts in a spot, none will be retained. Prevent viewers from leaving to grab that beer during the program break by using the first few seconds of the spot to keep them glued to the screen. If you're not lucky enough to be the first spot in a commercial pod, a strong opening will also bring viewers back if they haven't paid attention to the preceding ads. Use a technique that is appropriate for the audience and the program. The idea may be right on target, but if the technique is wrong, the impact is lost.

Appeal to Emotions and Make Every Second Count

Appeal to people's basic wants and needs and do it in a way that shows you understand them. Whether your spot is packed full of visuals or contains several dramatic pauses, make sure there is a good creative reason for each visual and word.

Emphasize the Product

Strong product identification is essential in any ad, and television spots are no exception. Many commercials, even those with the most clever concepts, fail because they do not register the brand name in a strong way. You may remember the spot, but you won't recall the product being sold.

Repeat the Major Points

Just as in radio, drive home the important stuff. This is not a printed page people can gaze at, pore over, and return to later. When the TV spot ends, the message is gone until it's aired again. The viewers must be left with the image and information you want them to remember.

Prepare the Storyboards Carefully

Sometimes it's difficult to explain a television idea to the advertiser before you actually do it, but you must be able to sell it before you can produce it. This is usually done through the preparation of storyboards, which are rough sketches of key frames, accompanied by scripts, illustrating what will happen in each frame. Storyboards should be detailed enough to be self-explanatory, but not so detailed that they confuse the untrained eye. Show the boards first to someone who is not television savvy. If he or she understands them, chances are good that the boards are right for presentation.

Execute Well and Address the Problems

The creative does not stop when the idea is decided on and approved. What follows is just as important to the outcome of the spot as the idea itself. Choose your people carefully. Select the right spokesperson, director, casting director, editor, music composer, and sound finisher. They are all part of the creative process and have enormous influence on the outcome. No matter what idea you choose, it must address your advertising problems and needs.

TV Guide: A Television Guide Promoted through TV

When *TV Guide* approached our agency in search of a new direction for its television advertising, many changes were occurring at the magazine, among them that it had a new look and new editorial features that reflected the guide's desire to be the authority on television. The mission was to let the world know that *TV Guide* was not just a listing of what was on TV for the week, with a few fluffy features about TV stars, but that it brought you *inside* the world of television—behind the cameras, so to speak.

It was a big story to tell, and it was complicated by *TV Guide*'s desire to run only 15-second spots that would cost-effectively get the frequency it wanted in every market across the country. We felt that a spokesperson, someone recognized as an authority in the world of television, was necessary. It also was crucial to create a visual vehicle for that spokesperson to be able to deliver a lot of information into each week's 15-second spot without making it look crammed. Finally, the concept had to be changeable on a weekly basis, without constant, costly reshooting.

We considered a number of high-profile TV celebrities. The spokesperson ultimately chosen was Bob Costas. He fit the bill for many reasons. For one, his appeal and popularity had grown enormously in the last couple of years, not only as a commentator and authority on sports, but as an engaging raconteur on talk shows, where he had appeared frequently. Costas had even hosted one. Moreover, with his clean-cut looks, charm, and wit, as well as his appeal to both men and women, he transcended the typical sports figure.

The visual vehicle that we created was perfect for the positioning we chose. Using the positioning tag line "Get Inside. *TV Guide*," the spots began with Costas in front of a seamless white background saying, "This is the new *TV Guide*. Just open it up and boom, you're there." The spot then cut to an open mock-up of the magazine with television panels inside showing the features of the current issue. This life-size magazine mock-up (see Exhibit 8–11) and Costas himself were shot separately against a green screen, so that new features could be keyed in every week, giving the impression that each spot was shot for that issue alone. This creative direction allowed us to make each spot current and to make last-minute changes easily, when necessary.

The impact from the new brand image for *TV Guide* has now become apparent: The magazine has shown significant increases in single-copy sales as a result of the TV advertising.

Exhibit 8–11
TV GUIDE: SCI-FI ISSUE/TV STORYBOARD

PRODUCT: *TV GUIDE*
TITLE: "BOOM, YOU'RE THERE" SCI-FI FANTASY ISSUE
PROGRAM: :15
STATION:

[1] This is the new *TV Guide*.

[2] Just open it up and boom — you're there!

[3] Inside the Science Fiction and Fantasy Issue.

[4] *X-Files, Space, The Star Trek Reunion...*

[5] ...and all the hot new shows, too.

[6] When you want to be there — Get Inside. *TV Guide.*

9 | Sales Promotion

"I think we're getting a little carried away
with this eyewear theme."

♦ ♦

IT'S EASY TO GET CARRIED AWAY in the spirit of promoting. Your advertising has broken, and you want to reinforce it through sales promotion—markdowns, price breaks, holiday specials, post-holiday specials, and events. There are also contests, sponsorships, and sweepstakes. The menu is large and the options seemingly endless.

Effective promotion requires concentrating on what you are trying to accomplish and properly deciding where your sales promotion money will best be spent. While seeking a balance, stay aggressive. Go after the business. If you have adhered to the marketing plan, the advertising will draw customers and sales promotion will strengthen the bond. When I was senior vice president of marketing for the May Department Stores, grand openings were the biggest sales promotion opportunities. These were instances where making a big splash, establishing the image of a new store, and converting customers into repeat shoppers were critical. A grand opening commences with heavy advertising weeks before the actual opening and continues with a bevy of events on opening day and more during the first week to draw customers. At May Company, crowds were big and the atmosphere was festive. Politicians cut the ribbon; actors, athletes, and beauty pageant winners were invited. There were bands, beauty makeovers, mimes, jugglers, and other entertainment appropriate to the store's demographics. And the contests and giveaways, many donated by vendors seeking the spotlight during the event, were substantial. Sometimes, even cars were given away. And don't forget the media. We always got covered by local newspapers, radio, and TV, sometimes live and on the spot.

The risk is in creating a circus atmosphere with too much promotion or creating a dud with too little promotion. Find a balance. When you see what works, use it again, but don't hurt the store through incessant promotion. When there are too many price promotions, customers become programmed to shop only on sale days. That's not what you want. When advertising builds image and promotion drives traffic, you'll have customers all year long. In this chapter, there's more about effective sales promotion and cases that help put things into perspective.

♦ ♦ ♦ ♦ ♦ ♦ ♦ ♦ ♦ ♦ ♦ ♦ ♦ ♦ ♦ ♦ ♦ ♦ ♦ ♦

AN ENGINE ON HYPERDRIVE

It may seem like a heap of clutter, but those coupons, samples, and post-cards offering discounts that flood your mailbox and spill out of magazines are often highly programmed and directed sales promotion strategies. They're short-term devices and incentives geared to jump-start sales and give customers incentives for purchasing. They are based on business and consumer trends, and each strategy can be targeted to specific audiences or shopper groups with distinct lifestyles and buying habits. The devices range from the sophisticated to the unsophisticated, but all must be created as an integral part of the marketing and advertising engine that drives business. They should not be arbitrary, isolated events.

PROMOTION: THE QUICK FIX OF THE 1990s

Unfortunately, sales promotion strategies have become the quick fix for companies desperate for customers, frantically assembled to adjust for economic swings, fashion trends, calendar shifts, and the weather, without taking into account the overall marketing plan. Businesses are being driven by incessant price promoting, and it has only been recently that some have learned that they must get off the needle. Why? Because there are long-term effects on the company's image and on customers. For one, sales promotion activities can overshadow the advertising efforts instead of reinforcing them.

Secondly, customers have been conditioned to shop only when there is a promotion. A price break, or a storewide sale, could trigger a big sales gain, but then the company could suffer a huge falloff the very next day. No one shops regular price anymore.

One company that has managed to maintain an upscale image while being very promotional is Bloomingdale's. "We are aggressive," says Bloomingdale's chairperson and CEO Michael Gould, referring to the chain's steady lineup of promotional events, including private sales, coupons mailed to customers offering 15 percent off, and contests to win trips to resort hotels. According to Gould, the company has retained its mystique by building "an umbrella" of special events, such as designer appearances and selling special and exclusive merchandise at regular prices more often. That umbrella, Gould says, "protects you, so that when you are aggressive, you do not give the impression that you are giving away the store."

Traditionally, sales promotions were done to create a big splash to launch a product or usher in a holiday. They are no longer reserved for such special occasions and, because of their overuse, have lost impact.

EFFECTIVE PROMOTION: THE UNDERPINNINGS

It's not easy to formulate a balanced and creative sales promotion calendar. It's not easy to know when to rev up the engine and when to turn it down. The trick to sales promotion is to run the right kind of events on the right occasions and to use sales promotion strategies that will appeal to the target market.

Among the most potent campaigns are those that cross-promote two companies pushing different products. It enables two noncompeting companies to tap into the other's customer pool. Del Monte and AT&T, two unlikely partners, teamed up in the early 1980s on a promotion called "Talk of the Town." In the promotion, consumers would redeem proof-of-purchase slips on Del Monte products for discounts on AT&T phone rentals. In addition, "Talk of the Town" ads in newspapers included coupons offering discounts on Del Monte apple and pineapple juices. The campaign, held during the summer, sparked sales of Del Monte canned foods at a time of year when such items are outsold by fresh fruits and vegetables.

Integrated promotions—those that seek to accomplish several goals simultaneously, such as stealing business from competitors, building brand loyalty, enhancing the corporate image, and entertaining customers—can also be very effective but are more complicated to construct. A highly ambitious, multipurpose campaign was tackled by the Lion Match Company of South Africa. In this country, formerly divided by apartheid, vast segments of the population had been separated from families and friends and forced to relocate. Lion, around 1994, instructed South Africans to write a message to a missing loved one on top of a matchbox cover and mail it to the company, which would then publicize the message on matchboxes or in advertisements. The campaign was spurred by displays in stores, and retailers who were unusually cooperative received plaques. Lion's promotion helped reunite thousands of people while boosting its sales, strengthening its position against competing cigarette-lighter and match companies, and enhancing its reputation as a socially concerned company. It was good advertising, good public relations, and excellent sales promotion all combined in one grand campaign.

Event promoting, which is not as intrusive as advertising, can also be very effective. In a promotion, the product name stays in the background but is seen by the audience attending the event and gets repeated exposure on TV when cameras are pointed in its direction. Seeking to appeal to a younger audience, Schlitz in 1984 sponsored the "Schlitz Rocks America" concert tour by The Who. At the concerts, there were huge Schlitz posters and banners, a videotape about Schlitz Rocks America preceded the concert, and The Who drank from Schlitz water bottles. There was also a sweepstakes with prizes of two free concert tickets, a cassette player and a Who cassette, and Who T-shirts. Posters were sold for $1 and $5. Who T-shirts, caps, buttons, and other paraphernalia were also given as prizes over the radio.

Executing a strong promotion can boil down to having the right handle. Some people might call it a gimmick or device, but it's actually more. It's a symbol of the product that resonates with the public in an intelligent, clever, and creative way. Having that right handle will catch the eye of retailers and consumers and spark interest. In 1995, Penguin USA came up with a unique and offbeat handle on a suspense novel called *The Weatherman*. The company created a little red umbrella with the book title on it, which became a point-of-sale display and a giveaway at stores. In addition, Penguin sent the umbrellas and books to television meteorologists, who in many cases plugged the book during their forecasts. This curious umbrella sparked curiosity about the book, and even though the author was an unknown, *The Weatherman* made the *New York Times* best-seller list.

Promoting Image

The art of promotion is not all about spurring sales. Promotions can also enhance the corporate image and convey to the community that a company is concerned about social issues and charities, without necessarily aiming for a forceful impact on revenues. For example, Motorola in Texas launched a program to portray itself as a company concerned about the environment. The company distributed to students "discovery packs" that contained recycled products, solar-powered calculators, and flower seeds. The packs were handed out during special classes covering environmental issues. The promotion grabbed the attention of the media, caught the eye of local politicians, and eventually became a regular part of the school curriculum.

Another campaign geared to polish the corporate image, not pump up sales, was orchestrated by Canon Business Machines. It started with a party thrown by the company. Everybody who came had to join the Club Commute program for carpooling. Club members received car-wash kits, notepads, sunglasses, and other promotional products in a campaign that generated excellent public relations and a spirit of cooperation and concern at Canon.

Promoting Product Launches

Such promotions, however, are few and far between. Generally, promotions have more pragmatic aims, such as to kick off a new product. A product launch should be jettisoned by sales promotion and strong advertising. The key is to get the product into the hands of as many consumers as quickly as possible—and as cheaply and effortlessly as possible. Make customers want to try it. It's time to really entice your customers with a big discount or special offer. Consider a sales promotion test in one market first, to judge reaction to the product. When McDonald's introduced its Mac Jr. sandwich in the mid-1990s, the rollout was gradual, starting first in the Midwest. For this regional promotion, the fast-food chain tied into the 100th anniversary of the St. Louis Cardinals baseball team by offering a limited-edition set of 55 baseball cards featuring the greatest Cardinal players of all time. With each purchase, a pack of 11 baseball cards was offered so that repeat purchases were necessary to get the entire set. McDonald's scored a home run with the promotion and rolled out the Mac Jr. to other regions of the country. It was a marriage of two great American pastimes—baseball and burgers.

At a time when Nintendo was scoring big selling video games to kids, Crayola needed its own Big Mac type of success story to get children back into some good old-fashioned coloring with crayons. The company's strategy was to launch a new product and generate excitement around it by staging a contest. Crayola developed the "Big Box," a pack of 96 crayons, including 16 that were unnamed. For the contest, children were asked to come up with names for the crayons and submit them to Crayola. The contest lasted eight months and two million entries were submitted from thousands and thousands of children. Sixteen winners got their color's name and their own name printed on the crayon labels. In addition, the winners were inducted into the Crayola Hall of Fame and got free trips to Hollywood. Crayola supported the promotion with in-store riser cards plugging the contest and a contest for retailers as well, offering them trips to Hollywood for the best displays.

Sampling

An effective method for getting new products off the ground is to distribute samples to the public. At the very least, consumers will take notice of the product. They may become interested and eventually be converted into real customers. To get customers to try one of its new products, Heublein used the sample method. It arranged free tasting events at bars so people could get a taste of its new line of premixed margaritas. In conjunction with the tasting events, stores gave out free bags of ice to encourage people to buy the margarita mix. Outdoor advertising and posters—along with displays and signs inside bars and supermarkets—supported the campaign.

The beauty of sampling is that there's no risk to the customer, other than leaving a bad taste in his or her mouth. When there's no charge for something, people will try almost anything. There's also no peer pressure to avoid the product, even if it seems goofy or maybe not the healthiest. If trying a new product means getting ridiculed for it, you can just say it was free. That's the excuse.

In today's health-conscious society, many people have stopped snacking. Frito-Lay decided to battle back against the trend by staging the "D-Day Doritos Day" promotion. It was more like an invasion and is considered by some to be the largest ever one-day sampling effort. Held in the parking lots of 10,000 stores, millions of samples and coupons were distributed to hype the brand's new Nacho Cheezier Doritos. The campaign was backed by radio advertising and a full-page ad in *USA Today*. The results: Many people who couldn't eat just one went home thirsty.

A Sampling Slipup

There's a real challenge to sampling. New products must include clear and concise information on what they are and instructions if necessary. Many products, such as Doritos, speak for themselves, but not all products do. Take the case of Sunlight dishwashing detergent. Samples were distributed in small yellow plastic bottles with a large picture of a lemon on the label. It resembled the Minute Maid lemon juice container. Although the packaging identified the product as dishwashing detergent, the lettering was small. Several people—not just kids—assumed the sample was lemon juice because of the large picture of the lemon. They poured it in tea and other beverages and got a nasty surprise. Sunlight could have kept the mishaps to a minimum by putting a wide band around the container that declared in bold print that the product was detergent.

Samples Coupled with Coupons to Spur Repeat Purchases

Companies introducing new products want customers to believe their product is better than the competition's. If it really is, then a customer will try it again. Give customers a nudge by including, along with the sample, a coupon that cuts the price on the next purchase. It's a matter of molding purchasing behavior—getting consumers into a shopping habit and getting those repeat sales. Repeat sales will recoup the company's investment made in research and product development and start to build profits.

Sampling can be used to spur repeat purchases. For example, in 1993, Blockbuster Video, seeking to offset competition from a blitz of summer movie releases, offered free boxes of snack foods, valued at about $10, to consumers who rented three videos. The boxes contained snack food packs from Kraft General Foods, Procter & Gamble, and General Mills and were bar-coded so the promotion could be tracked. Spot TV ads, radio spots, and point-of-sale materials backed up the campaign. Not only did the promotion boost rentals, but it solidified loyalty to Blockbuster and raised awareness of the snack foods.

IT'S HOLIDAY TIME: PROMOTE, PROMOTE, PROMOTE

The holiday season is the time to promote like crazy. It's when consumers are shopping—and presumably buying—and businesses can make the most profit, provided they move inventories effectively. Gear sales promotions to strike fear in the heart of shoppers. Notify them that the holiday is fast approaching and that they should buy quickly while there is ample stock of the best gifts. Urge them to get to the store before the crowds get too big and unbearable. Pour on the catalogs, sales bulletins, window displays, signs and banners, ad reprints, demonstrations, and premiums.

In 1981, MCI used the holiday spirit to promote its long-distance service. The company had only a slight percentage of the long-distance market and wanted to increase its share. To capture more customers, it set up booths in 160 malls across the country to demonstrate its service and offer a free three-minute long-distance call to "make it a happier holiday for your family and friends." In exchange, consumers gave MCI their phone numbers and addresses so service representatives could call on them. Hundreds of thousands of shoppers accepted the offer of the free call, and thousands signed up for MCI.

The best sales promotion tools match the interests of the target market. The more you know about the target market, the greater the chance of making the perfect match. Two months before Christmas in 1994, Northwest Airlines felt a sense of urgency. The company had become aware that a high percentage of its target market had begun using cheaper forms of transportation to get to the Mall of America in Bloomington, Minnesota, a key destination for Northwest. In particular, Northwest was feeling the pinch from bus companies that were stepping up efforts to take shoppers to the mall. So Northwest met the challenge by dropping its fares to practically bus-rate level. It began charging from $38 to $98 for same-day round trips. The results were great. About 14,000 tickets were sold in an eight-week stretch during the holiday season. Moreover, the fact that no money had been spent on advertising or support for the promotion made it even more profitable.

Holidays Are for Kids—Don't Overlook the Little Ones

In France, the manufacturer of nonstick pans called Tefal capitalized on a French holiday called Chandeleur, which children celebrate by eating crepes. Tefal created a story around a female character called "Tefy," who became the spokesperson for the "Fete des Crepes" holiday. Tefy was featured in store displays and point-of-sale materials, such as balloons, recipes, and pins, that attracted children. The children, naturally, asked their parents to buy Tefy pans rather than cheaper competitive brands.

Kids may not actually buy the product, but they definitely have an effect on their parents, the ones who hold the purse strings. Seeing the power of catering to kids, the Howard Johnson hotel chain increased family bookings in 1993 by loading up its check-in areas with comic books, crayons, and posters featuring Sonic the Hedgehog, a character created by Sega, the video game supplier. The hotel loaned the Sonic video games at no charge to the guests. Hotel staff wore T-shirts and baseball caps to support the promotion, which was hyped in company newsletters and American Express mailings. Reservations and the occupancy rate took a significant upturn and the atmosphere at Howard Johnson turned more festive.

Don't let up on the promoting after the holiday is over. Some people give gifts late, so it is possible to perpetuate sales of holiday goods the week after the holiday. The post-Christmas period is big business, primarily through post-holiday sales, when there are plenty of people returning merchandise to the stores. That's another opportunity to reach a lot of traffic. It is possible to warehouse such categories as trim-a-tree and religious ornaments for the next year, provided you have the storage space, but generally, products get stale quick and should be included in the end-of-season clearance. Special clearances should be supported by newspaper coupons, window signs, and advertising. Consider selling another item in tandem with the clearance product. Offer premiums to help move the clearance item; for example, give away a stuffed animal with the purchase of end-of-season children's clothes. The price of the clearance item, even at its final price, should defray the cost of the premium.

BUILD BRAND AWARENESS: IT GOES A LONG WAY

Promoting doesn't simply have to be geared to lifting sales on a short-term basis. The strategy can also build brand awareness for longer-term gains by distinguishing the product from the competition and heightening its visibility. In France, there is a brand of processed cheese called Tartare Or. In the early 1990s, it was languishing on supermarket shelves because of stiff competition from better-known labels (such as Boursin) and a disinterested French consumer. To change the situation, the company redesigned the packaging to resemble gold bullion, which helped the product stand out on the shelves. Inside the wrapping, there were code numbers that gave shoppers a chance of winning up to $5,000 in real gold. The new packaging and the chance to win gold encouraged tens of thousands of shoppers to buy the cheese, go home, and quickly unwrap the product and phone the company to see if they had a winning number. Not only were sales spurred almost immediately, but France—a country of cheese lovers—discovered another fine brand. The contest increased both sales and consumer loyalty.

Rather than holding a contest, JanSport, an American company that manufactures backpacks and outdoor gear, took an educational, event-driven approach to build brand awareness. It created a clever multi-pronged campaign to promote its products and stimulate mall traffic. The company set up mock 16-foot mountains in malls and staffed them with rock-climbing experts who gave seminars at the sites. To receive climbing instruction, an interested party only needed a ticket that had been distributed at participating stores. The event was bolstered with TV, radio, and print ads and store posters. Also, consumers could get free "Mountain Tour" T-shirts with a JanSport proof of purchase. JanSport picked up a mountain of business.

TARGETING PROMOTIONS FOR THE LOYAL AND SEMILOYAL

Loyal customers react positively to most sales promotions, such as coupons and deals that offer two items for the price of one. They also respond well to contests. Labatt Blue, a Canadian beer company, ran a contest to increase sales among loyal customers, many of whom were baseball fans. It put cards with baseball scores in beer cases and told consumers to watch the Toronto Blue Jays baseball games to see if the scores on their cards matched the score that popped up during a Labatt Blue commercial. If they had a match, they could win a new Pontiac Grand

Am. The contest required little of the contestants. All they had to do to qualify for the car was buy the case of beer and call a toll-free number.

There are customers who are loyal to brands but don't purchase very often. Through promoting, it is possible to get this group more motivated. A chain called Spencer Gifts had plenty of shoppers who typically visited once a season, but Spencer wanted them there once a month. To get shoppers to visit more frequently and to raise the average sale price, the chain ran a "Wild 'N' Crazy Card" promotion in 1994. Each time they showed the card, customers were entitled to 10 percent discounts for purchases up to $25, and 15 percent discounts for items totaling more than $25. They were also automatically entered in a sweepstakes for a trip to Sweden, a stereo, or other gifts. The cards had rub-off spots revealing numbers, and if those numbers matched the numbers listed on store displays, additional store discounts and gift certificates were given as prizes. The promotion was hyped by displays and store personnel wearing "Wild 'N' Crazy" T-shirts.

The best promotions to build regular shoppers into frequent shoppers entail price reductions, coupons, bundling packs, sweepstakes, price discounts, and frequent shopper points. For example, JCPenney has found success with a direct-mail campaign that offers 15 to 25 percent off all purchases bought in one shopping trip by customers with the letter in hand. By collecting the letter, JCPenney can also measure the response rate and identify both the customers who respond to the offer and the items these customers are purchasing.

Solidifying Loyalty: Events and Cross-Selling

For customers who are brand loyal, consider a special event promotion that solidifies relationships with consumers. A huge, two-day homecoming was staged by Saturn, a division of General Motors, in Spring Hill, Tennessee. The promotion, which was advertised on TV and at dealerships, drew roughly 40,000 Saturn owners to the site of the plant. They got the grand tour of the facility and enjoyed an array of entertainment including live music, an auto show, and an arts and crafts workshop for adults and children. Admission to the homecoming weekend was minimal: Adults paid $34 and children $17.

Another way to build brand loyalty is to tie one product to another for a promotion that supports both brands, a practice called cross-selling or cross-promoting. In an NBC-Kellogg cross-selling venture, the stars of NBC's new fall lineup appeared on Kellogg's cereal packaging. NBC also developed premiums that were available with proofs of purchase of Kellogg products. The program was supported by Kellogg coupons distributed in grocery stores and viewer contests offered family vacations and chances to eat breakfast with NBC stars. Kellogg sales and NBC ratings both rose significantly.

Similarly, Nestlé teamed with *The Simpsons,* a Fox TV cartoon show, in a 1994 campaign entitled "Who Laid a Finger on Bart's Butterfinger?" Five different wrappers were created for the Butterfinger candy bar. Each wrapper had a different clue and suspect. By collecting all five wrappers, consumers gathered enough evidence to determine the culprit and could mail in the answer to be included in a $50,000 drawing. The contest encouraged sales of the candy bar and gave great exposure to the TV show. The promotion was strongly supported with Nestlé point-of-sale displays, 30-second TV spots, print ads, radio contests for other prizes, concert tickets, and T-shirts for contestants.

Timberland and BFGoodrich, two solid brands with plenty of consumer loyalty, once teamed up on an innovative promotion to build market share. With the purchase of a set of light truck tires came a free pair of Timberland Eurohiker boots. Ads in outdoor and car magazines and free guides to safe hiking on trails were incorporated into the promotion and a contest for retailers offered a free trip in the backcountry. During the two-month promotion, thousands of tires were sold and thousands of pairs of free boots were given out. Goodrich also made a large donation to nature preservation.

TARGETING: THE FUTURE OF PROMOTIONS

Promoting to the Price-Conscious: They're Not Pushovers

Those who are price-conscious don't always jump from one brand to the next just to get the lowest price. Promoting price is not always enough to win over consumers, as the Travelodge hotel chain learned. Like other economy hotels generally charging $40 to $60 a night, Travelodge was competitively priced. However, Travelodge had a problem: While its prices were as low as those of the competition, its vacancy rates were higher. To reverse the trend, the company introduced a full load of perks such as packages that included tickets to amusement parks, zoos, and movies and gas allotments. And, for business travelers who stayed at least six nights over a four-month period, a dozen free long-stemmed roses would be delivered anywhere in the country. Such perks helped increase bookings substantially and gave the chain a reputation for having more of a personal touch, providing value, and going one step beyond just offering a low price.

If the goal is to get consumers to switch to a more expensive product, however, convince them that for a little more money, they'll get something that lasts longer or is more effective—or perhaps tastes better or is healthier. First make this message with a special, temporary lower price. That will catch consumers' attention.

Send out samples to let customers compare from brand to brand. They may prefer the new brand over the one they have been using. Raise expectations about the product. Your goal is to get customers to feel that a better product is worth spending a little more on. Remember to include coupons with the sample to spur that second purchase.

Promote to Show There's More to the Store

Consumers can have tunnel vision. They regard certain stores as good for only certain items. The idea is to alert them to what you have to offer. One of the best sales promotion tools for achieving this is to stage special shopping nights. Invite customers by mail to visit the store on an evening when it is closed to the general public. On these less-crowded nights, designated shoppers are able to accomplish more with less effort. Add discounts on a wide range of items, serve hors d'oeuvres, and book some entertainment: It's an excellent way to kick off a new season or upcoming holiday.

Other businesses can also do more to make their clients take notice. Sheraton Hotels was able to increase bookings at its hotels by cooking up a "business-to-business" promotion that enlightened travel agents about the company's $1 billion renovation program. Sheraton discovered that travel agents were not fully informed about all the work that had gone into upgrading its fleet of hotels and figured more guests could be attracted if the agents knew about the changes. Working with an agency,

Sheraton created two fictional travel agent characters, Ellen and Carol, who visited Sheratons all over the world and sent postcards back to real travel agents with information about upgrades and special features at hotels. Also on the cards were questions that agents were encouraged to answer for a chance to win a free weekend at a redone Sheraton, magazine subscriptions, and cosmetics. The three-month campaign was bolstered through electronic messages sent to agents' computers and proved to be a success. Bookings rose dramatically and agents showed they knew something about the Sheraton makeover.

Promote to Steal Customers from the Competition

Some consumers are inclined to explore many stores because they get a thrill from new shopping experiences and are open-minded. Enliven the experience for these shoppers through promotions focusing on new products tied, perhaps, to special events and in-store contests and premiums.

There's also a group that may never shop your store. Some consumers stay rock-solid loyal to the competition. They are probably not a target market or they may have no need for your offerings. There is virtually no way to convert these people.

Others may just be in the habit of shopping the competition. Try to break this habit through sales promotion. Give them a good reason to buy your product or shop your store. Habits are hard—but not impossible—to break. To grab attention, send product samples or invitations to a day of discounts or a day with a personal shopper. Budget Rent-A-Car went after customers using other car rental services by celebrating its 35th birthday with a string of promotions including a "free day" certificate that was mailed out to about 350,000 households. There were also $35 and $.35 promotions, and travel agents got 35 percent bonus commissions when they booked a Budget rental.

Dewar's Scotch wanted to expand its customer base to a younger audience that was in the habit of drinking mineral water or lighter drinks. Using the pitch, "It's time to take the training wheels off your drink," Dewar's set up tasting events and bartender contests to see who could mix a drink the fastest; it put up posters and banners, distributed drink recipes, and generated a lot of hoopla to bring in a younger set. A direct-mail campaign in seven U.S. markets notified the target market about the events, at which complimentary drink cards and incentive coupons were distributed. The result: About half of the targeted market sampled the drink and about half of that group actually bought the drink. All this helped Dewar's project a younger, hipper image.

In addition to offering discounts, promote services that make the company shine. That's what Nynex has been doing in this age of telephone wars. In 1996 Nynex sent postcards to its customers in a preemptive strike against rival phone companies that had been calling to steal its customers. Nynex didn't want to lose any customers, so on the postcards it encouraged consumers to ask soliciting phone companies such questions as "Do you have a plan that allows you to talk for as long as you want for a flat rate?" or "Do you have a low per-minute rate?" The Nynex strategy did two things effectively: It indirectly highlighted the company's own special services and thwarted the efforts of the competition to steal its customers.

CREATIVE PLANNING: FROM COUPONS TO CONTESTS

In sales promotion, the key is to plan carefully. Bear in mind the mission of the company, the marketing plan, and the goals to be accomplished through a promotion. Following are some fast facts on promotion methods.

Coupons

Coupons are very popular, but they can cheapen the image of a brand or company and reflect desperation to get sales, particularly if the company has no history of offering coupons. The most frequently seen are the cents-off coupons that supermarkets and pharmacies offer. Department and specialty stores typically offer percent-off coupons. Coupons can be mailed, distributed in the store, placed in newspapers and magazines, and included in a preprinted insert or package. The preprinted and mailed coupons, which have superior photographic reproduction and give a clearer picture of the product, project a better image of the company.

Coupons have a low rate (about 2 percent) of being redeemed. Even when not redeemed, they serve as mini-advertisements. When a coupon is coupled with a sample, it can generate a repeat sale. It is possible that after two tries, a customer will switch from one brand to another for good. Gatorade and Foot Locker scored big with a joint summer promotion in which Gatorade distributed coupons for $10 off a purchase of $50 or more at Foot Locker. Also, Gatorade 25-cent-off coupons were put in print ads and handouts. The coupon promotion was supported through TV and radio spots, magazine ads, Gatorade sampling, and $25 gift certificates to grocery store managers for every 50 cases of Gatorade sold. More than $5 million in Gatorade coupons were redeemed in the promotion.

Rebate Programs

Rebate programs have been used by a wide range of companies from air-conditioning firms such as Fedders to automobile suppliers such as Ford and Toyota. Neiman Marcus customers who charge more than $3,000 a year on their Neiman's credit cards receive special catalogs, services, and bonus points good for rebates on future purchases. Saks Fifth Avenue has a similar program. Both programs create a bond between the shopper and the store.

Contests and Sweepstakes

Contests and sweepstakes add glamour, glitz, and fun, stimulate brand interest and motivate more buying and visits, and generate customer involvement. In a sweepstakes that Peter Paul Mounds once ran, the names of islands were printed inside the packaging, right on the inner tray under the candy. If you collected six different island names, you could enter to win a $6,000 vacation. Some candy bars also had instant prizes, such as cameras, luggage, and Polynesian dinners. The promotion, while structured like a sweepstakes, also helped build sales since six candy bars had to be purchased to win.

In the cassette tape business, discounting is done frequently to move product. However, Memorex staged a contest in 1992 to generate greater sales without discounting during the important back-to-school season. The tapes were packaged with a protruding tab, and shoppers were instructed to pull it out. The tab indicated whether you won one of the prizes offered, which ranged from a $5,000 trip to a concert to a rack stereo system. The contest yielded sales that far exceeded goals, and the increased business came without squeezing profit margins by discounting.

There is a downside to these kinds of contests and sweepstakes. Customers may stock up heavily during sweepstakes time and not return for a long time. The upside is that a sweepstakes can spark interest in products that consumers didn't buy previously. Among the best-known sweepstakes is the one run by Publisher's Clearinghouse, which encourages consumers to subscribe to magazines and offers dozens of publications at good values, but does not require a purchase—just a lot of paperwork—to enter.

Bundling

Bundling is a practice that offers related products as a package that costs less than if the products were bought individually. Examples are razors and blades, notebooks and paper, and printers and ink cartridges. It can involve offering a product along with a service for one total price, such as a membership at a health club that includes sessions with the club's personal trainer.

Bundling reduces financial concerns and peer pressure. You can say, "It came as part of the package." Heinz and Ore-Ida frozen french fries offered free "Dino-Pour" bottle toppers depicting a dinosaur, with the purchase of a bottle of ketchup and bag of fries.

Refunds

Refunds work well with loyal customers and highly price-motivated customers. The downside is a lot of work is involved for customers. They may have to make several purchases and clip part of the packaging and refund offer to get the refund. Also, few people usually participate. However, since refunding is a form of advertising with an offer that few people take advantage of, it could stimulate sales at the full price, without the supplier having to discount the merchandise. Cereal brands and other types of groceries have often offered partial refunds for proofs of purchase. In a one-month promotion, Healthy Choice, a frozen-dinner supplier, offered $3 instant-redeem coupons that skyrocketed sales. Toro, the snow-thrower maker, once offered refunds of from 50 to 100 percent of the purchase price, if there was little snowfall in that season. The idea was to encourage sales to people who wanted the machine but feared there would not be enough snowfall to warrant buying one. The deal specified, for example, that if the snowfall in your area was only 20 percent of the annual average, then you could keep the machine and get a 100 percent refund. If there was a 50 percent annual snowfall, you could keep the machine and get a 50 percent refund. In its ads, Toro used the tag line, "If it doesn't snow, we'll return the dough."

Premiums

Premiums are generally freebies and can be offered in different ways, such as through the mail in return for a specified number of proofs of purchase or a combination of proofs of purchase and some money to speed the process. Dinty Moore once offered a free Ford Explorer toy truck with 10 proofs of purchase, which boosted sales by more than 20 percent. Mail-in premiums have a redemption rate of less than 1 percent. Premiums are great for promotions tied to holidays or special events such as a movie release or the Olympics. McDonald's, for example, offers videos at low prices to customers who purchase certain combo meals. One of the most famous premiums is offered by Crackerjacks, with its inside-the-box tiny trinkets and toys.

INTERNET, MTV, AND CNBC: NEW MEDIA OPPORTUNITIES

Burger King originated the television coupon. On TV, Burger King asked consumers to create coupons and bring them to the store to receive a dollar off a meal. The response was fantastic. The hamburger chain received coupons from children as young as 3 to adults over 60. The campaign was a breakthrough in using the mass media to communicate and interact with customers rather than just inform and motivate.

Similarly, some cable TV programs have been encouraging viewers to call in questions, requests, or answers to surveys posed by the program. These are also methods to forge links between the medium, the product, and the consumer and to track buying behavior. Cable messages can be monitored to see how many people watch a particular show or phone in for a special offer.

Another hot new medium for sales promotion is the Internet and World Wide Web. Through a Web page, a company can attract consumers, disseminate information, and monitor buyer behavior and usage on the Web. A choice of premiums or free time on the Web can be offered. For example, *Popular Mechanics* magazine, in conjunction with *Redbook,* did a sales promotion on a Web page. If a reader hit the Web site and answered some questions, then the customer would receive a prize in the mail. That gave the magazines some data on how many of their readers "surf" the Web and a better idea of the medium's potential.

Pillsbury has used Prodigy, the on-line service, to promote its Green Giant brand. Five screens on Prodigy showed recipes and photos of dishes that could be printed out. In addition, Pillsbury e-mailed thousands of Prodigy users to encourage them to visit the recipe pages. The promotion was tied into Green Giant food demonstrations in stores, newspaper inserts, and radio spots. Soon television companies will help us to access the Internet on cable channels, opening up the information superhighway to virtually everyone and cementing the Internet as a consumer medium.

Ragu put together a friendly Web site that doesn't just push product. It created Mama Cucina, the quintessential Italian grandmother, who conveys an eat-drink-and-be-merry attitude. She dispenses advice on life and provides recipes for spaghetti and meatballs, among other dishes. Ragu's Web site is unusual because it has distinct personality and also because it gives recipes for desserts that do not include Ragu products; it even has information available on Italy and Italian art and antiquity.

GIVEAWAYS: TEMPTING SHOPPERS OR TRASHING THE STORE?

Before you give something away, make sure that a new teddy bear or lipstick shade is something the target market really wants. The purpose is to build foot traffic and pull in the target market, as specified in the marketing plan. Lots of giveaways end up in the garbage or scattered on the floor of the store and do little to attract customers and enhance the image of the company. As with premiums, the free gift should be of interest to the customer and should raise the profile of the product or the store name and increase sales. Many people accept a free gift just to be polite. Others may throw it back, figuratively speaking, in your face. Test-market the giveaways. Consider a cash gift. McDonald's did it in England, stuffing cash—anywhere from 5 to 50 pounds—inside "lucky" straws, provided the Extra Value Meal was purchased. McDonald's gave away 500,000 pounds, a hefty amount—though a mere drop in the bucket for the fast-food giant. The chain's sales picked up 11 percent.

CREATING A CAMPAIGN STEP BY STEP

Develop a Budget

Base the budget on objectives. Compare it to estimated returns. If the return does not cover the costs of the promotion, reconsider the format and examine less-expensive strategies or think about other goals possibly being achieved that can be assigned a monetary value. Give the impression of being generous but not giving away the store. Make customers feel good about the company and make sure you don't overspend the budget.

Identify the Goals

The goal could be to inform, motivate the public to visit the store or buy the product, introduce new products and services, or reward customers. The goals should be stated in measurable terms, such as increasing by 5 percent the number of people who can accurately describe the company and its offerings and having this expanded awareness translate to a 4 percent upturn in sales. Or the goal can simply be to generate sales. NyQuil in Canada, for example, set a goal of boosting volume by 30 percent during a 1994 promotion. So it mailed to more than 2,000 pharmacists a pack of samples, tissues, and information about colds and followed up by having representatives visit the pharmacists. There were also TV spots and point-of-sale displays to support the campaign. The company far exceeded its volume goal.

Set the Message

Determine what products or services will be spotlighted. Match the message to the target market and the sales promotion method. Emery, the air-freight carrier, perceived that businesses were not aware of its services and that it needed to refine its service message to attract more customers. So it tied a lengthy message about all of its service options to a 50-percent-off promotion on trial shipments and pumped up revenues over a three-month period in 1992.

Timing Is Critical

Pick the right time of year and set time limits—such as 60 or 90 days— for the sales promotion campaign and measure the effectiveness at 30, 60, 90, 120, and 180 days. Often, promotions have residual effects, so don't stop monitoring them prematurely.

Coca-Cola, for example, once sponsored Julio Iglesias's U.S. concert tour. The tour began in June, just when the peak season for drinking soft drinks commences in the United States, and lasted three months. Citicorp once gave out free coupon books with $2,500 in discounts for those buying $600 in traveler's checks. The promotion was held from June to August—perfect timing since summer is vacation time for the masses and people need traveler's checks. Many vacationers bought more checks than originally intended, just to get the coupons.

Focus on a Target Market for a Special Promotion

Use different information and promotion methods to target different markets. Schlitz, for example, wisely chose to sponsor The Who's concert tour to reach out to customers in their early twenties at a time when Schlitz had primarily an older clientele.

Subway, the sandwich chain, capitalized on children's fascination with dinosaurs, which was fueled by Steven Spielberg's blockbuster movie *Jurassic Park.* In 1993, Subway ran a six-week promotion built around Dino, the friendly dinosaur from *The Flintstones.* The company put up signs in the restaurants and offered premiums (such as Flintstones coloring books and Dino patches) on kids' meals. The promotion was so successful that Subway subsequently staged another dinosaur-themed promotion, this time licensing monsters from *Land of the Lost.* Other marketers, including *Family Circle* magazine, have seized on the dinosaur craze by tying in with Barney, the PBS character.

To target adults, specifically educated and ambitious women, Sara Lee sponsors the Frontrunner Awards each year to honor women who are high achievers. Among past honorees were the poet Maya Angelou and the U.S. Attorney General Janet Reno. To target its audience, Sara Lee places ads in such publications as the *New York Times, Working Women,* and *The Wall Street Journal,* among others, which all have highly educated readerships. The promotion is geared to give women a positive image of Sara Lee brands, including Hanes Hosiery and Coach, which is important considering women make up the majority of Sara Lee's customer base and workforce.

Unlike the Dino promotion, the Frontrunner campaign is not geared to have an immediate influence on sales; it's more of an image campaign. But the two promotions actually have more similarities than differences. Both are targeted to certain audiences, sophisticated in their execution, and successful in breaking through the heap of commercial messages that bombard the American public. It's not just more clutter.

Know the Limits of Sales Promotion

Sales promotion can accomplish many objectives. It can reach new users, introduce new products, build purchase frequency, and reinforce a brand's advertising. Sales promotion cannot develop a long-term consumer franchise or build brand loyalty. Sales promotion cannot reverse a declining sale or overcome consumer resistance to an inferior product. It is better to check problems in pricing, packaging, and quality and to reevaluate the total marketing plan before adding another sale to pump up volume and make this month's sales goals.

10 | The Merchandising Arena:

Point of Purchase and Personal Selling

"I don't think our customers want to see
Fabergé eggs displayed this way!"

THROUGH THE MEDIA AND THE MAIL, you've developed a wave of advertising and sales promotion communications directed at the consumer. Don't let up. It's important to keep the flow going inside the store with an effective sales force and point-of-purchase displays, whether you're selling luxurious Fabergé eggs or dispensing diapers. The marketing plan will guide the character of these communications so that they are consistent with the media advertising.

Point-of-purchase (POP) displays provide the last opportunity to communicate to customers. Signs, coupons, posters, display cases, samples, and interactive kiosks are some of the options. POP is the final chance to dress up the merchandise arena and win a sale. Make it count.

My many years of experience in retail trained me to always look for new point-of-purchase opportunities. So when I became head of an advertising agency, I continued to think that way working with my clients. For example, in 1992, Crystal Brands came to Ziccardi & Partners with a new plan to separate the famous Izod/Lacoste label into three distinct lines. Izod would be primarily moderately priced sportswear and golf wear; Lacoste would cover mid-priced tennis wear, including the famous crocodile tennis shirt; and Chemise Lacoste would be a new line of fashion sportswear catering to a more upscale tennis customer.

The marketing challenge was not only to explain the three new lines to the trade but to be well-defined in representing the product on the selling floor without creating confusion. As part of a comprehensive retail marketing strategy, we designed three distinct shop concept plans. Taking our lead from the marketing plan, we showed in detail how the individual lines would be displayed at the retail level in distinct ways. We included not only the shop design but signage with new logos, hang tags, window displays, counter cards, and other point-of-purchase materials. When the shops opened, they delineated each of the new lines clearly, all in tandem with the launch advertising to the trade and to the consumer.

The stores embraced the point-of-purchase ideas because they made the transition—from one name to three—clear on the selling floor and provided expanded selling opportunities with Izod/Lacoste. To the consumer, the famous Izod/Lacoste brand name was expanded, not diluted, and the result was that Izod, Lacoste, and Chemise were launched successfully in stores across the country.

This chapter provides a rundown on POP options, several illustrations on some of the best, and a perspective on how to pull off enticing in-store communications to rope in customers.

PERSONAL SELLING: BUILDING THE SALES FORCE

Advertising and sales promotion are the first commercial messages hurled at consumers through the media and the mail and on the streets via billboards, posters, and flyers. The next wave of communication gets propelled in the store, through the merchandising arena of point-of-purchase displays, special events, and personal selling. Like advertising and sales promotions, the merchandising arena is a vital and active weapon, firing at consumers messages that encourage purchasing. Both waves of commercial communications—in store and out of store—should be created to reflect the total marketing plan. That way, they reinforce each other and are doubly effective.

Whether marketing paper clips, coffeemakers, or Christian Dior cosmetics, personal selling is decisive in moving products at the wholesale and retail level. Other promotion methods are aimed at markets, or groups of people. Personal selling is precise, enabling marketers to closely target the most promising sales prospects. However, developing a strong selling force can be the most expensive part of the promotion mix when you factor in salaries, benefits, and incentives. Hiring qualifications, salary ranges, and payment methods (salary, commissions, or combinations thereof) should be spelled out.

A retailer could choose a self-service environment, keeping costs low and sales staff minimal. Likewise, manufacturers could choose to use a third party, or sales representative, rather than an in-house sales force. If a sales force is created, it must be managed effectively by a sales manager who sets sales objectives for salespeople over specified time periods. These help motivate the sales force and set the standards for evaluating and controlling it.

For a retail company, objectives can be measured by comparing the number of total visitors to the store with those who have contact with a sales associate, the number of total visitors with those who try on an item or witness a product demonstration, and the total visitor count with those who buy something. For manufacturers, objectives can be measured by comparing the number of companies contacted by a salesperson with the total dollar and unit sales per salesperson. Objectives can also be measured by comparing sales achieved by a salesperson with the number of clients scheduled for future meetings.

Building a sales force is not just a matter of developing happy and helpful salespeople who know something about the products they are selling. The sales force should monitor the sales strategies and products of the competition. They should learn about new products under development and learn to emphasize the advantages of their products over others. They should also develop a list of potential customers, a process called *prospecting*. The customer list is compiled from referrals, trade shows, data banks, and mailing lists. Everyone on the list is evaluated and ranked based on ability and willingness to buy.

Before making a sales presentation, a salesperson should develop a relationship with a client, rather than just push the product outright. Get to know the client beforehand by calling on him or her for lunches and informal meetings. This will help you find out about the client's needs, his or her personal characteristics, the brands the client has been using, and his or her feelings about these other brands.

Salespeople should learn how to size up the personalities of customers, who can fall into different personality profiles in the shopping environment. For example, some are more focused on the products and its attributes, while other customers may be more feeling and focused on the salesperson. If a salesperson can be perceptive enough to pick up on the personality, then he or she can choose the right approach with which to engage the customer. The salesperson could be chatty or take a more serious and immediate approach to discussing product. Armed with good information, a salesperson will be able to develop a presentation that strikes a chord with the prospect.

Sales Presentation Tactics

The best presentations evolve into a dialogue, with both sides listening and asking questions, in which the product is demonstrated and tried out by the prospect. Anticipate questions and concerns about the product and consider addressing them even if they haven't been raised during the presentation. This approach can be risky, however, because it flags issues about the product that the prospect might not have otherwise thought of.

In the next step—the closing—the salesperson asks the prospect to buy the product but does it without seeming heavy-handed or pushy. For example, ask the potential customer whether any particular colors are desired, about preferred financial terms, or about a quantity that might be purchased. Reactions to such questions usually indicate how close the prospect is to buying.

After the closing comes the follow-up by the salesperson to make certain that every detail of the sale was properly executed. Then comes the follow-up to the follow-up. Place the phone call and write the letter to the customer to solidify the relationship and foster future transactions.

On the retail selling floor, the key is to be equipped with the right script to follow, one that leaves plenty of room for improvisation. It's a script based on consumer behavior, human psychology, and simple etiquette, as well as product and store knowledge. Here's how the selling scenario should unfold.

Scene One: The Engagement

The scene opens at the entrance to the store, the gateway of lost shopping souls. There's the greeter, a kind of traffic cop with a charm school personality who is there to welcome, orient, and direct customers. But the selling action really starts when the customer arrives at her destination. There's a salesclerk on the floor, discretely observing what she is handling. He's fixing displays, but from the corner of his eye, he notices that she is eyeing those black lug-sole boots. No, she just shakes her head and moves over to the red pumps. After a few moments, the salesclerk approaches the shopper. He's ready to engage. He has memorized plenty of opening lines and now must come up with the right one. The objective: to make his presence known without putting pressure on the customer. This store clerk has a veritable warehouse of information stored in his brain. He knows about special sales, new product arrivals, fiber content, best-sellers, and hot items; he also has a mental road map of product locations, including those well outside of his department. He knows he must be on his toes in order to quickly assess the situation.

Most importantly, the clerk knows he should refrain from uttering those fateful words, "Can I help you?" Those words often result in defeat—curtain time.

Typically, shoppers answer the "Can I help you?" line with "Thanks, I'm just browsing." You don't want that. The salesperson knows that shoppers often need help, but many resist it. He knows that shoppers can be like drivers who refuse to ask for assistance, driving in circles for miles before admitting they're lost and finally asking for directions.

He has a better opener. "What type of shoe are you interested in?" And the customer replies, "A black, low-heeled, comfortable business shoe, one I won't break my ankle in." Then he says, "Great. Let's just walk over to that display." With that, the clerk is fully engaged. He has combined action with words. While ambling over to the display, he discusses other displays and brands that might satisfy the customer's needs. He also mentions the special promotions offered in the shoe department that week.

Scene Two: The Chosen Ones

Now the customer has selected a few pairs of shoes. The salesclerk, quick on his feet, notices the items, sees her hesitation, and quickly heads back to the display area or stockroom to find some alternatives. She looks at what he's brought over. "What do you think?" he asks. And she responds, "No, I don't think so."

Rejected but not defeated, he comes back with some questions. The answers lead him to a clearer understanding of the customer's needs and desires. He's learning what the customer wants so he can make further selections. As she talks about her favorite pair of shoes at home, what she wears to work or to go out at night, this salesclerk demonstrates a thorough knowledge of brands, including the quality, prices, and advantages and disadvantages of each. He has a handle on the products.

Scene Three: The Customer Becomes a Client

Now, the customer is entirely comfortable with the sales associate, and she's listening to his opinions. She's no longer just a customer. She's a client, meaning that she'll come back to see him again when she's ready to buy more shoes. And he is no longer just a salesclerk. He's an adviser, maybe even a stand-in for the friend who couldn't be there with the customer on this shopping excursion. He's also ready to accompany her to other departments. Well aware that one sale can lead to another, he says, "We have some great hosiery, perfect for those shoes." But perhaps she declines, saying, "That's all right. I have to go." The salesclerk then hands

241

her his business card. The curtain closes. But there's an epilogue. She phones him a week later to buy another pair of shoes. The item is not in stock, so he puts in an order to have it shipped from another branch location and will call her when it arrives. She just saved herself a trip to the store.

In the merchandising arena, there are ways to measure whether customers' expectations or needs are being fulfilled. Target has used the "guest satisfaction report card," on which customers grade the service and other components of the store. Pizza Hut has used a 24-hour hot line customers can call to voice opinions and get immediate feedback from the company. And Prange Way has encouraged shoppers to send letters to the president of the chain.

In 1993, 3M started asking customers about its sales force. The company had previously sent out customer surveys, but now, for the first time, the focus was on selling practices, not just product performance. According to the company, sales training is based on what customers say in these skills assessment surveys.

Body Language: Part of the Selling Dialogue

Words convey information. So does body language. The best salespeople not only pay attention to what customers say but also notice facial expressions, posture, and movement. A successful salesperson once said that it was easy to sell: All you had to do was repeat back to the customer what his or her face was telling you. If the customer likes the goods, it shows on the customer's face. The salesperson should notice that and tell the customer the item is perfect.

Many salespeople agree with customers no matter what and ascribe to the old "the customer is always right" school of selling. But there are customers who are never right and are the cause of product failures. They are uninformed, overly demanding, and abusive to products and store personnel and are not worth satisfying because the costs to the company would be too high.

Reassurances can help sell products, but honesty could go further in building a long-term client relationship. A good way to agree and disagree is to tactfully tell the customer that the item fits well, but there are other choices. If the customer is dissatisfied with the product, consider other items in the same color but a different style or in the same style but another color. This way, it's possible to determine what the customer likes and dislikes. Once you nail down the attribute most important to the customer, it's easier to find the item that will sell.

If the customer is unhappy, it shows on his or her face. Now action will speak louder than words. Bring many items to the shopper to provide alternatives. Bring a sample of each type of product in the department to help narrow the search and learn more about what strikes the customer's fancy. If the customer begins to show interest in some of the items, then bring out more in that style. Use inventory, but don't overdo it.

A good salesperson listens to the customer and knows how to convert information to suit the needs of that shopper. Not every shopper requires the same information. Each customer wants to have questions answered, not hear a mere rote listing of the product's attributes. Questions posed by customers provide an opportunity to suggest more of the product's benefits and how it fits into their lifestyles.

Speed the Transaction

Once the customer has decided to buy the product, a good salesclerk will do everything possible to speed the transaction. Lead the customer to the closest checkout counter and ring it up pronto. The quicker change is made or a credit purchase agreement is signed, the less time there is for the dreaded buyer's remorse. That's when the customer gets cold feet and starts to think twice about buying something. It's that little voice inside saying "reconsider, reconsider" just when the sale is being rung up and the paperwork completed. It's even more likely to happen when the clerk is no longer beside the customer and must find a superior to sign a form or finish the ring. Don't let the customer listen to that voice. Stay close and tell her how great she looks in the shoes. Tell her she has a great product. Maintain the engagement.

If the customer really wants to buy a product, but it's sold out, the salesclerk should fill out a want slip (a record of a customer's request for a stock item). After the customer has left to take care of other shopping requirements, the clerk can call other stores in the same chain or call the store's buyer to ascertain the ability of the store to obtain that item.

Sales Skills Can Be Taught

Many good sales techniques can be taught. They are variations of every-day social skills and can be honed to close more transactions. Nordstrom, for example, "would rather hire nice people and teach them to sell, than hire salespeople and teach them to be nice," according to the book, *The Nordstrom Way*. "Nordstrom, it is said, 'hires the smile and trains the skill.' "

Good sales techniques center around greeting the customer, asking questions, listening, offering solutions, having a dialogue, and showing respect. A good salesclerk has a willingness to be trained and a talent to persuade, must possess an intuitive sense of what customers want, and is alert to body language indicating that customers either want assistance or reject it. The salesperson must have enough restraint to avoid saying, "Can I help you?" A confident and reassured manner and an ability to shrug off rejection are definite assets. A good salesperson has a skillful approach to people, neither hovering nor straying too far, and keeps in mind sales goals for the day, week, month, or year.

Another important tool that some stores use is the customer book. The book lists the customer's size (including whether the customer is a difficult fit), record of purchases, phone number, address, family members, occupation, and any further information that could guide the selling. Even phone numbers of other stores should be listed in case items are out of stock at your store and you need to contact another branch to get them. Nordstrom salespeople maintain customer books but also frequently use the telephone to tell clients about new products just arrived or an order that has been received. Patrick D. McCarthy, a top Nordstrom salesperson, writes in *The Nordstrom Way* that his customer book includes 40 executives from one corporation. It's critical that he keep a record of what he sells to each one so that none of the executives show up at work wearing the same outfit on the same day.

What makes a poor sales associate? A poor sales associate is one who is not around when a shopper needs help or is ready to make a purchase, bears little product knowledge, lacks social and selling skills, and shows scant concern for the customer and the products. It's a wonder how many sales associates lack what it takes to do the job.

LET IT POP: IT'S THE LAST CHANCE

Just as a stage can't set the scene without props, no store can convey a mood without point-of-purchase displays and advertising. They fall into five basic categories: merchandisers, which are displays that set a product apart from the regular fixturing or shelving; signage, which shows a store name or logo; glorifiers, which highlight the product and put it in a context or environment that enhances the product; organizers, which help control inventory and make products easy for shoppers to select; and in-store media, which include ads on shopping carts, in-store sound systems, interactive kiosks, coupon dispensers, and televisions at checkout lanes.

POP display and advertising, roughly a $12 billion to $15 billion industry, achieved a 7.7 percent rate of growth in 1995. That's a greater growth rate than network TV advertising (2.8 percent) and national newspaper advertising (5.6 percent), according to *Advertising Age*.

POP displays represent the last opportunity to reach the customer. They can influence a consumer at the very last moment of decision, when he or she is ready to reach for the product or hold back. It's a significant and final factor in the last few feet of a brand's marketing campaign, particularly among time-pressured shoppers who may not have put together a shopping list. The on-site advertising can jog people's memories of things they need to buy.

Almost every square inch of a retailer's space is an opportunity for POP. Displays can be installed in the front or rear of the store, in the lobby, in the aisles, in a specialized area (such as an in-store shop featuring a single designer), or perhaps in the bakery (on shelves, suspended from the ceiling, or in the windows). Consider any place that does not disrupt the traffic flow but takes advantage of it.

Effective POP displays coordinate with the advertising conducted outside the store and therefore serve to reinforce advertising and sales promotion messages. POP displays are easy to assemble, load with product, and set up on the selling floor, without requiring a lot of work from the retail staff. Paper Mate, for example, has "power wing" displays that include a brand mix, featuring all the hot new products (as opposed to a specific product) for the back-to-school selling season. A sign in the front of the store might advertise a specific new product. According to some reports, Paper Mate displays can be set up in seconds.

The function of POP, as with advertising and promotion, is to sell product. However, the POP displays or fixtures that house the product must not overshadow the product itself. "We design and manufacture POP solutions that make the product—to paraphrase David Ogilvy—the hero, and not the display," says Jim De Simone, vice president/group manager of Thomson-Leeds Company, Inc., a leading manufacturer and designer of displays, merchandising materials, and retail environments.

> We try to keep the design simple, using symbols and not words, whenever possible, to convey a brand's message. Words add to the visual clutter at retail and require more time for a consumer to process. Symbols and recognizable icons help a display to instantly communicate the brand and product being sold, capturing the consumer at the crucial instant when the purchase decision is being made. Integrating POP advertising with a brand's image advertising and coordinating the program with both the advertiser's sales supports and the retailer makes sense. However, POP effectiveness can vary by product category and region, so it is very important for marketers to understand the dynamics of POP advertising relative to specific, market-by-market conditions.

De Simone adds that marketers must be able to prove to retailers that their profits and sales will increase if their brands are given special exposure by using POP materials and situating their brands in prime locations in the stores. That could involve showing results from other stores where the POP has and hasn't been employed.

Each project Thomson-Leeds works on has an account team consisting of people in design and engineering, production, account management, traffic, and administration. At the heart of the team is the account manager, who works with the retail or manufacturer client to define the objectives and come up with a program. Thomson-Leeds dispatches "investigative teams" to stores that sell their clients' products and those of competitors. These teams study the selling environment, observe shoppers, take pictures, and ask questions.

Evidence That POP Has Pop

Industry studies show that more than two-thirds of consumer purchasing decisions are made inside the store. In 1995, the Point-of-Purchase Advertising Institute, a trade organization, conducted a study of consumer buying habits. It revealed that an even higher rate of purchasing decisions are made in-store. At mass merchandisers, for example, 74 percent of brand purchase decisions are made in the store. At supermarkets, 70 percent of brand purchase decisions are made in the store. Furthermore, shoppers spend at least 12 percent more than they expected on each trip to the supermarket and 5 percent more at mass merchandisers. This is evidence that purchase decisions can be influenced through the use of POP displays and advertising and that it makes a great deal of sense for manufacturers to develop these selling tools and to work with stores to ensure that POPs are placed where they will be noticed by customers.

For a balanced presentation, higher-quality products should be displayed with more sophisticated and high-end POP materials. An example of a simple, inexpensive POP display suitable for a more basic item is a cardboard poster (placed beside, beneath, or atop the product) that shows the same picture seen in the ads. That's a low-key approach. A POP display that lights up or swings can grab more attention to the product. Signs that stand out from the shelf draw attention but must be placed so shoppers don't get bumped as they walk by. It has been found that any technique that lends movement or novelty can draw more attention to the product. Among the other POP props that emphasize products are wobbling signs set on springs, electronic signs arched over aisles to spotlight new products, pamphlet and brochure dispensers that display the product and list its benefits, and end-of-aisle or "end-cap" displays (special merchandising racks that highlight the products at the end of the aisle or in a heavily trafficked spot).

New Balance, in 1995, wanted to update its display in an end-of-aisle location in the Sports Authority, but the retailer would not alter its existing fixture to accommodate New Balance. So a unit was developed that worked into the existing fixturing, enveloping it but also converting it into a compelling "boutique within a superstore." The POP display featured large, eight-foot sports graphics, a big New Balance logo, and powerful halogen lights hanging from the ceiling that spotlight the display and illuminate Day-Glo shoe shelves. There are also peg holes with hooks to merchandise socks with the athletic shoes.

Additionally, POP can help create an aura around a product and reinforce a brand image while increasing sales. For example, Rolling Rock beer set up a modular, three-dimensional display called the Latrobe Company Store with a green awning—an imitation storefront devised to draw attention and set a country-style mood. The storefront was rigged with branded memorabilia, such as caps and mugs, and a catalog of merchandise was created. The setup reportedly sparked sales of Rolling Rock by 10 percent in 1994.

A key point about POP is that a creative design can solve problems, such as lack of space, in the merchandising arena. When Hunter Douglas introduced its line of Silhouette window treatments in 1993, the company needed a POP display that was small enough not to crowd window treatment stores, which are generally small specialty shops. But the display also had to be big enough to have some impact, since the product was being launched.

The second challenge was to create a POP display that would let consumers try out the new product. The manufacturer worked with Thomson-Leeds to develop a display that not only exhibited a long sample shade but let consumers feel the fabric and work the opening-and-closing mechanism. It also had the unique feature of allowing people to see how the shade would look from both inside and outside. On one side of the display, an outdoor scene was depicted, simulating a window view. This display showed the customer that you couldn't see through the shade into the room. The room side of the display demonstrated the shade's ability to permit light into the room while still providing privacy. The frame took up little space on the selling floors, yet had a dramatic presence.

Space and image were also important considerations for Sony when, in 1991, the company introduced a new cellular phone. The challenge was to show it in a way that would educate consumers about the phone and allow them to handle it. Sony also wanted to display the phone on counters or right off the selling floors. To meet these objectives, two base columns, a tall one and a short one, were developed for counter and floor display. Second, the head of the display was developed so it could be installed on either column and was illuminated from the inside so information panels could be noticed and read easily. Third, the phone was attached to the headpiece by a telephone cord so it would be hard to steal but could be picked up and handled. It was a high-tech POP design that captured the quality and advanced look of the Sony phone and provided some merchandising options for retailers.

Taking the high-tech concept even further, interactive POP is also becoming more popular. Interactive POP includes coupon-dispensing kiosks and information-based interactive computer shelf systems that are used for products such as cosmetics, food, liquor, and wine, for which it is important to distribute information. Also, since liquor and some other products, such as cigarettes, are restricted by law from advertising in certain media, POP for such products becomes doubly important. Other interactive POP technologies generate store traffic and solicit customer opinions. Companies such as Clairol, Kraft, and Coppertone have used shelf computers to provide information, dispense coupons, and attain consumer information.

Not only do manufacturers provide the POP displays, developed by firms such as Thomson-Leeds, but they also pay fees to the store to rent space for the display, just as many stores collect shelf fees from manufacturers to display the products on the shelves.

Setting the Stage at the Point of Purchase

When the doors to the store open in the morning, it's like the curtain going up on a Broadway show. There is a similar feeling of excitement and anticipation. Retailing is the theater of consumption. People go shopping not only to purchase goods that they need but also to have a social experience. It is a way to see what everybody else is wearing, check out the latest fashions, and show off new clothes and hairstyles to friends.

A store is the stage for products that can be enhanced through lighting, fixturing, and props to create an atmosphere. A store can have a central theme that each department customizes to suit its products.

Shoppers can be drawn through the store by presentations of innovative and tempting products. The smell of fresh baked bread or chocolate chip cookies wafting through the bakery can help boost sales of pots and pans. Svelte models in activewear demonstrating exercise equipment can spark sales of both categories. Allow customers to try the stairsteppers or the bicycles and offer videotapes that demonstrate proper use of the equipment. Product extensions can build sales volume. All the activity and the right assortment of related products can spur impulse shopping and generate more volume.

However, the most theatrical sections of the store are in designer clothing and higher-priced cosmetics. Higher-priced clothing departments are marked by elegant fixtures, in-store shops with lots of space to display product, deep carpeting, cushiony chairs, and large dressing rooms. It's a setting of comfort and service catering to customers buying expensive items.

The setting of mystery and magic can be more intense in the cosmetics department. Some stores have special rooms with reclining chairs for relaxing facials. During the facial, you will hear about all of the emollients you need to maintain a brilliant complexion and healthy skin coloring. Cosmetic departments are filled with photos of the world's most glamorous women, such as actresses Isabella Rossellini and Elizabeth Taylor, who put their names on fragrances and cosmetic lines and sometimes make store appearances. These products sell the promise of beauty and glamour and are therefore promoted in highly theatrical settings.

The merchandising arena is energized by fashion shows featuring appearances by designers or through informal modeling sessions with wardrobe specialists from design firms. If possible, stage full-fledged, narrated, fully accessorized fashion shows to draw large audiences of both couture customers and the general public, all of whom are intrigued by the color and action and are ready to enjoy the show.

Special events can increase the traffic of the target market and bring in a new audience. Fashion shows can attract women, men, and teenagers of both genders, depending on the designer. Male teenagers may take an uncaring stance about their appearance, but choosing the right role model for fashion can make all the difference. If Michael Jordan introduced a line of clothes to go with his shoes, his fashion shows would be standing room only. Some men are extremely fashion conscious, whereas others rely on women to outfit them. Knowing the lifestyles and habits of your target market will help you determine who the decision makers, buyers, and users are within each of the target markets.

By envisioning the entire store as a theater, excitement from one department will carry over to another department. For example, a fashion show in a women's fashion department should be coordinated with a special event in accessories, such as a demonstration on how to fold a scarf or how to accessorize a wardrobe to make the same outfits look different. Research has shown that by moving customers through more of the store, you will increase the amount that each person buys.

If your theme for a fashion show or event is regional or foreign in flavor, several departments can participate. For example, if the store is staging a promotion of imports from France, then French fashion, cooking, furniture, culture, food, and cookware should be carried throughout the store to the give it a theme and new energy for the season.

Children's merchandise and events draw adults to the store. Visits from comic-book and television superheroes (Power Rangers or Ninja Turtles), sports figures, and music stars can draw a multigenerational crowd. In the 1990s, the Barbie doll has reemerged as a popular collector's item among girls and their mothers. At F.A.O. Schwarz, Barbie accessories were popular Valentine's Day gifts for adult women. They started at $40 for a key ring and exceeded $200 for a crystal powder case. When the interests of adults and children overlap, as with Barbie, special events are a natural. You can place attention on clothes that a small and larger Barbie would wear, and you can use Barbie as a role model to create entire children's and adult's wardrobes. Not only can your daughter dress like Mom, but she can dress just like Barbie, using the same outfits.

11 | **Public Relations:**

The Art of the Spin

"Our official position is that
this is <u>not</u> a hostile takeover."

CALL THEM SPIN DOCTORS, media hounds, whatever. The media may not always buy into the "official position" of the corporate flack, but public relations is still an integral part of the marketing plan. PR is on the front lines when it comes to positioning your store or your product to the trade, the media, and the public.

So even though you have used magazines, newspapers, TV, radio, and point-of-purchase display advertising and just about every sales promotion technique known to hype product, price, and image, it's necessary to deliver the message through public relations. Be aware that you can't always control how the media interpret the message. The key is to minimize the risk of distortion and maximize your chances of having it told as you see it, or at least as close to your view as possible.

One of the keys is to play up the creative angle. PR stories have to be unique and imaginative. They require more than just issuing press releases. You have to think creatively to capture the attention of the world. In Ziccardi & Partners's first PR campaign, we wanted to stand out from the agency pack. We discovered a clever premium, customized it, and allowed it to do the trick. It wasn't just another PR gimmick. It was a desktop-size canetary arch made of small wooden blocks. The blocks were made so the arch could be constructed around a center foundation; when complete, the foundation was removed and the arch stood by itself, seemingly defying gravity. On the blocks, we put our logo and slogan, "Build your business around Ziccardi & Partners and stand alone among the competition." The blocks accompanied all of our press releases and new business mailings. As we made our follow-up phone calls, we found that almost everyone remembered our blocks. They became a great conversation opener and positioned us as creative thinkers. It personalized the agency. This led to dozens of favorable stories on the company in newspapers and trade publications and was directly responsible for scoring several new clients that year.

But be forewarned. Public relations is not an exact science. There are no guarantees. This chapter outlines the purposes and pitfalls of PR. It makes the case for being preemptive—telling your story before someone else tells it for you.

THE PURPOSE OF PR

Public relations is geared to do more than sell product and pump up the stock. It can be a very effective tool in communicating the marketing strategy to consumers, shareholders, suppliers, the competition, and the government. It's the voice of the company addressing the groups that care about the business, have a stake in it, or can have an impact on it. These constituencies need to know how the company is being positioned, where it is headed, what it stands for, and how it is performing.

Public relations serves other purposes beyond disseminating information. In communicating strategies, it will also help shape the company's image, as does advertising. The key difference is that advertising is paid for and can be tightly controlled. The message of the public relations department, whether it is conveying an executive change, an acquisition, or a record-setting quarter, is subject to interpretation by the media. The message sent by the public relations department can enhance the value of the business and generate interest in the company and excitement over events happening there. It can also reduce interest in the company and depress its value. The key to effective public relations is to have accurate information and know where to go with it.

According to Matthew Evins, a public relations executive, there are three key goals to public relations: to achieve market visibility, market awareness, and market presence. First, a PR campaign should put the product in the public eye: make it visible. Second, it has to be understood. The public's knowledge of the brand must go beyond its name to what the product stands for. Third, it has to have a market presence. It has to fill a niche "and own it," Evins says.

The PR strategy must be oriented for both short-term goals and strategic, long-term goals. Sucrets took both of these into consideration in 1994 when the company decided to put a new face on its packaging and retire the 62-year-old tin pack. For a smooth transition, it staged a retirement party in the Rainbow Room in Rockefeller Center in New York to officially donate the tin to the Smithsonian, and to launch the new packaging. It also offered prizes related to the retirement to stimulate sales. With the tin positioned as a collectible, sales surged immediately after the party and kept way above the previous year's level for many weeks.

Thus, both short- and long-term goals were accomplished. The old tin was phased out and the new tin integrated easily into the market.

Easing the Mind of the Public

The public relations department is responsible for easing the company or product through transitions and strategic moves by helping to create a positive image of the company. When the Ohio Bancorp was considering offers to be taken over by other companies, it feared a replay of what had happened during a previous takeover attempt, when customers withdrew millions of dollars in deposits. This time, however, no one was left in the dark: Ohio Bancorp's public relations firm held a news conference announcing its plans, then subsequently met with community groups, reporters, and editorial boards of newspapers. In addition, an employee newsletter was started up and the president of the company sent out a letter to customers. News coverage was generally positive. The decision was made to merge with National City Corp. An overwhelming majority of shareholders voted for the merger, and only a minimal amount of deposits was lost. Often, a change of ownership generates tremendous concern about employment and the economy. The public relations team must formulate the message and deliver it so that the community stays calm and reassured.

Changing the Mind of the Public

It is the role of public relations to update or correct public opinion about a company or product. For decades, aspirin has been universally accepted as an almost natural antidote for a variety of aches and pains. Yet aspirin started to lose market share in the early 1990s when new alternative analgesics such as Advil became popular and reports were surfacing about potential side effects of taking aspirin, such as stomach problems. So the Aspirin Foundation of America hired Ketchum Public Relations to reverse the trend by spotlighting newly discovered advantages of aspirin, as well as previously known benefits, and its relative harmlessness. Seminars were held with the medical community, the foundation's advisory board went on a media tour and made itself available for inquiries, and a toll-free phone number was set up. The capper came around tax time in 1990, when Excedrin started an offbeat promotional campaign. Research indicated that people suffered from headaches more frequently during tax season when they were filling out tax returns, so the company formed the "Excedrin Tax Team." With giant inflatable bottles of Excedrin as props, models in Excedrin shirts and sweatpants distributed samples to people mailing their tax returns. Thousands of samples were handed out at post offices, Excedrin sales rose significantly, and the theme "Excedrin Headache #1040" played on Excedrin's highly successful "Excedrin headache" commercials of the 1960s. The campaign was extended into the early 1990s.

In another instance of PR helping to change perceptions, the designer Valentino wanted to reimage his couture house into one with greater visibility and appeal to a younger audience, while still hanging onto the older socialite set. A "Thirty Years of Magic" retrospective for Valentino was organized, featuring Bette Midler, Placido Domingo, and Aretha Franklin singing happy birthday to Valentino. A collection of lower-priced commemoratives was developed to sell at Saks Fifth Avenue and Neiman Marcus, and proceeds from the sale of the items were donated to AmFar, the charity for AIDS research. The promotion culminated in actress Sharon Stone parading down the runway during Valentino's ready-to-wear show, creating a major media event. As a result of these activities, Valentino's customer base was broadened with a fresh new image and the business was revitalized.

PR For Pushing, Plugging, and Launching a Product

A company may invite the press to cover a special event. It could be for a new product or promotion and could center around an event or a celebrity endorsing the product. Monsanto's Chemstrand division, working with the Doyle Dane Bernbach agency, hyped its Acrilan acrylic fiber (used in rugs in the Empire State Building) at Lincoln Center openings, bull-judging contests, beauty pageants, shopping center openings, even a party at Barbra Streisand's apartment—any red-carpet occasion. Sometimes the Acrilan name was plugged and sometimes it wasn't, but the events were photographed and used for public relations purposes. As a result, the product became associated with festive occasions.

Launching an Uplifting Product

There are other reasons for calling in a public relations specialist. Any kind of launch requires the attention of the communications department, whether it's for a new product, a new division, or a new store. The firm of Marina Maher launched Sara Lee's Wonderbra with enormous success, even after similar products had already been introduced in Britain. The Wonderbra was deemed the "original dramatic cleavage bra" and launched in a manner resembling the arrival of the Beatles for a U.S. tour. An entourage was created with men dressed as secret service agents guarding the product as it was rushed into a fashion show and models unveiling the product. In different cities, the entourages arrived by different means—San Francisco's used a cable car; Los Angeles's flew in by helicopter.

PR to Smooth Over Financial Changes

Changes in a company's financial structure—such as an initial public offering, calling in bonds ahead of their call date, a stock split, or employee cutbacks—require the expertise of a public relations department. PR should know the answers to pending financial questions and quickly get the information to the media.

In 1992, Coors's PR machinery was ready for action. Coors was about to spin off its nonbeer businesses, but before the big move, Coors's PR firm created a new logo, press kit, fact sheet, video, and slide show and arranged meetings with stock analysts. Because Coors's PR team, along with Coors's executives, had all the information about the spin-off at its fingertips and was prepared to field all questions, the company came off looking confident and ready. Consequently, coverage of the event was positive.

In the mid-1990s, Eastman Kodak had to reshape its employee benefits package to save money. Before the announcement, it had the internal communications team meet with management to learn about the cuts. Then human resources and managers were briefed and trained to communicate the changes to employees. The announcement was then made to thousands of employees, and finally the press was notified. Because Kodak made the effort to be open and to communicate effectively, there was little backlash to the changes.

The public relations team must know why the company has taken such steps, what the repercussions will or could be, and what groups will be affected by the decision, including present and potential investors. Government agencies such as the Securities and Exchange Commission (SEC) may also be interested in financial changes within a company. Public relations is generally not the primary contact for the government, though the PR department, as well as the legal department, will be looking for feedback from government agencies to convey information to management. PR staff from major national retailers, including Kmart and The Limited, are constantly monitoring the U.S. Commerce Department on developments in international trade and tariff negotiations that affect the cost of importing merchandise (and ultimately retail prices) and minimum wage legislation, which affects labor costs. The PR departments might be involved in lobbying efforts and issue releases seeking to influence public opinion.

Coping with Crisis

When Federated Department Stores went bankrupt in 1990, the situation was desperate. Consumers and suppliers thought the company would go out of business and that many stores would close. At that time, few suppliers and consumers understood what a Chapter 11 bankruptcy meant—specifically, that the firm would continue to operate as it worked out a plan of reorganization that would satisfy its creditors. Federated held a press conference with the trade press to take the message to suppliers, the CEO sent a letter to thousands of suppliers explaining the situation, and top executives visited many manufacturers. Information sheets were distributed explaining the reasons for the bankruptcy and why Federated still had a future as a viable business. In addition, interviews were held with reporters. The key message that had to get out was that Federated was not closing and that, fundamentally, its business was still viable.

In Federated's case, PR played an important role in the company's survival. In a situation involving fashion designer Louis Dell'Olio, PR helped prevent his image from being sullied. When he left Anne Klein, there was speculation that he was leaving unwillingly. Had the rumors reached the media, Dell'Olio's reputation would have suffered. But Anne

Klein's PR agency, Evins Communications, Ltd., saved the day by preparing a straightforward media message—that it was time for a change at Anne Klein and that Dell'Olio's departure was not a nasty dismissal.

Next, the format for conveying the message was established. Frank Mori, owner of Anne Klein, Dell'Olio, and Dell'Olio's successor, Richard Tyler, together conducted about 20 interviews with trade and consumer press to present a united front. The result: Most of the press described the situation as a "mutual parting of ways." According to Matthew Evins, the men were able to "tell the truth in a positive way so they could walk away with their heads held high."

Responding with a Single Voice

In Anne Klein's case, a single voice responded to the media. A course of action was developed in response to the crisis. If the details of the situation had leaked out without a plan in place, it would have been too late to come up with a strategy. A good public relations department is preemptive. Just as the Marines are prepared for action before a crisis arises, a PR squad should be able to handle a problem and have contingency plans in place. Disaster planning is crucial. If a crisis occurs, a savvy public relations department can make the difference between a company surviving or falling apart. You may never need to respond to a disaster, but a formulated scheme (similar to a well-rehearsed fire drill) should be in place. If you have to stop and assign duties to everyone, you will be lost in the crush of news media chasing a story. If a company in crisis does not take an active role, chances are greater that erroneous information will be reported. And then control will be totally forsaken.

Legislation: Cause and Effect

Public relations must be alert to indications that government officials are considering legislative changes. If the legislation is positive, the company wants to make changes in strategy to take advantage of new opportunities. Strategies should be timed to take effect just after legislation is passed. Evaluate public reaction to new legislation to gauge how quickly to move.

Coppertone, the suntan lotion company, kept abreast of a decision by the National Weather Service to provide daily forecasts of the ultraviolet index. Responding to rising public concern about the potential dangers of sun exposure, Coppertone wisely promoted the index with new TV and print ads. In old Coppertone ads, a dog tugs at a girl's bikini bottom to reveal her dark tan line. In the new ads, the girl wears a T-shirt and hat and carries a bottle of suntan lotion; the dog tugs at her T-shirt. Through this campaign, Coppertone helped educate the public about the ultraviolet index and helped itself as well—sales increased.

Along with this type of educational effort, the public relations department can mobilize public opinion by placing editorials in the media to convey the corporation's perspective. Special-interest groups with the same point of view should be recruited to lend another voice. These groups can mobilize their memberships to write letters to the government.

GETTING OUT THE MESSAGE

There are different ways to get the news out. The most common is the press release, created by the public relations department and usually requiring the sign-off of upper management and the parties mentioned in the release. Make it easy to read and informative and bear in mind the style of the media you are writing for.

The Press Conference—the PR Theater

When the news is highly significant, call a press conference—but be judicious in deciding when to call it. It is more than just a conference, it's theater, and the company must perform its best act. Typically, public relations opens the show, delivers an opening statement, and then turns things over to the other executives or experts. Each should give a short speech but also allow time for questions, photos, and product demonstrations. Distribute press kits, which may include a compilation of story information, case histories, the company history, background on product development, and an anecdote that might humanize the story. They should be inviting, entertaining, and useful for journalists.

To publicize the 30th anniversary of the Oscar Mayer wiener song, Ketchum Public Relations created a media kit with a computer chip that played the song. Biographical information on the composer and his daughter, who sang the song in the original 1963 TV commercial, was also provided. The kits were distributed to the press before an employee party celebrating the anniversary, which was taped for the media and interspersed with clips of people on the streets singing the song. The tape also included some of the better Oscar Mayer commercials. Millions saw the campaign, helping to strengthen Oscar Mayer's position in the hot dog market. This was one kit that really did the job. Remember, though, that once the information is in the hands of the media, it is beyond your control.

For companies introducing new products, public relations departments set up press conferences and keep the market aware of the launch date. It is important to stimulate positive word of mouth and purchases of the product as soon as it hits the shelves.

A press conference should highlight the best features of a new product. Public relations must be able to answer all questions about the product, particularly those related to health or the environment, and how it might be used with other products. Distributing samples is an excellent idea: Let the media experience what's being sold. If the product is good, there's a better chance of getting a rave review.

Press conferences save time and money because they gather many members of the media in one room. This way, company executives and PR executives will not need to answer the same questions repeatedly, as happens with individual interviews. A press conference is particularly effective with a national story for which widespread coverage is desired. TV and radio stations also benefit, since a press conference creates the impression that the station is on the scene of an event in the making.

Keep in mind that press conferences must be about something new, not overly commercial, and not filled with technical jargon—if some technical terms are absolutely necessary, they should be explained. Also, it is important that press conferences be scheduled to meet deadlines and be complete with information to answer many questions, provide perspective, and suggest the big picture behind the details of the story.

The Press Release—Well Articulated and Well Timed

Press releases should follow the same criteria as press conferences. In addition, they should be researched, well written, thorough, factual, and not opinionated; they should also include a source to contact for more information during business and nonbusiness hours.

Use double spacing and try to limit the release to a couple of pages. If it goes any longer, let the reader know—using large notation—that additional pages follow. Compare it to sending out a résumé that will have to compete with many others for attention. You have 20 to 30 seconds to make an impression. Make it attractive and easy to read, with a strong opening.

An example of a bad press release was one issued by Dillard's in March 1996. The company was closing two of its regional offices and firing hundreds of employees. The announcement was made at 5:30 on a Friday afternoon, when reporters might have already gone home and when Dillard's executives were unavailable. The release was short, lacked necessary details (such as where all the other regional offices were located), and succeeded in frustrating reporters. It appeared that Dillard's wanted to bury the news. By holding back on information, Dillard's image was damaged and it seemed to be a company with operational problems. It was a poor public relations effort.

A better public relations effort was made in 1996 by Charming Shoppes, a women's specialty chain that had been experiencing executive upheaval. In 1995, a new CEO was appointed, and massive store closings were announced. In 1996, a new chairperson was appointed, underscoring the lack of stability at the company. When the chairperson was announced, Charming issued a brief release. Executives used the occasion to reach out to the press in phone interviews and explain the company's new strategies for survival. As a result, press reports were balanced. They detailed the company's financial woes, while indicating the game plan initiated by the new regime.

Bear in mind that a public relations effort that is forthcoming with information will do more to enhance a company's image than one that lacks detail. For example, *Architectural Digest* magazine in 1994 issued an excellent release about a survey it had sponsored. The release cited the survey's major conclusions and its methodology and explained its relevance. A key finding was that U.S. consumers were becoming more enlightened, with elevated aesthetic sensibilities, and the conclusion was that they are now prone to spend more on higher-quality products. The press release indicated that the survey, conducted by Yankelovich

Partners Inc., had identified a "powerful, new attitudinal demographic which while not necessarily affluent, will readily spend more to buy the best." *Architectural Digest* called this group "the people who know the difference" and said that within four years, it would comprise 11 percent of the U.S. population and by the year 2010, possibly more than half.

The release was provocative and informative and drew coverage in the media. Significantly, even though the news in the release did not directly pertain to *Architectural Digest,* the magazine's reputation as an arbiter of good taste and an authority on lifestyle was enhanced through its association with the survey. The release could have been totally ignored. The magazine certainly had no guarantees the release would get picked up, but because of the way the news was handled, media interest was piqued.

In essence, public relations can be like a crap shoot. You roll the dice and pray things turn out your way. Once your press release moves from public relations to the media, there's no telling how the story will be told. The public relations version will be edited, chopped up, reinterpreted, rearranged, rewritten, and possibly altered beyond recognition. Expect the media to perform major surgery. There are, however, ways to increase the chances for a smooth operation.

WORKING WITH AND WITHIN THE COMMUNITY

Public relations can also research what customers are thinking and saying about the business. The business may be a good one, marrying the right products with the right customers and fulfilling their needs and desires. However, if community members are unhappy with some aspect of the business, such as its creation of pollution or traffic problems, they will complain. The job of public relations is to monitor the complaints and find solutions.

Before the new Baltimore Orioles baseball stadium opened in 1992, there was wide concern that nightmarish traffic jams and parking problems would result. Few people had used public transportation to get to the old stadium, and studies showed that the downtown area and interstate highway system would be clogged by traffic to the new stadium. In response, the Maryland Stadium Authority hired a public relations firm to encourage fans to take public transportation. The Authority knew old habits wouldn't be easy to break, but with the firm's help it devised a campaign based on the theme "Route, route, route for the home team" (from the song "Take Me Out to the Ballgame"). The campaign was taken to local radio shows, presented to community groups, and broadcast through a TV public service announcement. Meetings with editors were arranged, and new transit signs were posted. The use of public transportation increased dramatically.

The Dangers of Not Communicating

It is important that a company on the growth track or launching a new product bear in mind the potential effect on the community. If a company just blindly proceeds without regard for others, it may run into opposition and never get to complete its plans. For example, in cases in which concerns about traffic are not dealt with satisfactorily, the community may start litigation to restrict the business by regulating parking or forcing the business to purchase land to increase parking. The company could be forced to restrict store hours on certain days to keep traffic down or create a park as a buffer between the business and the residential area.

A classic case of a company not communicating with the community involved Bristol-Myers Squibb Co. in Syracuse, New York, where there was a toxic spill from the company plant. Even though the plant was a major local employer, the spill spawned intense negative press and enraged the community for several years. Its future was further imperiled by the company's refusal to respond to the negative press and community questions. Some locals wanted the company to shut down its plant.

Under pressure, the company reversed its no-comment position and opened its doors to the public. It disclosed its projects for the next several decades, launched a science camp, and held an open house so that people could get an inside look and have their fears allayed. The result: The community developed a more positive opinion of the plant, and media coverage became less focused on environmental issues and Bristol-Myers. The company also promised to work harder to prevent additional spills.

A Natural Disaster and the Need for Community Concern

A case in which a company showed community concern was in 1995 when Bullock's department store reopened in the Northridge section of San Francisco, which had been leveled by a devastating earthquake the year before. Rebuilt with a sturdier design and angular walls, the new store was launched with great fanfare and with the theme of celebrating heroes, both real and fictional. Direct-mail pieces reflected the hero theme, and many parents brought their children to the opening, which attracted a crowd of 2,000 and exceeded volume expectations. Marvel comic characters appeared as part of the hoopla, a giant Spider-Man balloon floated overhead, and Stan Lee, the creator of the comic-book heroes, attended as a special guest. Firefighters, Red Cross workers, and others involved in rescuing victims of the earthquake were honored at the opening. Their presence served to show that Bullock's cared about the community and wanted to be a part of its recovery.

False Assumptions and Long-Term Goals

If upper management is oblivious to community concerns, strategic plans may be built on false assumptions and long-term goals may be impossible to achieve. BP Lima Chemicals in Ohio once had to win the community's trust to continue a wastewater disposal process in an underground well. The plant would have had to close because of new, toughened environmental regulations. There was some concern that the process was hazardous to the environment, but through public relations, a broad educational program was developed. Included were videos of BP Lima's technology, plant tours, meetings with community groups and politicians, and open discussions with employees. BP also established an exhibit of the geology of the areas of the waste disposal rock core to help demonstrate the safety of its system. Public hearings were held and BP Lima was able to maintain its operations. In the end, the EPA dropped its new requirements.

Sometimes, if the media portrayal is inaccurate, you have to restate the truth. In early 1996, Kmart was plagued by persistent rumors that it was planning to declare bankruptcy. Kmart public relations officials kept denying the rumors, and the chain's CEO sent a letter to vendors saying that the company was turning around and had no plans to file bankruptcy. A copy of the letter was also faxed to the media. In addition, the company repeatedly stated it was negotiating a new arrangement with lenders—one that would give the company more time to pay back debts. Finally, the company announced that the deal had been completed, giving it some breathing room.

In this case, it was necessary to restate the company's position and actions to help deflate perceptions of a looming bankruptcy among several constituencies, including suppliers, investors, employees, and the media. Although beleaguered by endless negative press and poor market perceptions, Kmart restated and restated its position. As a result, rumors of Kmart's imminent demise ceased, the stock price picked up, and speculation shifted to whether Kmart has what it takes for long-term survival. For the time being, Kmart was okay.

NATURALS FOR PR

Groundbreaking Events

Other kinds of company activities are perfect public relations events. Breaking ground for a new building, laying the cornerstone, and the grand-opening ceremony are all photo and interview opportunities. The Rock and Roll Hall of Fame had delayed its groundbreaking a couple of times and the project was losing credibility. Something other than the normal hard-hat groundbreaking was decided on to restore confidence. A weeklong celebration, organized by a public relations firm, included a ceremony for new stamps commemorating music legends and a luncheon featuring interviews with dozens of music giants and politicians. Groundbreakings for store openings are often considered nonevents, but in the 1990s, a period of intense store closings, they have once again become newsworthy.

Promoting New Projects

Even blueprints or sketches of new projects can make a story. Chanel's new flagship store on 57th Street became a major story in *Women's*

Wear Daily in early 1996, even though the building was still under construction and the luxurious interiors could only be seen in sketches. The construction plans were unique, since they included a separate "suite"—double the height of the other floors—for fashion shows, charity events, trunk shows, and parties, as well as Chanel's first fine jewelry shop in New York City.

A Meeting as a Newsworthy Event

For large companies and unions, sales meetings and annual shareholder or analyst meetings could be public relations opportunities. The meeting site itself is important and plays a part in projecting the firm's image. In a time of austerity, don't hold your meeting in a swanky resort. But don't wait for the annual meeting to find out what the public is thinking: Consider it on a routine basis.

Preemptive Strikes

Political and legislative initiatives can start without warning. Events can be staged to help sway public opinion and tighten the bonds between company and community. For example, before it opens a new store, Nordstrom dispatches hundreds of employees to work for a charity in the area. Try to fund local environmental projects, cultural events, and events with holiday themes. The role of public relations is to learn what residents of the community are thinking and how to help them, while enhancing perceptions of the company.

Dow Goes Environmental

Around 1990, Dow Chemical Co. was taking heat for its plastics production and was becoming known as a major environmental polluter. Working with Ketchum Public Relations to create a more positive public image, Dow decided to team up with the National Park Service on a recycling program in the parks. Dow also paid for educational materials that were distributed to park visitors on the recyclability of plastics, and news conferences publicizing the program were held at park sites. This served two purposes: Dow became identified as a company concerned with a cleaner environment and sensitive to community issues, while the national parks were better able to clean up a great deal of waste. Millions of Americans visiting the parks participate in the program, helping to cast plastics as a recyclable product.

Business-to-Business PR

The Takeover, a story about a Wall Street leveraged buyout, was written by Stephen W. Frey, a young investment banker with a lot of spunk and personality. Penguin, the publisher, sent him on a three-week trip to meet with wholesale clients. It also staged pizza parties for truck drivers and successfully brought the author into contact with those involved in the distribution and selling to help get the book placed efficiently and properly in the stores—or as Maryann Palumbo, vice president and director of marketing at Penguin USA, says, "on a higher level." Palumbo adds that Frey's charisma enabled him to connect well with the truck drivers, warehouse workers, and others integral to the distribution process, and as a result, "They felt as if they were part of the process and wanted to be part of the success."

Donna Karan has another type of charisma. She is one of Seventh Avenue's great schmoozers. She is constantly in stores meeting customers and salespeople to generate excitement and find out what people like—and hate—about her products. She's also there to ensure that stores follow through on the way she wants her collection displayed. She's hyping the line, pumping up business, creating an in-store event, and getting the message out, all at the same time.

PR MISFIRES

The Failure to Act Preemptively

The *QE 2* was renovated and scheduled to be relaunched in 1994. When the launch date arrived, the ship was not ready. Work on the ballroom and the kitchens was not complete, and construction equipment was scattered everywhere. Cunard, however, didn't want to delay the voyage and failed to notify passengers that there would be some inconvenience.

The company could have turned a bad situation into an interesting story by depicting the passengers as intrepid, willing to set sail despite the unpleasant conditions. Alternately, the company could have chosen to delay the launch. But it feared that either scenario would make the company look inept. So Cunard tried to cover up the situation, never informing the passengers that the boat was still under construction, and did little to make the passengers more comfortable. One passenger filed a class action suit, and the company reportedly issued refunds to some passengers, while others accepted an offer for a free cruise. The company suffered a big loss of credibility.

Cunard, however, learned a major lesson: A company must demonstrate it has the interests of its customers at heart. The stark reality—that the company had failed to get the *QE 2* ready in time for its relaunch—was hardly the issue. Because Cunard had not been aboveboard with its passengers, they perceived Cunard as not doing the right thing. It is the perception of the company caring about its customers, not merely the product itself, that people buy.

Poor Sam & Libby

Ruth Schwartz, president of Ruth Schwartz & Co., the public relations firm, once set up a meeting between Sam & Libby, the shoe company, and the *New York Times*. The goal was to generate publicity for the shoe company, and arranging the meeting was no simple feat considering the demands on the *Times*. But not only did the *Times* reporter spend two hours with the shoe executives, the group ate lunch together, too. The reporter returned for a second interview. According to Schwartz, it seemed like a courtship, but a story on the company never appeared.

This scenario is not unusual for public relations. It happens to companies all the time. There's also a variation on the theme—in which the reporter interviews executives up and down the corporate ladder, then publishes a story that barely quotes anyone. PR people ask themselves, "What's gone wrong?" In many cases, the reporter either didn't get the necessary information or got far more information than desired. The job of public relations is, in part, to make sure the reporter doesn't waste his time or the time of those interviewed.

Galeries Misses Gorby

A big PR blunder happened at Galeries Lafayette at its former location on 57th Street in New York. One day in May 1992, Mikhail Gorbachev was in Manhattan to raise money for the Gorbachev Foundation. The Secret Service called the store to say that Gorbachev and his wife Raisa were planning to drop by. Galeries then got its PR machinery into action and called the press to rush photographers to the store. It would be marvelous publicity. That afternoon, Galeries employees stood by the entrance in the Trump Tower atrium, gifts in hand, awaiting the couple. The head of the store had French earrings and a pin for Raisa. They waited and waited. When the Gorbachevs finally arrived at Trump Tower, they rode up and down the escalators, stopping in the Harry Winston store, but never making it to Galeries. The headline in *Women's Wear Daily* read, "Gorby's End Run Leaves GL Waiting."

SPIN CONTROL

Developing a Relationship with the Press

Things often don't go as planned. Public relations may envision a story very differently than a reporter would. The reason is not always obvious and may be even more obscure if you don't know the reporter well. In fact, a story pitched by public relations may not even qualify as a story at all in the eyes of a reporter or from the perspective of an editor who can kill it.

Building a relationship with the press is critical. Don't simply communicate with them when you have a press release. Become a source. Provide reporters with information and tips on companies other than the one you represent. Become a resource, also. Provide information on trends and industry occurrences. It all helps. The reporter will pay closer attention to the information in your release. When you know the reporter, you are in a better position to place a story and can mention that it has been awhile since your company has had any space or airtime in that medium and that you have something great to discuss. Larger companies generally have more clout when it comes to nudging a reporter, but a good story from any company can be successfully pitched.

Putting Out Fires

Certain situations demand tight control over the information going out to the press. In 1979, a major fire broke out at Macy's Herald Square on the second floor. The store was evacuated, and a firefighter was killed. "The Seventh Avenue side of the floor looked like a burned-out shell," said Ruth C. Schwartz, who ran Macy's public relations department before starting her own firm. She was one of the few to view the damage, and only she and Macy's chairperson Edward Finkelstein gave information to the press. Television news crews and reporters were prevented from visiting the scene. "It was a tragedy and we didn't want the wrong story to get out. The tight communications structure helped a lot," Schwartz said. She said the coverage was fair and accurate. The smell from the fire had penetrated other floors of the store, but by the next day the media had sniffed out other stories. For Macy's, the less media coverage about the fire, the better for the store.

Nudging as an Attention Getter

There are times when you want press coverage, but the media ignore your calls. When this happens, don't feel slighted. Certainly, the Washington, D.C. based Skits-O-Phrenic Productions, a comedy troupe, didn't let months of rejections get it down. The troupe was eager for critics to review its show, but the critics just didn't think the show rated a review. The troupe called, wrote, and sent invitations to the critics, but they were unmoved. The troupe grew more determined. It rewrote its material, expanded the mailing list, drew larger audiences, and kept the heat on the critics. The troupe implemented an unusual and clever public relations drive. During the show's intermission, it distributed postcards that the audience could use to send messages to two influential critics, urging them to see the show. The critics received stacks of postcards, but still to no avail. The troupe used the setback as comic material and publicized its failure, thereby generating more publicity and sentiment around town.

271

The mailing list grew, the audiences almost doubled, and finally one of the critics caved in and came to the show. The ice was broken. Soon other critics showed up, reviews were published, and the audiences continued to grow.

Crafting the Message for Many Constituencies

Public relations messages don't necessarily have to go through the press, though publication is the most efficient way of getting the word out. The message can be taken directly to the people, and in some situations, that's the best route. Curad, when it released a new adhesive bandage in 1991 called Curad Kid Size, embarked on a nationwide public service campaign that also served to boost sales. The public relations agency on the account, G.S. Schwartz, consulted with school nurses and created a campaign with "Carrie Curad." Carrie appeared in a brochure instructing children how to take care of minor injuries, and Geraldine Shepperson, the 1990 nurse of the year, went on tour as the spokesperson for the bandage. Curad distributed thousands of brochures across much of the country and saw significant growth as a result of the campaign.

Better Your Chances for Getting Coverage

The press owes nothing to public relations executives. You can't buy news coverage in the way you pay to place an ad, but there are ways to increase your chances of getting coverage. Examine your script carefully. Craft the information so that it doesn't just focus on the market buying the product or service. Employees, stockholders, potential investors, the government, and the community should be considered part of the audience. The sphere of influence is wide. Many sectors of the population are affected by your company and can have an effect on it.

In 1992, the city of Wahoo, Nebraska, wanted to take over the investor-owned Minnegasco natural gas system in order to generate revenues. The PR firm of Padilla-Speer-Beardsley, which had handled other municipal takeover threats, was called into action to defeat the upcoming city referendum. First, some quick research was conducted and it was learned that 7 of 10 citizens would vote in favor of the takeover. The firm developed a message that would hit different constituencies, including city leaders and employees. It said the company had the experience, know-how, cost-effective methods, and community links to do a better job than the city. The message was carried forward at a country fair and at employee meetings (so employees would tell their friends and family how to vote) and delivered door-to-door to the general population. A citizens' group was created to advise Minnegasco, to show that the company was listening to community concerns, and to gauge the population's reaction. At the referendum, the town voted against the takeover.

The Minnegasco message was strong, clear, accurate, and apparently persuasive. In 1994, Dell Computer took its case to the public in a similar manner. A perception existed among consumers and Dell stockholders that the company didn't know what it was doing. People were not satisfied with its products and the company's reputation was taking a fall. Nevertheless, using the public relations firm of Fleishman-Hillard, Dell launched a campaign for its new Latitude notebook computer and went directly to the people with it. Dell CEO Michael Dell staged the launch at JFK International Airport and lent some of the battery-powered notebooks to passengers flying to Los Angeles. He hopped on the flight and demonstrated the new product to convince the public that Dell had finally delivered something special and effective. The company also announced that customers would be surveyed about its products to help work out concerns. As a result of these efforts, the stock jumped 17 percent in a week, and Dell gained standing among consumers.

The Tylenol Tragedy: Exemplary Spin Control

The perception of a company caring about its customers played a major role in one of the most significant public relations dilemmas of the century. Tylenol was keenly aware of customer perceptions in the 1980s when its product was tainted by cyanide and one person died. The company did not hesitate to act. Tylenol did not wait for the government to force a recall; it immediately examined the production lot number and warned the public about the possibility of being poisoned. The company also requested that Tylenol be returned for a refund. A spokesperson expressed the company's deep regret over the tragedy and stated that it would vigorously investigate how the cyanide got into the capsules.

In addition, Tylenol kept querying customers to see how they viewed the situation, as the company continued to scrutinize its manufacturing process. The company concluded that the capsules must have been tampered with and that Tylenol, not just the person who died, was also being victimized. The company knew it was not at fault and, by telling the truth, impressed on the nation that the company itself was responsible and caring in its handling of the situation. A company doctor went on television news programs to try to calm the public. Each time new information was uncovered, he presented it to the public.

After it was established that tampering had occurred, Tylenol developed a triple-seal container to reduce the possibility of a reoccurrence. Tylenol announced a product giveaway for people who called a toll-free number, ensuring that only those who were comfortable with the steps taken by Tylenol would get the coupons. Within about two months of the tragedy, the Tylenol brand was back on store shelves, regaining lost market share. By acting quickly to reduce the risk of more people being poisoned, Tylenol showed that it cared about its customers and was able to bounce back.

Staying Power

As an ongoing function, public relations departments should be working on ways to get favorable coverage for the company or product. Public relations specialists should have strategies geared to pump up sales and products and have a measurable effect. For its first 12 years, the National Veterans Wheelchair Games had no way to measure its success from a public relations point of view. For the 13th annual games in 1993, a comprehensive plan was developed to increase interest in the games and to determine whether the games' popularity had grown. Among the efforts, the games staged its first-ever press conference, rigged up a satellite hookup to send out news stories, published a daily newsletter and posters, and issued news releases. As a result, scores of media stories were generated, and a telephone survey conducted after the event revealed that almost 90 percent of the community knew about the games compared with 13 percent previously. In addition, attendance grew roughly tenfold from earlier years, to more than 5,000.

However, it is not always possible to measure the impact of PR efforts. For example, the famous Macy's Thanksgiving Parade is held on Thanksgiving Day when the store is closed so there are no sales results. However, the event creates enormous goodwill, which can't be measured.

There are other stories created by public relations that don't generate goodwill or business. Nike, which usually generates enormous publicity, fell flat in 1995 when it tried to publicize the groundbreaking for its 57th Street NikeTown store in the Trump Tower atrium and the raising of its big swoosh logo. It attracted a handful of photographers, several construction workers, and a few onlookers, but no major sports celebrities came and little news coverage was generated. A Trump Tower employee even told one journalist who passed up the event, "You didn't miss anything." It was a case of poor PR event planning—a company chasing the media without pitching a rich enough story or even planning a party.

It's important not to sink into the role of what is called the media hack, where PR people chase the media with stories that lack substance and campaigns that have no purpose. When a public relations person is called a *flack*, it usually stems from a fabrication of information purely designed to get notice. Hollywood flacks were notorious for creating situations around actors or actresses that put them in the news, in an attempt to jump-start their careers. Romances were fabricated between people who had little to do with each other but were seeking to get into the news and become part of the gossip.

PR: DETERMINING ITS WORTH

Just because information has passed out of your hands into the media's doesn't mean your job is done. The next step is to monitor the results of your efforts, beginning with the budget. Most companies have a limit on the amount of money spent to enhance public perceptions. The public relations firm and the client agree either on a monthly fee or a set fee based on the project. The client can be billed for the creative effort and out-of-pocket expenses. Public relations is notorious among other fields for padding or marking up expenses. It has become almost an accepted practice, but it doesn't make for good working relations.

Measure Results against Preestablished Goals

Goals such as increasing the number of people who know about the product or company, getting a piece of legislation passed, or surviving a crisis while retaining 50 percent market share are important to know up front. Measure those results against the budget to decide whether the goals attained were worth the expense.

Public Opinion Polls

To determine whether a PR campaign has been effective, poll the person on the street. The poll can be conducted by the PR firm itself, though it would not necessarily be objective. Better yet, use an independent polling agency. Gauging reaction to a campaign and what's being publicized will help direct efforts on how to change perceptions in the future.

Image Surveys and Additional Questionnaires

Image surveys are questionnaires used to gauge feelings about a company. An image survey is different from an effectiveness survey, which asks people to rate the company's activities and place in the community. The two surveys should be reviewed to help determine the effectiveness of the public relations efforts. Also, review news articles to see what's being reported about the company. This technique, known as a content analysis, is another tool for gauging public relations—and it doesn't require interviews.

PR Audits

In another technique, called a public relations audit, the perceptions of employees and those from outside groups—such as investors, customers, and government officials—are evaluated. It's an extremely thorough examination, used in very important public relations campaigns.

Remember, the clearer the objective measure, the easier to judge whether the public relations program was a success. You should be able to report that you made your plan. Not only did current and potential customers have a better opinion of the company, but you also achieved that double-digit percentage gain.

12 | Doing It by the Numbers:

Budgeting, Timetables, and Measuring Results

"Next time, let Higgins
bring him the ad campaign results."

D<small>ON'T GET HUNG UP ON YOUR ADVERTISING BUDGET.</small> Indeed, setting its size and deciding how to distribute the dollars come down to the mission and the realities of the season, such as product launches, media switches, plans to outadvertise and upstage the competition, sales goals, and how much money there is in the pot.

But don't forget the big picture—the corporate profile—that drives your business. Are you cost-driven, driven to be close to the consumer, or driven by an entrepreneurial spirit, regularly propelling new products into the marketplace? Those issues should have a strong bearing on the scope and shape of the advertising and the budget for it. The amount of money you have to spend will also shape the campaign but don't let the bean counting subjugate the creative process. Nike, McDonald's, and Sears Roebuck have built empires off cultures that support spending handsomely on advertising and marketing, while maintaining a focus on the dollars. If they were to pull back and shift gears, a different message would be sent to consumers and a new attitude would seep through the organization, altering the cult of the company.

In setting the ad budget, there are choices to be made based on black-and-white realities, but there's also room to take an intuitive course. It's like being an artist and an engineer at the same time. That's the essential message of this chapter—maintaining your budgets and your schedules—and attaining the results you truly want out of your marketing plan.

BUDGET: BIG OR SMALL?

Flexing to Meet Opportunities and Solve Problems

To determine the size of the advertising and total marketing budget, you need to consider many issues. A few of the areas that must be covered before constructing a well-planned, effective budget are what the competition spends on personal selling incentives, how much of a share of time or space in different media you need to deliver an effective message, and what sales promotion results are essential to your strategy.

There are several different methods—or a combination thereof—that you can use to come up with an initial advertising budget. Some of these methods have intuitive appeal along with serious disadvantages. The "spend as much on advertising and marketing as you can afford" method rarely parcels a sufficient portion of the total company budget for advertising. Usually, the advertising portion of the marketing plan receives the amount left over after every other department and plan is funded. Often, this off-the-cuff approach is not a good way to go.

Percentage of Sales

One common method is based on a percentage of sales or profits. This is objective because it specifies the percentage of last year's sales or profits to be used for advertising this year. The disadvantage is that sales and profits should not define how much is spent on advertising and marketing. First, advertising helps drive sales and profits, not the reverse. Second, in a period of declining sales or profits, one would be consigned to spend even smaller amounts on advertising. However, this may be precisely the time when the message should be gaining a higher rather than lower profile.

Competitive Method

The competitive method requires an estimate of what the competition spends on advertising and other marketing; then that amount is matched. Again, it is a fairly simple method to implement. It considers the amount of advertising in the industry and the competition's market share compared to yours and designates a specific amount for advertising and marketing. The disadvantage is that it has no connection to your marketing objectives. A competitor's objectives may be to merely maintain sales, reduce costs, decrease advertising, or any number of different strategies in which you have no interest. It also assumes that others in the industry have some special knowledge that makes them experts on budgeting advertising. However, this method is sometimes an improvement over the percentage of sales/profits, especially for a firm introducing a product or retail category. Use the track records of competitors as an estimate for new product advertising.

Market Share Method

Similarly, use your market share as an indicator of how much to spend on your share of media time and space. To increase market or voice share, increase the advertising budget by an estimate of the desired share increase. The catch here is that it is difficult to determine what others are doing. If they increase ad spending at the same time you do, there will be no comparative increases at all.

Inertia Method

As the name suggests, the inertia method involves keeping the advertising and other marketing expenses constant and maintaining market share. It suggests changing little or nothing about the general theme or expenditures, as certain companies or products have done. The company that produces Tide laundry detergent, for example, has presented the same message for decades, while improving the packaging to meet changing times and advancing the product's effectiveness by upgrading the soap ingredients. Tide has been able to stand the test of time by presenting the consistent message that its performance is superior and by using ordinary people to promote the notion that Tide out-cleans other brands. This focused strategy allows for minor annual cost changes to provide for inflation in media rates.

The disadvantage to this method is that unless you link budgetary needs to goals and strategy, the budget may be too low or too high in any given year. While having more money is not a problem, it's important not to waste it.

Prior Year's Analysis and Computer Models

Lastly, compile several years' data using your past ad campaigns, sales promotion efforts, selling incentive programs, and other merchandising programs and their success rates or sales increases. Use that information to evaluate a proposed strategy for its efficacy and apply the appropriate costs. Computer models can simulate several advertising campaigns with different budget levels to help configure the best budget for the company.

Reduce the Budget to Writing

With all of these methods, budgets must be acknowledged with *reserve allowances* (specific amounts of unallocated money held for contingent emergencies) built into the totals. You do not want to reach the fourth quarter with only an eighth of the budget left to spend. With good planning, you can project a realistic budget with sufficient flexibility to accommodate any unforeseeable changes in media.

Each budget should be broken down into broad categories. Sales promotion, publicity, merchandising, and research are included in the total marketing mix. If there were personal selling costs, they should be included in this budget as well. The total marketing budget is calculated against the planned sales objectives, and at a minimum, the marketing budget as a percentage of sales should be compared to last year's ratio.

From the budget, a timetable is formulated reflecting when the moneys will be spent. The flow chart provides a visual overview of the amount of noise you will be making in the marketplace, by medium and by month. From this chart, you can calculate planned expenditures by month and the planned expense as a percentage of planned sales. Last year's monthly expense ratios and specific industry ratios should be compared to next year's plan. Any major variances should be fully explained and justified.

How to Budget a New Product Launch

When a publisher is ready to launch a new book, the company makes a sales projection based on the author's reputation, the subject and title of the book, last year's sales, and other factors and typically budgets 7 percent of that figure for marketing the book, according to Maryann Palumbo of Penguin USA. "Seven percent of sales for marketing is the average in the industry and it sort of works in terms of the company's budget and profitability," she says.

However, Palumbo will make a case for increasing the marketing budget if she feels the 7 percent figure is inadequate. "Every book is a different product," she explains. "We look at the nitty-gritty. We have to consider if we have a long-term contract. If the author is new. Do we need to build [the reputation] of this author? Is this a one-shot deal? Is this a major author with [potentially] a big image we need to create? Is there a big market for this? Is this a trend? Then I come up with a budget. A lot of times, we are way above the 7 percent. We have to make the determination whether this book is something we really want to blow out, or whether it will find an audience on its own. If the author is not publicizable, we look at promotional efforts, such as point-of-sale, point of purchasing, and bookmarks."

Co-op Advertising Can Fund Part of Your Advertising

A company does not have to provide all the money for the advertising budget. Co-op advertising is advertising in which the costs are shared by the manufacturer and retailer of a product, such as when Bergdorf Goodman advertises in the *New York Times* a $3,655 alligator handbag by Judith Leiber or The Wiz runs an ad that includes $400 Aiwa boom boxes and $900 Panasonic televisions. A co-op venture can also involve two consumer products companies. In 1981, Pepsi teamed with No Nonsense panty hose on a co-op sales promotion and advertising campaign. It was a great pairing because Pepsi was looking to gain market share among women with its Pepsi Light and diet Pepsi lines.

Experts estimate that more than $2 billion is spent on co-op advertising in the United States each year. If the manufacturer and retailer agree on responsibilities and authority in producing a joint-venture program, co-op money can be used for advertising, in-store demonstrations, and direct-mail literature, including catalogs.

Co-op advertising increases consumer awareness of both the brand and the store. It is a tremendous aid to consumers in making them aware of a product's availability and price. In our time-pressured society, this information helps simplify the product search by consumers, allowing them to more easily find the products they want. Co-op money is available for all media with the majority—generally about 65 percent—targeted to newspapers. The remainder of the money is typically divided as follows: direct mail, 11 percent; television, 10 percent; radio, 8 percent; magazines, 3.5 percent; and others, 2.5 percent. Co-op is another tool to add budget flexibility. It can increase the impact for both manufacturer and retailer by tying together two or more well-known brands.

MEASURE THE RESULTS

At the point when progress is measured and compared to the specific objectives delineated in the advertising strategy, consider whether the target market's perception of the store has changed, and if it has, in what way. Have you increased the buying rate? Are there more repeat sales to individuals? What is the sales volume in units and in dollars? How does that sales volume compare to six months ago and a year ago?

A & U Studies

A commonly used device to project and measure levels and changes in awareness of a product and use of the product is A & U (awareness and usage; sometimes called ATU—awareness, trial, and usage). This study surveys consumers' awareness of the product and relates the overall level of use to the level of awareness. Once the relationship between awareness and use is established, projections regarding the expected return on additional marketing dollars can be made. Then follow-up studies are conducted to measure the additional marketing dollars spent with actual changes in product or total store usage.

Awareness

Awareness is usually measured on both an aided and unaided basis. In measuring unaided awareness, consumers report some level of familiarity with the product or service without prompting. In measuring aided awareness, consumers report some level of familiarity with the product or service only after being prompted by some stimulus. While aided awareness is always higher than unaided for the same product, unaided is usually judged to be more valuable because it is believed to relate more faithfully to consumers' true level of familiarity with and commitment to a brand.

Trial

The trial number is the number or percentage of consumers who report being aware of a product or service *and* also report having tried it. Because it is the first indication of conversion from awareness of a product to interest in its use and is usually the precursor to general usage, trial is a very important communications variable.

High levels of trial generally indicate that the marketing program has successfully generated consumer interest in the product and/or it enjoys a good positioning. Another common reason for high levels of trial is a significant amount of dissatisfaction in the category, hence, a high degree of brand switching. As consumers continually seek alternatives to current competitive offerings, they are more likely to try other products. Low trial usually indicates an ineffective marketing program, poor product positioning, or a category in which current products provide an acceptable level of consumer satisfaction.

Usage

Regular use of a product or service is called its usage. Conversion from trial to usage implies consumers' favorable reaction to the product's actual performance—it delivered well on its promise or consumers' expectations.

Sales Projections versus Actual Results

If it can be determined that a certain level of marketing investment will cause a known change in awareness and the relationships among awareness, trial, and usage can be estimated, marketers can project the return on their marketing investment and make judgments as to how best to spend their available marketing funds. A postanalysis of actual results can then be compared to projections to determine what successes and/or failures were actually realized.

Set Goal Timetables

Determine when you should start seeing sales results from the ad efforts and define the time limit. Sales strategies want to see an increase in sales in 24 hours; image advertising requires 6, 9, or 12 months, or longer, and companies usually monitor sales at each quarter to ascertain whether they have met the plans. With more frequent sales measurements, more accurate and rapid revisions of the strategy can be made to meet the goals. So choose to evaluate the advertising program at frequent intervals—as often as it takes for you to know (or at least have a sense of) at any given time whether your ad dollars are paying off.

Consider the Competition's Responses

One reason for sales falling short of the goal may be a counterstrike by one or more competitors. Others may have lowered their prices, increased services, extended the hours that they are open to the public, or changed their product mix. They may also have altered their advertising strategy—by, for example, saturating the market with new ads—to steal the thunder from your ad campaign. Increasing ad frequency to compete with saturation is expensive. Don't react too hastily. Unless your competitor's budget has been increased, the ad bombardment can't last for long. Consider waiting it out and maintaining your course.

Product Innovation Can Affect Ad Results

There are other reasons why ad campaigns could flop. The competition could respond to your advertising campaign by changing products and services or engineering a breakthrough in technology or product innovation. Under those circumstances, it would be surprising if your target market continues to shop your product, even if it's highlighted in advertising. When competitors have reacted to an advertising campaign with a genuine product improvement, it's critical to determine whether your present advertising strategy will work in the next six months or if it's doomed. This may be the time to cancel or modify the campaign and devise a new strategy highlighting a different competitive advantage or to modify and improve your product to match the competitor's.

Does the Target Market Get the Message?

If the progress of sales is satisfactory, abide by your advertising and marketing game plan. With luck, the campaign will exceed all expectations. If, however, sales diminish or do not rise as much as planned, evaluate why. It may be that the target market is not picking up on or understanding the campaign, as was the case with Barneys's ad campaign for its expansion, which featured illustrations.

Barneys

Before Barneys New York declared bankruptcy in January 1996, the chain went through a period of major expansion and Barneys executives determined that a new umbrella advertising campaign was needed to carry it through the growth period. They had to come up with something different and catchy that would spotlight Barneys in the minds of consumers, particularly in markets it was entering, such as Beverly Hills, where consumers were unfamiliar with the store. In 1992, meetings were held to generate a concept. Attending were Barneys owners Gene Pressman and his father Fred, as well as Ronnie Cook, creative director, Glenn O'Brien, a Barneys copywriter, and Simon Doonan, head of public relations.

At the time Barneys was brainstorming, Doonan recalls, "People in the industry weren't talking about advertising concepts. They were talking about which photographer you were using. Who is shooting your ads? Everybody was asking, 'Are you using Meisel? Are you using Avedon?' " referring to the famed fashion photographers Steven Meisel and Richard Avedon. "Photographer ads were all over the place. We were disenchanted with that. We were searching for something new because we had a big story to tell and to reduce this message to the work of one photographer, to be emblematic of what we were doing, would be hard."

The store broke out a witty color illustration campaign grouped around themes such as "Sometimes" or "Private Lives." The ads used funny, fleeting scenes of people, presumably the Barneys cult of shoppers, at a party or a day at the beach, with a singular thought coming from a central figure. In one ad Virgil and his date pass some bodybuilders on the beach, and Virgil is thinking, "Quality is more important than quantity." Another illustration shows a group of women at a birthday party, presumably for Ingo, with the line, "They called Ingo a guru. He called himself a consultant." Detailed information about the clothes depicted in the sketches was listed in the ads.

The campaign was effective on some levels. Says Doonan: "We used about five focus groups and Coopers & Lybrand to validate our feelings that we weren't saying as much as we needed to say. It was cool and hip, and the illustrations suggested there was this club of people in the store, and people were responding to the ads. But the problem was there was a limit to how much information we were conveying to our new customers. It was too oblique, too off-putting." After several seasons, the campaign was abruptly dropped.

What Else Could Be Wrong?

It is also possible that an ad campaign proves nothing other than it's possible to spend money on ads and see no rewards. The target market may simply not be seeing the ads. The wrong media may have been chosen. The sales promotion being offered may not be right for your customer. Or if the target audience does see the ads, maybe the information is too complex to understand. Perhaps the information is packaged in an unappealing presentation that makes it difficult to process. Maybe the point-of-purchase displays are not appropriate for the customers' attitudinal mind-set.

In its postanalysis of a marketing campaign, Penguin, the book publisher, analyzes sales figures and promotional efforts after three weeks, a couple of months, six months, and a year to determine why a book sold or didn't sell. In some cases, "you never really figured out what happened," Palumbo says, adding that the success of the book could simply mean that it was well written, seized on a trend, or was right for the market. "Word of mouth is a most critical element in affecting sales," she says.

Other times, she says, the analysis is much clearer. For example, a book that bombed could have been hurt by poor packaging and a cover that did not convey the essence of the book or perhaps retailers were not receptive to the concept and felt it was not exciting enough. A book could have bombed because a competitor introduced a similar product at the same time and cut into your sales.

Palumbo noted that when Penguin is ready to launch a new product, it will try to pick a month when the competition is not steep. "You don't want to publish Danielle Steel, Stephen King, John Grisham in the same month. Why not share the wealth?" she advises, adding that talking to the competition beforehand to learn their schedule is smart, though not everybody in the industry is always willing to share that kind of information.

Choosing the right media for publicizing the book is also important. In one case, a book bombed because the author plugged it on TV, though he had previously plugged his books on radio and was really a radio personality. "Unfortunately, when you switch mediums like that, with the same kind of budget, you don't have the same kind of reach," Palumbo says. "It showed in the sales. The next book, we went back to radio."

Again, now would be the time to dissect the problem and research why the response has been nil. Look to revamp the advertising campaign and any of the other marketing strategies only when there is certainty about what is truly causing the disappointing results.

Conclusion

MARKETING: THE GREAT MISSED OPPORTUNITY

Ask 10 business executives to define marketing and you will probably get 10 different answers. Ask 10 others what's involved in formulating a marketing campaign and you may get blank stares. Consider yourself lucky. If you have made it this far through this book, you have what few executives in retailing and manufacturing have: an understanding of marketing.

You've learned about the importance of the right approach and how to break through the clutter and create a winning marketing campaign—and that it takes work to get to that point. Marketers must set the corporate mission, stake out the right territory and customers, deliver the right goods and services, and execute forceful advertising and promotional strategies to accomplish, and perhaps even exceed, the financial objectives.

It is rare to find a company that has gone through all the stages of self-examination, explored the competitive landscape, and kept all of its marketing components—advertising, sales promotion, and public relations—working in concert to create a strong identity for its services or products. But that's what it takes to successfully position a company so that it stands out from the pack, casts a clear image of itself, and generates a healthy bottom line.

Why do few companies develop a really comprehensive, effective marketing program built on a thorough review of company strengths and weaknesses, the competition, and the target market? Why is it that few companies develop a campaign that creates an umbrella of consistency for selling the products and services?

The answer is simple. Few companies have the leadership and the drive to get down to it. It's like trying to write a book. It takes a highly organized and disciplined approach and a lot of work. It boils down to making the commitment, gathering the resources, and then just doing it. It's like climbing a mountain. The task seems enormous, but you take it step by step and set realistic goals along the path. That way you can measure the progress, draw satisfaction from the gains, and sustain motivation.

Marketing is critical to the success and survival of any business, and the subject is hotter than ever. That's because the world is changing faster, with new forms of communication and technology rapidly emerging and seismic shifts in demographics and consumer attitudes anticipated well into the 21st century. Marketing strategies must be worked and reworked to adapt to the turbulent and cutthroat world and doggedly revisited and revised. Creating a great marketing program is not a one-shot deal. It's a work in progress that has to keep pace with swings in society.

However, most marketing strategies spawn from eleventh-hour reactions, knee-jerk responses to the changing environment. Sales slow, profits slip, morale dives, and then companies move into action. Businesses tackle problems with single-minded approaches that don't provide long-lasting solutions. They fail to realize that taking a proactive approach and developing short- and long-term strategies to solve immediate problems and anticipate trends on the horizon creates an environment for a better future.

Marketers are up against a tough world. People are less interested in shopping, turned off to many stores, and skeptical of the messages of advertisers. But we are still living in a material world where marketers must satisfy the basic needs and wants of society. The most successful marketers will go beyond the basics and take it one step further.

GETTING STARTED

In a nutshell, formulating the marketing plan entails many steps. Start by conducting a business review. Define the business in broad strokes and clearly focus on where you want to take the company and for what it should stand. List all the products and services, draw the customer profile, and include a discussion on management style and the financial health of the organization.

Don't think of your competitors or consumers as statistics on paper. Think of them as personalities. React to them emotionally and intellectually and get a feeling for their essence. What makes them tick? React viscerally: Gut reactions are often the right way to go.

Review decisions of the past—good and bad—to help judge customer reaction. Use market research to see whether your vision of the company and what it should stand for match what customers think. Learn what makes your customers tick and what they want. You may be selling apples, but customers think you sell oranges. Or your apples may be inferior to another brand's.

It's likely that perceptual problems and shortcomings will be unearthed. Don't get discouraged. From problems come opportunities for new solutions. If, for example, you find that only an older audience is buying your product, it's an opportunity to consider how to sell to a younger crowd. If you discover that only part of the store is being shopped, it's an opportunity to examine strategies for steering traffic through the store. Find points of departure from the competition. While conducting the review, keep a record of any ideas for the marketing plan that pop into your mind. Consider developing a mission statement, something to rally the troops, but remember that the business review is not the time to come up with specific objectives and strategies.

POSITIONING THE COMPANY

Next, wear a new hat. Become an outsider looking in. It's time for a complete diagnosis, the top-to-bottom evaluation of how the company is doing. What's selling; what's not? Which services work; which don't? Review the advertising and gauge the response. Take a look at some old campaigns and break out fresh ones. Learn from the past. Examine the skills of the sales force and the management.

In taking stock of what the company has and doesn't have, consider outside help to get objective opinions or bring in fresh blood in full-time positions, people with no ties to the old ways and a readiness to shake things up. Set a new plan and devise a sweeping new marketing agenda. Don't wait for the company to sink so low that an outside director or shareholder group gets on your case. It could be too late by then. Many

CEOs have been pushed out of office for not being on top of things. Many companies have fallen into bankruptcy because they waited too long to act.

KNOW YOUR CONSUMER AND COMPETITOR BEFORE WRITING THE GAME PLAN

Examine the profile of the end user. Manufacturers and retailers should learn about their customers and how they spend their time and dollars by asking questions, taking surveys, using focus groups, and being on the selling floor. Consider what stages of life the customers are in. Consider their occupations, leisure activities, and religion. Income alone does not suggest customers' interests. Once you know what they stand for and what they want, focus on that and *stay* focused on it. But also concentrate on the children and grandchildren of the target customers. That could lead to brand extensions, additional product lines, and new marketing strategies. All activities of the marketing program should reflect the target customer and the target customer's family. Maintain a consistency in the look, price, quality, and style of the products. All must ring true with customers, and one product should support the sale of related products. Multiple sales from each customer is a prime objective.

In addition to learning what customers do and do not buy from you, find out where else they shop and what they buy from the competition. There may be more potential to sell to this customer group. However, don't try to sell everything to everybody. Be aware that buying habits are hard to break. Determine how fast the market is growing or shrinking. Comb the streets and selling floors to see firsthand who the customers are and to hear what they say.

Shop the competition. It's the best way to launch a defense. Enter enemy territory and examine inventories, prices, catalogs, customers, signage, merchandising methods, and service strategies. Take a field trip to the mall and size up who shops the competition. It's called intelligence gathering. Digest it, evaluate it, and then act fast and furiously on counterstrategies and innovations before the competition gets wind of your new approach.

Be aware that the competition is going to do to you what you do to them. Watch out for corporate raiding parties. The competition wants your talent. The talent you need to retain should be well-compensated and involved in fulfilling assignments. The competition wants your best products. Watch out for deals undermining your partnerships with suppliers. Always innovate and update the product line. Keep one step ahead. Time sales to beat theirs. Don't fear the competition. Strategize off it.

THE MARKETING PLAN

Goals are what you want to attain, so make them quantifiable (e.g., sales up 20 percent in the first year); objectives are the blueprint for getting there. Set new sales and profit goals and objectives. Revise them periodically, depending on the level of the success, the competition's level of success, the economic climate, and industry trends.

Sales goals can't be subjective and open to interpretation. You can't say, "Let's bring sales through the roof." Do it with numbers and definitive statements. Don't commit to pie-in-the-sky numbers. Reach for the stars and settle for the treetops.

Develop an appropriate time frame to meet the objective. It shouldn't be more than a year. Explain why these goals are attainable. Financial targets must be realistic and attainable and based on real demographic information, the competitive landscape, and the amount being spent on advertising and promotion. Seeking a 40 percent gain in sales doesn't make sense if you are only increasing the advertising budget by 2 percent.

Consider the risks of reaching for higher goals. For example, a quest for a greater sales gain in a year may entail markdowns and cutting margins to drive volume. Monitor the results on a short-term basis, each month, every two months, and quarterly, to maintain realistic objectives, control costs, and determine progress.

CREATING AND DEVELOPING THE BRAND IMAGE

In positioning your company or brand, don't try to be all things to all people. Position yourself against the best. Remember, playing in a better field will elevate your game. Don't confuse image with positioning. Image sets the attributes. Positioning sets the brand apart. To position a Rolls-Royce, for example, the message might be that it is for an older, more established audience. It's the most expensive car in the market and more stately than anything else out there. The Rolls might be pictured next to the Parliament in London or by a château in the countryside. The positioning strategy should be a simple mission statement. People have to be able to get it—and get it without thinking about it. Positioning is also set in the sales promotion tactics, pricing, level of service, selling policies—all things relative to the competition.

FORMULATING THE CREATIVE; MEDIA PLANNING; CREATIVE ADAPTATION FOR THE MEDIA

Before creating the advertising, examine the major trends out there. Ads in the mid-1990s are bigger, bolder, slicker, sexier, more high-tech, more special effects–oriented, a lot more expensive, and bent on price promoting and repeating old themes. Break out of the mold. The message of the advertising should capture the attention of the target market. It has to reach out, grab, and suck in without being too gimmicky or falsely representing the product.

The end goals of advertising are multifold. They can be geared to boost sales instantly, reshape or differentiate a company's image, launch new products, clear out old ones, position a brand or help define its image, give it a personality to attract a target market, stress a product's attributes and advantages, or instruct on how to use it. You must decide on the goals of the advertising.

Creating ads is not an overnight process. Advertising must be done in the framework of an entire marketing plan, not based on a creative whim that someone in the company may have brainstormed the night before.

Search for the big idea, or the central message, attitude, or underlying theme that runs through the ads in the campaign. Aside from the visual excitement of the advertisement, the main and most difficult goal is getting the big idea, the proposition that is going to sell the product. It requires a great deal of research of the product and objectives, some time to absorb all the research, some thinking, and some incubating; from the

I-have-the-idea stage comes the morning-after stage when you find that things are all wrong. That's the time you have to think of creative teamwork and be open to alternate suggestions. That's what makes a good idea into a great one—its ability to be molded and shaped from its original form. It can be stated through words or pictorially. It's the platform for presenting the products. It's what shapes the components of the ads, including the headline, copy, emotional content, photo, colors, and size.

When the advertising is in place, don't change it too quickly if there isn't an immediate reaction. Don't treat it like a change in lipstick. Don't expect all ads to have a positive instant effect on sales or store traffic. Give an ad program time to kick in. Set reasonable goals for the campaign. If they are not met, consider pulling the campaign and revising it. Is all the right information in the ads? Are the ads being placed in the right media? Some ideas become instant successes. Those are few and far between. Be patient, do research. Maybe it's the product or the sales force rather than the advertising that's faulty.

In developing ads, a tone and style must be chosen. A straightforward, factual approach works when advertising price or special promotions. But for an image or positioning campaign, ads can be humorous, witty, or dramatic. It's a matter of selecting the right tone and emotion for what's being advertised and for the targeted audience. Know that ads cover the range of human emotions—fear, humor, frustration, anger, hopefulness, nostalgia, despair, love, generosity, caring, hate, and jealousy. They can also appeal to ego and logic.

Focus on what message you want consumers to hear to determine what to say in the ads about the product. Consider later how you want to say it. The headline and the visual have to be arresting. The ad must have impact. Talk the language of the target customer. Incite curiosity. Most importantly, work as a team. Be open to alterations and suggestions to the ad from different members of the team. Someone's great idea is still his or her own great idea, even if it gets edited and refined during the creative process.

Decide where the ad will appear—in newspapers, in magazines, in the electronic media, or on a blimp. Those decisions are based on the target market, the nature of the ad itself, the advertising budget, and the quality of reproduction desired.

In planning the media strategy, think of the five Ws: Who is the target audience? What is the creative message? When does it need to be told?

What media does it need to be in? The *why* becomes the rationale for the media strategy. Always make sure you are getting the right amount of impressions per medium and in the total plan. If you can do only one TV spot, you're better off doing 20 radio spots.

SALES PROMOTION; THE MERCHANDISING ARENA: POINT OF PURCHASE AND PERSONAL SELLING

Sales promotion is a tricky yet integral part of the marketing plan. Strategies should blend into the tone and style of the advertising and the character of the business or brand. Strike a balance between promotions that push markdowns and those that promote image, charities, contests, and new products.

In a tough business climate, the temptation is to drive sales through steep markdowns and incessant price promotions. Don't run too many of these. They can alter the character of the company, destroy price credibility, and, in the long run, shoppers will avoid the store or brand when there isn't a sale. Be aware that certain kinds of promotions, such as coupons, rebates, contests, and sweepstakes, change the mood and image of a business. Build strong sales promotions by cross-promoting two brands in the same promotion. Offer promotions that strive for more than one goal, such as enhancing a company's reputation or providing a public service, while generating more sales.

Smart marketers test-market before rolling out a sales strategy on a national basis. They time promotions with peak selling periods and creatively mix tactics to achieve a variety of goals. They distribute samples and coupons in the same promotion to spur repeat sales and develop brand loyalty, time the distribution of premiums (such as T-shirts) with product demonstrations or educational events to gain product awareness, and stage special events to solidify relationships with customers. Other strategies include sampling and then selling at a temporarily reduced rate to induce people to buy or using the Internet and other new media for tying information from Web sites with store demonstrations and mailers. Identify the goals of the promotion. Do you want to inform, to encourage the public to shop or buy the product, or to reward customers? State goals in measurable terms, such as upping sales by 10 percent or increasing by 5 percent the number of people who know about a company or brand.

Selling the brand requires a sales force that does more than sell products. They should monitor the competition and their products, "prospect" customers, and develop sales presentations and selling styles that engage clients: Be on the scene, but don't hover over clients. Don't push the sale too hard or too soon; listen to customers and learn about their needs and wants. Pay attention to body language. Keep a client book that contains such information as birthdays, sizes, family members, occupations, and past purchases. Engage in a dialogue and don't rush to make the sale. Follow up with phone calls and letters to solidify relationships and raise chances for further selling in the future. Know your products and their advantages and disadvantages.

Point-of-purchase (POP) displays must integrate with the advertising, store ambiance, and total marketing plan. But don't use displays that are more dramatic than the products they help to sell. POPs should enhance the product and help convey a message—not overshadow the brand. That doesn't mean that the POP display has to be subtle. It shouldn't be, since many purchasing decisions are influenced at the point of purchase. POP displays can be imaginative, colorful, illuminated, or high-tech.

Consider POP a problem solver. It can help educate customers about a product's benefits and effectively display product even though space in the store may be limited. Think of POP as an essential ingredient of the merchandising arena, which in turn can be thought of as an active and interactive theatrical selling environment filled with product demonstrations, fashion events, product launches, and appearances by celebrities, authors, and fashion designers. The goal is to get people into the store and moving through it.

PUBLIC RELATIONS: THE ART OF THE SPIN

Publicity through the media is one of the better forms of getting your message out because it comes from an unbiased source. But remember that nothing in life is free. You lose a certain amount of control with respect to the frequency and the nature of the message. Developing relationships with the press and making sure you are always forthright can help minimize changes in the message. Make sure when you talk to the press that you have a real story and not a yawner. Don't be a media hack.

Don't think of PR as a substitute for advertising. On the other hand, if the budget is very low and you can only afford to do a little advertising, PR may be the way to go.

One final note. Be sophisticated and street-smart at the same time. There are major phases in the marketing plan when you have to forgo the MBA in you and think of business as life. Remove yourself from the academic and corporate mentality. Become a consumer.

DOING IT BY THE NUMBERS: BUDGETING, TIMETABLES, AND MEASURING RESULTS

Figuring out how much to spend on advertising and the rest of marketing is not an exact science. There are many formulas, ranging from basing the budget on a percentage of sales or profits to estimates on what the competition spends, your last year's expenditures, and your best judgment.

Flexibility in budgeting is key. If you think you have a great idea, go with it, but hold some funds in reserve to handle emergency requirements, such as clearance advertising to compensate for a disastrous selling season. Also, be aware that co-op advertising can broaden the scope of the ad program.

Set goals for the advertising: Determine the kind of sales gains you want to see and evaluate the program. If the sales aren't coming, something is wrong. Maybe the message isn't being heard. Or maybe it's misunderstood. Or perhaps the advertising was just poorly timed. Advertising is not an exact science, either: It must be regularly monitored to see whether it's working.

References

American Association of Advertising Agencies. *Guide to Newspapers.* New York: American Association of Advertising Agencies, 1994.

Anderson, Carol. *Retailing: Concepts, Strategy and Information.* Minneapolis/Saint Paul: West, 1993.

Berman, Barry, and Joel Evans. *Management: A Strategic Approach,* 5th ed. New York: Macmillan, 1992.

Book, Albert C., and C. Dennis Schick. *Fundamentals of Copy & Layout,* 2d ed. Lincolnwood, Ill.: NTC Business Books, 1991.

Bovée, Courtland L., and John V. Thill. *Marketing.* New York: McGraw-Hill, 1992.

Bovée, Courtland L., et al. *Advertising Excellence.* New York: McGraw-Hill, 1995.

Brivic, Allen. *What Every Account Executive Should Know about Co-op Advertising.* New York: American Association of Advertising Agencies, 1989.

Guzmán, Isaac. "A Cram Session For Cars." *Newsday,* November 25 (1995), p. A4.

Kotler, Philip. *Marketing Management: Analysis, Planning, Implementation, and Control,* 7th ed. Englewood Cliffs, N.J.: Prentice Hall, 1991.

Ogilvy, David. *Ogilvy on Advertising.* New York: Random House, 1985.

Predmore, Carolyn E. "Control and Power Equity in a Sales Interaction: Good Business and Ethics." Annual Conference of Society for Consumer Psychology, February 1996.

———. "The Effect of Reinforcement on Paralinguistic Synchrony in Dyadic Sales Interactions." Master's thesis, Baruch College, 1985.

REFERENCES

————. "Re-Energizing the Salesforce with an Old-Fashioned Ethical Approach: Listening." Georgia State University Center for Business and Industrial Marketing 1st Annual Conference on Transfiguring the Salesforce: The Leading Edge of Business Selling, January 9, 1995.

————. "Relational Communication and Personality Traits: Effects on Telemarketing Sales Success." Ph.D. diss., City University of New York, 1991.

Predmore, Carolyn E., and Joseph G. Bonnice. "Finding Good Telemarketing Sales and Service People." *Journal of Professional Services Marketing,* in press.

Pride, William M., and O. C. Ferrell. *Marketing: Concepts and Strategies,* 9th ed. Boston: Houghton Mifflin, 1995.

Siebert, Lori, and Ballard, Lisa. *Making a Good Layout.* Cincinnati: Northlight Books, 1992.

Young, James Webb. *Techniques for Producing Ideas.* Chicago: NTC, 1994.

Index

INDEX

INDEX